I AIN'T RESISTING

I AIN'T RESISTING

The City of Greensboro
and the Killing of
Marcus Smith

IAN McDOWELL

Scuppernong Editions
Greensboro   2023

I AIN'T RESISTING

CITY OF GREENSBORO
FOR IMMEDIATE RELEASE

Subject that Collapsed in Police Custody Later Dies at Hospital

GREENSBORO, NC (Sept. 8, 2018)—At 12:45 AM Greensboro Police located a disoriented suicidal subject running in and out of traffic in the 100 block of North Church Street. Officers worked with the subject for several minutes in an effort to give him assistance. EMS arrived at the scene at 12:50 AM. While officers were attempting to transport him for mental evaluation, the subject became combative and collapsed. Both EMS and on scene officers began rendering aid. The subject was transported by EMS to a local hospital for additional treatment. The subject passed away at approximately 1:50 AM.

This incident is currently under investigation by the Greensboro Police Department and the State Bureau of Investigation. The officers involved will be placed on administrative duty, as according to policy of the Greensboro Police Department.

# # # #

The last 18 minutes of Marcus Deon Smith's life are on YouTube.

On the channel CityofGreensboroNC, there are 20 videos depicting how he died in the early morning of September 8, 2018. His name is nowhere on them.

The only text is the titles, consisting of "Video", a number and "November 30, 2018." That date is when the videos were posted, not when the incident happened two months and 22 days earlier. Only by noting the timestamp can a viewer with no prior knowledge of the man's death tell when it took place.

Nor is the location identified. Anyone unfamiliar with the mostly unoccupied buildings between 113 South Church Street and 111 North Church Street, an unprepossessing 407-foot strip on the lower east side of downtown Greensboro, would find it difficult to tell where Marcus Smith died.

Eighteen of the 20 videos are from the body-worn cameras, or BWCs, of the eight Greensboro police officers who laid hands on him. Several are represented by multiple videos, due to them turning off their cameras when entering patrol cars or mounting their ATVs, and on after emerging or dismounting. One video is from the dashboard of the lieutenant parked blocks from the scene, and another is from the bodycam of a corporal who arrived after the ambulance departed for Moses Cone Hospital, where Marcus Smith was declared dead.

One claim about what happened on those two blocks can be found on the City's channel. "November 30, 2018 Compilation Video" features clips from some of the individual body-worn cameras edited into a chronological narrative. Produced by the City, it is introduced by former Police Chief Wayne Scott, who retired in January of 2020.

In his five-minute-50-second introduction, Scott says he will describe what the videos show. He makes at least one inaccurate statement and two disputed assertions, which will be described later in this book.

While the name of the 38-year-old Black man who died in police custody does not appear in any text, Scott speaks it aloud. "Unfortunately, you will witness an individual, Mr. Marcus Smith, and you will witness some very disturbing images of him." Several of the unedited videos contain even more disturbing images of what appears to be his actual moment of death, but that footage is not in the compilation.

After the Press Release

1 THE CITY WHERE HE DIED

Greensboro, where Marcus Smith lived the last eight of his 38 years, is the third-largest city in North Carolina. Its demographics are different from those of the majority-white state capitol Raleigh, where African-Americans represent 28.9 percent of the population, or Charlotte, the state's largest city, where they represent 35.4 percent. In Greensboro, 42 percent of the municipal population is Black.

In the 2020 census, that population numbered 299,035, making Greensboro the largest city in North Carolina's Piedmont Triad region. Its environs form the apex of the Piedmont Crescent, an area of continuous urban development curving upwards and west from Raleigh and down to the Charlotte metropolitan area near the South Carolina border.

The Piedmont is the plateau between North America's Atlantic coastal plain and the Appalachians, stretching from New York to Alabama. Before colonial expansion, plague, and genocide, the low country belonged to the Tuscarora and the high country to the Cherokee. Between these indigenous nations lay the tribal lands of the Saponi and the Saura.

By the late 17th century, their populations were greatly reduced by European diseases and by the wars in which the Saponi fought other tribes alongside the colonizers who brought those epidemics to North America. After Virginia military leader Nathaniel Bacon massacred over 200 of his former allies, the surviving Saponi were pushed into what is now North Carolina. There, they traded and intermarried with the

Saura, who occupied the land that would become Guilford County and its county seat of Greensboro.

In the first half of the 18th century, the remnants of both tribes were pushed west or simply lost their cultural identity as their declining populations intermarried with refugees from other tribes. By 1768, the indigenous population of what is now Guilford County was estimated to be less than 60.

The Piedmont's first wave of European colonizers were primarily Scotch-Irish and Germans who came down the Great Wagon Road from Philadelphia. The former were predominantly Presbyterian, the latter Lutheran and Moravian. The second wave was English, and largely Quaker.

In their new home, emptied of its original owners by European encroachment and microbes, they grew corn and wheat and tobacco, and built stores, gristmills, sawmills, and tanneries. By this time, Africans were transported to the North American colonies to replace enslaved indigenous people who had either succumbed to disease or escaped west, but Quakers largely resisted the growing commerce in human chattel. Members of the Society of Friends were not prohibited from owning slaves, and some did, but their faith forbid buying or selling them.

The Quakers who farmed what would become Greensboro named their settlement Capefair. With more coming from as far away as Nantucket, Capefair became North Carolina's most important Quaker community. In 1771, that community became part of Guilford County, named after Francis North, 1st Earl of Guilford.

In 1781, the Battle of Guilford Courthouse was the fiercest conflict of the American Revolution's southern theater, with Cornwallis' pyrrhic victory over Major General Nathanael Greene's troops costing the British general 25 percent of his army. In 1808, Capefair was renamed Greensborough in honor of the general who made Cornwallis pay such a bloody price, with a new central square replacing Guilford Courthouse as the county seat.

Elsewhere in the North Carolina Piedmont, slaveholder agrarian oligarchs were not as prevalent or powerful as in neighboring states.

However, Stagville, located in Durham County 63 miles from Greensboro, was one of the largest plantations in the South.

In 1861, North Carolina became a grudging and uncooperative member of the Confederate States of America, one deeply distrusted by the Richmond aristocrats who ran the CSA. Because sustenance farmers were not protected from the draft by the "Twenty Negro Rule," which exempted the sons of rich planters from forced conscription, the region's corn and wheat growers were more likely to shoot at Virginia troops sent to forcibly recruit them than at Yankees, especially when the Virginians dragged men as young as 15 and old as 55 off their farms and into the killing fields of Gettysburg, leaving their crops to rot in the fields.

"The NC Piedmont was a hotbed of militant Unionism," wrote historian Victoria Bynum, a specialist in Southern resistance to the Confederacy. "Piedmont Unionists were well-organized and armed, as exemplified by the Heroes of America."

That secret society, also known as the Red Strings, was a southern guerilla organization dedicated to destroying the Confederacy from within. The Heroes harbored spies, helped POWs escape, and spirited runaway slaves to free states.

By 1884, Greensborough's population was 5,538, and it had a newspaper and two colleges. This attracted attention from northern industrialists, including Moses and Caesar Cone of Baltimore, whose large-scale textile plants changed the village to a city. After its name was shortened to Greensboro in 1895, it became a center of the Southern textile industry, with factories producing denim, flannel, and overalls.

The elections of 1898 restored a Democratic majority in the state legislature. Just as 19th-century Democrats supported slavery, 20th-century ones opposed Black voting rights until Nixon's "Southern Strategy" realigned the two parties. Restored to power, North Carolina white supremacists instigated the Wilmington Massacre, the most successful and brutal coup d'état in US history, which overthrew the multi-racial government of that coastal city and killed or exiled most of its formerly majority Black population. In North Carolina and across the

South, Black voters were disenfranchised, with many reduced to a state of de facto slavery that would persist until the Civil Rights era.

One landmark of that era was the 1960 lunch counter sit-ins at Woolworth's in downtown Greensboro. This peaceful protest by David Richmond, Franklin McCain, Ezell Blair Jr. (Jibreel Khazan), and Joseph McNeil, four Black students from North Carolina Agricultural & Technical State University, commonly known as A&T, sparked similar sit-ins across the South. What was once the downtown Woolworth's building is now the site of the International Civil Rights Center and Museum (ICRCM). During Greensboro's Black Lives Matter rallies following the murder of George Floyd, protesters regularly chanted not only Floyd's name, but that of Marcus Smith, as they marched from the museum to where Marcus died two blocks away.

While the ICRCM commemorates the 1960 Woolworth's sit-in staged by A&T students, it contains no exhibit or gallery devoted to either the 1969 Siege of A&T or the 1979 Greensboro Massacre. The former is described in three sentences on the Wall of Remembrance, but there are no images of what Martha Biondi, author of 2012's *The Black Revolution on Campus,* called "the most massive armed assault ever made against an American university."

The Greensboro Massacre is not mentioned at all.

The Siege of A&T started on the campus of James B. Dudley High School and moved to that of the historically Black state university attended, nine years earlier, by the four students who began the Woolworth's sit-in. On May 21, protests erupted at the high school after senior Claude Barnes, a hugely popular write-in candidate for student council president, was denied his landslide victory due to this involvement with the Black Power movement. After Dudley students boycotted classes, the Guilford County school superintendent replaced the school's Black principal with a white administrator, and stationed riot police near the school.

Dudley students then turned for assistance to A&T, which had become a major center of the Black Power movement in the South. Over the next four days, the protests spread to the A&T campus, resulting in its occupation by the National Guard.

Hundreds of students were arrested and one bystander, sophomore honors student Willie Grimes, was shot dead. Grimes had been walking to a late-night restaurant when he and friends were fired on from a passing vehicle. Whether it was a police car or one driven by white counter-protesters remains a matter of dispute. Among those arrested in 1969 was A&T student activist Nelson Johnson who, a decade later, survived the deadly white supremacist assault on a pro-labor and anti-Klan rally he organized.

The 1979 Greensboro Massacre was an attack on a "Death to the Klan" march led by Johnson and other members of the Communist Worker's Party, which had been attempting to unionize the mostly Black workers in Greensboro's textile mills. While the violence was described for years in local media as a "shootout" between Communist labor organizers and a coalition of KKK and American Nazi Party gunmen, the historical consensus is that it was an act of domestic terrorism by the Klansmen and Nazis. One of the key findings of the 2006 Greensboro Truth and Reconciliation Commission Final Report was that the Greensboro Police Department "showed a stunning lack of curiosity in planning for the safety of the event," and the massacre probably would not have happened if the GPD had done its job.

Johnson, who cofounded the Beloved Community Center of Greensboro 12 years after the massacre, would go further in his criticism, stating in 2019 that the Klansmen and Nazis, who killed three of his friends, an attending physician he did not know, and a young woman he considered family, belonged to "a North American death squad facilitated by the Greensboro police."

In a 2023 interview, Johnson described being told "your name is on the lips of every Klansman and Nazi in Greensboro; you're not going to stay alive unless you work with us." He didn't recall whether it was the FBI agent or the cop who said that to him at three in the morning after the Greensboro Massacre.

"My injuries weren't life-threatening, so after they patched up my arm where the Nazi knife went through it, I was sent straight to a four-by-four cell without bond, and that's where I woke up with them standing over me. When I got up and turned my stool into the corner and didn't reply, one said something like 'we'll rip these bandages off your arm,' but I just sat there. That's when I knew the FBI was a part of what happened, but what really got me was that they wanted me to be their agent, the way we later learned Edward Dawson had been."

The degree to which the Klansmen and Nazis were "facilitated" by the city and its police was made public in a 1985 civil suit, when a Christie Institute legal team, led by Greensboro attorneys Lewis Pitts and Daniel Sheehan, Durham attorney Carolyn McAllister, and Flint Taylor of the People's Law Office of Chicago, won the only liability award to result from the massacre. Taylor and Pitts are recurring figures in this book, although only Taylor was still a practicing attorney when Marcus Smith was killed.

The five murdered marchers included former Bennett College senior class president Sandra Neely Smith, who was shot between the eyes while trying to get a group of children to safety; James Michael Waller, shot in the back while running for cover; César Vicente Cauce, struck from behind with a club while fighting with his attackers and shot through the neck while he lay on the ground; Michael Ronald Nathan; and William Evan Sampson, who drew a pistol and returned KKK fire, but was shot in the heart.

The jury in the 1985 civil suit imposed no financial penalty for the murders of the four Communists, but found two Klansmen, three Nazis, two Greensboro police officers, and a police informant liable for the wrongful death of Dr. Michael Nathan, who was not a Communist, and for injuries to survivors Dr. Paul Bermanzohn and Tom Clark.

The Klan-Nazi caravan was led to the scene of the march by Edward Dawson, a founder of the North Carolina Knights of the Ku Klux Klan turned FBI informant in 1969 as part of the agency's Counter Intelligence Program (COINTELPRO). In the fall of 1979, he was also working as an informant for the Greensboro Police Department. Prior to the march, he was given a copy of its intended route by his GPD handlers. Dawson shared that map with the Klansmen and Nazis with whom he was embedded, but then, according to his later testimony, became frightened by the potential for violence. When he alerted his handlers that the armed caravan of Nazis and Klansmen was moving towards the march, GPD officers followed at a distance, then pulled back and essentially allowed the massacre to happen.

For decades following the 1969 siege and 1979 massacre, Nelson Johnson was vilified by Greensboro's white conservatives, including some members of the GPD. In 2019, a former GPD deputy chief posting on the Facebook group Greater Greensboro Politics claimed the only injuries Johnson received in the massacre happened when Johnson "dove under a TV van" to escape gunfire. In reality, Johnson was stabbed while using a stick to fend off an attacking Nazi's knife.

Flint Taylor of the People's Law Office of Chicago, who co-litigated the lawsuit, had previously been instrumental in changing the public narrative about the police assassination of Black Panther Party chairman Fred Hampton. He would later join Greensboro attorney Graham Holt in Mary Smith's suit against the City of Greensboro, the eight officers, and the two paramedics involved in the homicide of her son Marcus.

In 2006, a group of North Carolina private citizens founded the Greensboro Truth and Reconciliation Commission. Modeled after the 1996 Truth and Reconciliation Commission assembled in South Africa after the end of apartheid, it began an investigation into the causes and consequences of the Greensboro Massacre. In its final report, the GTRC noted the importance of the Greensboro Police Department's absence from the scene of the attack and condemned not only the KKK and the American Nazi Party, but the Greensboro Police Department and city government as responsible for the massacre and its subsequent cover-up.

In October of 2020, the Greensboro City Council passed a resolution apologizing for the 1979 massacre and acknowledging that police and city personnel "failed to warn the marchers of their extensive foreknowledge of the racist, violent attack planned against the marchers by members of the Ku Klux Klan and the American Nazi Party with the assistance of a paid GPD informant," and "failed to divert, stop or arrest the members of the Ku Klux Klan and American Nazi Party, whom police knew were carrying a cache of concealed weapons."

The resolution concluded by stating that "the City of Greensboro hereby expresses its apology to the victims, the survivors, their families and the members of the Morningside Homes community for the events that occurred on November 3, 1979 and the failure of any government action to effectively overcome the hate that precipitated the violence, to embrace the sorrow that resulted from the violence, and to reconcile all the vestiges of those heinous events in the years subsequent to 1979."

I AIN'T RESISTING

2   THE MAN WHOSE LIFE MATTERED

"You see brutality on TV and you have compassion for those people, but you never ever think it's going to walk up on your door," said Mary Smith during a press conference at Greensboro's Shiloh Baptist Church on December 3, 2018, when she took the podium to the address a roomful of people who had just watched police videos of her son's death.

Then she talked about his life.

"He was the most compassionate, loving, kind person you would ever meet. If anybody here is a teacher and he was your student, you would love him. Not only was he special in Greensboro, he was special in our community. He was a great basketball player, a poet, and a writer, and a kind son."

In 2019, Mary elaborated on what she'd said about Marcus the previous December, again describing his academic and athletic accomplishments as a child and teenager, emphasizing his tight bond with his siblings and parents.

"No matter how bad things were with him, he always wanted to know about us. He was a great brother to Kim and Len and a great son to me and my husband, and always very supportive. He was a math wizard; no form of calculating was any kind of problem for him. He dressed well. Even when we were going through bad times, he was always a great advocate for our family, just as he was when his own times were hard. He didn't like to talk about what was going on with him when it was bad, and we knew it often was, but he always wanted to know what was going on with us. No matter what some on Greensboro City Council say, everybody loved him in our family."

Mary was referring to a remark made by Councilmember Marikay Abuzuaiter, who, after hearing 35 members of the public call on Council to investigate Marcus' death, said "I cannot judge Mr. Smith on why his family may not have been around."

The first member of Marcus' family to speak that night was not his mother Mary, but his sister Kim. "My brother and I, we were one year apart," she said. "His birthday is January 30 and mine is February 2. In school, we told people we were twins, until he got really tall while I stayed really short. He was very funny. He would make you laugh. He would turn any situation upside down. As you guys heard, he was a poet. That was something he wrote maybe 15 years ago."

Kim was referring to "Heart of Granite," a poem Marcus wrote in 2003, which he later recorded, with Kim singing backup vocals. The recording was played at the beginning of the press conference, so the people who'd come to support his family could hear his living words before listening to his last breath. It begins:

Vacant thoughts flowing through my head,
Got me thinking, what is life when your heart is dead?
I guess you're heartless and the darkness starts to cloud some thoughts
Only security that you have is to face your loss
That's how it works, and though it hurts, you must continue on

In December of 2018, members of the Smith family were not the only ones to describe their fond memories of the man whose death the state medical examiner had recently declared a homicide. Speaking to Greensboro City Council the next evening, Prasafany Outlaw talked about how Marcus helped her when she herself was homeless in Greensboro.

"He was a really good friend of mine, and he did a lot to help me and my children when I first moved here to Greensboro from East St. Louis, Illinois. I don't know if you know anything about the area, but it wasn't one that I wanted my kids to grow up in. So, I came here, and had to experience homelessness for a while, and while I did, Marcus was there to look out for me, and now, who's going to look out for him? He loved everybody, he was always kind and giving, although things may have been hard for him. He wanted to better himself, he wanted to help other people, he cared for other people, but unfortunately, he's not going to be able to do those things anymore."

Marcus Deon Smith was born January 30, 1980, in Clinton, South Carolina, a town of 8,596 located 200 miles southwest of Greensboro via I-95. He was the third child of textile mill workers George and Mary Smith, after his brothers Len and JJ. He and his younger sister Kim would become particularly close.

The Greensboro-based *News & Record*, since 2007 reduced to a shadow of its 20th-century self by waves of staff cutbacks, devoted its most substantial reporting in recent years to how Marcus' family reacted to his death. Veteran reporter Richard Barron became close to members of the family and interviewed them several times.

"She and Marcus, they just had an extra touch for one another," said George Smith about his son and daughter when interviewed by Barron at a family get-together in 2019 held at the Charlotte home of Marcus' brother Len Butler.[1]

In the same interview, Mary Smith spoke proudly of her son's cheerful and friendly personality and his prowess at Little League Baseball, where he regularly hit home runs. George described the family as tightly knit. "We didn't have much money, but togetherness was a big thing for us."

Kim remembered Marcus as being very protective. "We played basketball, so we would travel on the bus. The girls played first. He would make sure he took time to come and watch me play. We would get back and we would walk back home together." His brother JJ told Barron that Marcus was very intelligent and that "all the teachers loved him." Mary Smith showed Barron the Student of the Month certificate Marcus earned in middle school.

While he seemed that way to Kim, Barron's article described Marcus as "not especially tall." In his autopsy, his body was listed as having a "length" of 71.5 inches. People are typically longer when lying down than they are tall when standing up, and postmortem measurements are an inaccurate indication of someone's height. It's safe to say that Marcus was much shorter than most NBA all-stars, but taller than 5-foot-9-inch Isiah Thomas of the Charlotte Hornets. Still, he excelled at the sport, making up for his stature with muscular athleticism and a competitive nature.

Things changed for him when he was around 15. George Smith described to Barron "an incident" in which his son "had gotten with the wrong crowd and he got in trouble." His coach dropped him from the basketball team, and he began to rebel. According to his South Carolina legal records, he was arrested for dealing cocaine a few days after his eighteenth birthday.

Mary Smith couldn't help but worry about her son but told Barron, "Even when he was at his lowest point, he still was positive," and "he gave me words to live by: *Mama, don't worry about it.*"

Like many in their early twenties, he felt his hometown too small and slow, and told his mother he longed for the space and surprise of bigger cities. His urge to see new places took him to Jacksonville, Florida, where he worked construction, but also committed larceny to support his drug use. When Mary and George could get time off from their long shifts in the mills, they would drive five and half hours to be with him in court.

"You cannot turn your love like a light on and off," Mary Smith told Barron. "Mine always stayed on. No matter what he did, I was glad to see him."

In April of 2002, Marcus' son Marquis Zyquarius Smith was born in Laurens, South Carolina. His mother was Kendra Scurry, who in May of 2019 filed a letter with the North Carolina Clerk of Superior Court stating that Marcus was the father. Scurry requested that her son be part of any settlement of the lawsuit over Marcus' death. He and Scurry never married, and Marcus never signed the birth certificate.

In 2006, Marcus was charged for unlawful use of a car. A year later, he pleaded guilty to assault and battery. There were other arrests, and time in prison, during which he earned his GED.

In 2009, he moved in with his brother Len in High Point, which is 18 miles from Greensboro and has about one-third the population. A year later, he moved to the city where he later told his sister he wanted to spend the rest of his life.

"He was living in High Point with Len," Mary Smith said. "Somehow or other, I guess he wanted to spread his own wings and go to Greensboro. I don't know what kind of decision made him want to do that, but he did, and was there for seven years. He had girlfriends, friends, whatever. He wasn't sleeping on the street."

During his decade in Greensboro, Marcus had convictions for a variety of misdemeanors, including public intoxication, soliciting alms, misdemeanor larceny, carrying an open container, and resisting a public officer. While he spent a few nights in jail, he did no more prison time and had no pending charges at the time of his death.

A year or two after his arrival in his final city of residence, he started showing up at the IRC, or Interactive Resource Center, a day center for people experiencing homelessness. It became his address of record.

Mary Smith expressed some discomfort with the word "homeless," stating that her son often stayed with friends or girlfriends. Marcus Hyde, an activist with the Homeless Union of Greensboro and former AmeriCorps volunteer at the IRC, explained that the Department of Housing and Urban Development defines a homeless person as "an individual or family who lacks a fixed, regular, and adequate nighttime residence."

Hyde then noted: "This definition practically means that less than half of the people I approached when I volunteered were able to be counted. If you were doubled-up in grandma's basement, or were illegally squatting or staying in a motel, they train the volunteers not to count those people. Hence, HUD estimates Greensboro has about 500–600 people experiencing homelessness, while the Department of Education, which uses a much better definition, counted over 3,000 homeless students last time data was available."

Hyde expressed "complicated feelings" about the word "homeless," but acknowledged that "for all practical purposes, Marcus Smith would meet the definition, as he did not have a stable place where he resided."

"[The IRC] is a safe space with a low-barrier approach, and there's a lot of dignity and trust," said Michelle Kennedy, former executive director of the IRC. "There are a number of resources on site. There's medical care, a computer lab, phones, laundry, showers. It's a place to come during the day to access services that someone might need and it's open to anyone. On a typical day, there are people taking showers, doing their laundry, picking up their mail, or just sitting in the day room because they needed a place to be for a period of time. The main part where you can see people is a large day room, and there's a whole front bay of windows and a really large, open space where folks gather and hang out."

Speaking at Shiloh Baptist Church in December of 2018, Mary Smith praised the IRC and said Marcus loved the place. "He really did. Not only did the police officers take Marcus from us, they took him from the people there. A lot of those guys depended on Marcus for smiles, a haircut, a conversation, a joke. If Marcus had it, you had it."

Mary said she and her husband visited Marcus there as often as they could. "Mostly on the Fourth of July, when we got off work for a week. He would take us all around town. He loved the Water Park. If I brought a thousand dollars with me, I left with 50, because I would spend the rest on him."

Kennedy said Marcus was a fixture at the Center when she became its executive director in 2014, after previously working for two other nonprofits, Los Angeles-based Strategic Actions for a Just Economy and the Greensboro Housing Coalition.

The earliest reporting on Marcus as a human being rather than a fatality was by award-winning journalist Jordan Green, now a staff reporter for *Raw Story*. At the time of Marcus' death, Green was a senior editor at the Greensboro-based alt-weekly *Triad City Beat*. In a September 2018 article for that weekly, Green quoted Tiffany Dumas, volunteer coordinator at the IRC, saying Marcus had become "like family" to both staff and clients. "I have never loved anybody in my life the way I loved him, because he had so much potential. There were so many things that got in his way. He wanted greater for himself and his children."[2]

Dumas told Green that Marcus had a teenage son in South Carolina, a 2-year-old daughter in Greensboro and a 1-year-old in Raleigh (statements by others somewhat contradict that chronology, although not the basic facts of his fatherhood). She also spoke of his parents. "I would talk to his mom and dad; they would come to visit him. He had a very supportive family. He was taught by his father to make better choices."

Like Marcus' parents, Dumas spoke of Marcus' basketball prowess, with the additional detail that he became extremely depressed after being sidelined by a torn ligament in his senior year. She told Green that when Marcus moved to Greensboro, he "didn't want his family to know that he was experiencing homelessness," as he feared it would disappoint his mother. But eventually, his parents learned of his situation.

Dumas also described Marcus cutting hair for other male IRC clients, something he both enjoyed doing and was good at; he became known as "the IRC barber."

She spoke highly of his character.

"Every time I got depressed, he gave me encouragement. He was so intelligent. He treated you with dignity, whether you were gay, straight, or transgender. He was a very inspirational leader in this community. I'm upset because he gave so much to everyone else, but he could never get to the greater for himself."

Mia Dixon, the IRC's fundamental services coordinator, called Marcus "a real gentleman," of whom "anybody who came across him knew he came from a good family." [1]

She remembered him as a welcome presence at the IRC. "Everybody liked Marcus. I don't know many people who didn't. He knew he had some issues. He would talk about it, but he didn't let it define him."

Dixon added that Marcus could become "a different person" under the influence of drugs. "You knew when Marcus hadn't been doing anything and you knew when he did."

She cited an incident from a couple of months before Marcus' death, when he was very agitated and started ranting, although she emphasized that he never became violent. "That was not the norm," said Dixon, who added staff called for an ambulance to get him treatment and he went willingly. The only conflict she could recall anyone at the IRC having with him was when he forgot to sweep up after cutting someone's hair, and then he took her gentle scolding with good grace.

According to Mary Smith, another person her son was particularly fond of at the IRC was its director. "Right before he introduced me to her, Marcus told me that he loved Michelle Kennedy."

Kennedy saw Marcus five days a week for four years and four months, from her first morning on the job in June of 2014 until two days before his death. She described Marcus as "a smart, funny guy who cared a lot about other people," called him "honest, about both good and bad things," and said she and her staff would miss his jokes and the poetry he wrote to express more somber feelings.

"He wasn't perfect, he would have told you that, but none of us are. He was working through some of the harder things in his life, to try to start moving in the right direction. He was a father, and proud of being a father."

Kennedy was present at the birth of Marcus' youngest daughter, as she had been at the pregnancy diagnosis.

"My strongest memory is [the mother] finding out she was pregnant. It was a mixed bag. She was excited to be pregnant, but they were in a pretty tumultuous relationship, so she was nervous about that. But there was a lot of excitement around that pregnancy, all the usual stuff with having a baby. She would always update me when she'd been to a doctor's appointment. She came in the day she had her ultrasound picture and gave me one of her slides. It was overall a happy time as far as she was concerned."

Kennedy said Marcus and the girl's mother were not in contact at the time of the birth, and the woman was not in Greensboro in the months leading up to Marcus' death, as she "was not at a place in her life that she could continue custody."

As for Marcus, Kennedy said he "had struggles with romantic relationships" and "I'd describe him as single when he died."

Kennedy also said she wasn't sure if Marcus had ever seen his youngest daughter in person. "I know that he had seen pictures and videos, but I don't know that he had ever met her. He spoke of her, he talked about all of his kids. He would show baby pictures and talk about how cute they were, the things that every parent does. Talking about who looked like who and things like that."

Marcus suffered from a diagnosed mental illness that produced anxiety, paranoia, and delusions. Like many people with those symptoms, he sometimes self-medicated with drugs.

"Behavioral issues are not a linear thing," said Kennedy. "They happen when they happen. You don't always know when you're going to be triggered, or something is going to throw you into an episode. It shouldn't be hard for anyone to understand that—when you're experiencing real poverty, and also experiencing behavioral health problems—self-medication is a norm. Most people who are housed self-medicate when they have behavioral health issues. The classic example is the mom with three kids who drinks a bottle of wine every evening. She doesn't get held out as an alcoholic. But if a houseless Black man is drinking boot juice because he's having an issue, then he's painted in a completely different light. Whatever happened, and whatever was in his system, is irrelevant."

She called self-medication an increasingly typical response in a state that has gutted its mental health services. "When you dismantle the mental health here and start dumping the responsibility of being mental health crisis responders into the laps of police officers who are not trained in that way, you're opening a Pandora's box. Those officers are there to process criminalization, not to offer therapeutic interventions for someone having a psychological break. When you layer in institutional racism, and issues of poverty, it just gets worse."

Kennedy called it inevitable that people experiencing poverty would seek out any way they could find to temporarily feel better, regardless of whether they were also dealing with mental illness. "A lot of times, that's through street drugs. How long would it take you or I, if we were living on the streets and all that goes along with that, before we would be reaching towards anything that might give us some relief? I just don't think you can judge that."

Kennedy said that Marcus' episodes of mental health crisis varied in duration and frequency. "It wasn't daily or even weekly, but every few months. It probably happened three or four times over the year before he died. If we noticed that things seemed different with him, we would try to intervene at the earliest point. We didn't want him to get to the place where he was in full-blown paranoid anxiety. There were a lot of times where it was caught early on."

While she described the worst instances as resulting from "a combination of his mental health state and whether or not he was self-medicating," she also said his episodes could come without substance abuse.

"There was no real rhyme or reason, and that is common, as it has to do with the ebbs and flows of mental illness."

She described that the worst episodes included a lot of paranoia, general distrust, and an intense feeling of being unsafe.

"There could be anger, but most of it centered on fear for his own safety. Through the years we'd have several of those instances, where he'd be at the IRC and think that somebody was chasing him, and would be extremely panicky, sweaty, nervous, anxious, paranoid. There were times you could de-escalate that, and times we had to call for EMS support. But never in any of my interactions with him was I afraid or was he dangerous. He was a person in crisis."

She was adamant that he did not fit the stereotype of either a homeless person or a mentally ill one.

"His big thing was fashion and the way he looked. That mattered a lot to him."

She said that's how, in a phone conversation with GPD Chief Wayne Scott, she correctly identified the man whom Scott said had suffered "an incident" downtown, although she did not yet know the incident was fatal.

"When I was told what the person who died was wearing, I knew immediately who it was. People have this image in their head of what people experiencing homelessness look like, in terms of how they dress. Marcus would never have been somebody you would have picked out off the street as homeless, because of the way he dressed. He took it really seriously and was big on how his outfits looked. He was never the guy who was going to come in with messed-up clothes. That's not often common with the population we served."

Kennedy will always remember his love of basketball and freestyle (improvisational) rap. "It was so often. When you think of a typical day there, that was kind of part of it, and I mean on a weekly basis. There was no accompaniment, it was straight up spinning rhymes."

This was one of many things he was loved for there. "The IRC is very much a community, so anybody with a talent or skill who was doing it around other folks in the community, they got a lot of support and enjoyment from everybody involved."

The basketball was also a constant.

"We used to have a goal in the front parking lot, or sometimes in the warehouse if it was rainy, and shooting hoops and pickup games were a regular thing, just like you were in a park. He was always part of that. The scene in our lot when there was a pickup game was the same as if you rolled into any city park and saw folks just playing one-on-one, three-on-three or whatever."

The only games that could be played inside the center were checkers and chess. "He always seemed to be around those tables. I don't remember if he actually played much, but he definitely watched and was part of the scene."

I asked her about the last months of Marcus' life, which she called "an interesting time."

"[In the last months] he was working with our staff on getting into Prestige Barber College and was pretty happy about that. It was a transition period that he was excited about, and he was looking forward to what was going to come next."

"He needed to have a little more stability to be able to do it successfully, but he was working on those things. It was hard, but he really, really wanted it and was trying to figure it out. I think he was excited about being able to do that as a career. He was really good at it and it would have been a great path for him."

Kennedy saw him hours before he died.

"I saw him downtown on that Friday night but would have seen him at work the day before. We closed early on Friday because they were blocking off the street for the North Carolina Folk Festival, so Thursday, September 6, would have been the last full day at the IRC before his death. On Friday, he and I saw each other through the downtown crowd, and we threw up our hands and waved at each other, acknowledging each other like folks do."

She was happy to see him happy and didn't think about him again until she got an early morning call from the police chief.

③   "MARCUS, MY NAME IS MARCUS!"

The first nine of his last 18 minutes:
12:40:47 a.m. to 12:49:50 a.m., September 8, 2018

At approximately 40 minutes after midnight, police officers Michael Montalvo and Christopher Bradshaw parked their ATVs near the intersection of Market and Church streets in downtown Greensboro.

Like the other six officers Marcus would encounter that night, Montalvo and Bradshaw are white men, a demographic that, at the time of Marcus' death, represented 63 percent of the force. That year, 418 of Greensboro's 661 sworn officers were white men and 59 were white women. 137 were Black men and 34 were Black women, meaning that 72 percent of the police force was white and 20 percent was Black, in a city where 45 percent of the population was white and 42 percent is Black.

That Friday was opening night of the first North Carolina Folk Festival, a free three-day spin-off from the National Folk Festival held in various US cities since 1934. For the three previous years, the itinerant national fest was in Greensboro, where it featured a definition of "folk" elastic enough to include not only locally born Grammy winner Rhiannon Giddens and Japanese Taiko drum master Seiichi Tanaka, but R&B/Gospel superstar Mavis Staples, hip-hop DJ Grandmaster Flash, and Afrofuturist jazz ensemble Sun Ra Arkestra. One purpose of the touring national festival is to inspire host cities and states to sponsor an annual local festival after the national one moves on. That's what happened here.

In 2015, the National Folk Festival brought over 110,000 people to Greensboro. In 2018, the first North Carolina Folk Fest brought an estimated 150,000. While Friday's festivities officially ended before midnight, hundreds of cars were still exiting city lots well into the early morning.

As part of the Greensboro Police Special Events Team, Montalvo and Bradshaw were patrolling the festival perimeter on their ATVs. Policing special events on the four-wheelers, which can traverse parks and sidewalks as well as streets, is considered special duty, often outside an officer's normal working hours and districts, for which they were paid time and a half. Their shift, and that of the six other officers who soon arrived at the scene, was from 8 p.m. until 5 a.m.

Sergeant Bradshaw was team leader; Corporal Douglas Strader, who would arrive four minutes later in answer to Montalvo's call for assistance, was assistant team leader. A fourth ATV team member, Lee Andrews, pulled up seconds after his partner Strader. The two pairs of officers had cruised the perimeters of the festival's eight stages, which were spread across ten city blocks. In his deposition, Bradshaw described the team's primary task that night as protecting festival property. At the time they encountered Marcus, Bradshaw and Montalvo were patrolling an area about four blocks long and two wide.

At around 12:40 a.m., Montalvo turned right from the eastbound Market Street corridor onto the 100 block of South Church Street, with Bradshaw about 20 yards behind him. While most festival pavilions were several blocks west, on Davie and Elm Streets, Church Street included a major downtown parking deck very near three of those stages.

Two blocks south of that deck, the officers encountered a Black man in a white t-shirt, white pants, and a blue New York Mets cap, a white bookbag swinging from his left hand as he ran back and forth in the middle of the street, his mouth open in shouts they could not hear through helmets and engine noise.

This was Marcus Smith.

In his deposition in the federal civil rights lawsuit over Marcus' death, Montalvo recalled not seeing Smith until passing him. The absence of traffic in the cordoned-off far-right lane allowed him to turn his head and get a better look. Pulling a tight U-turn, he parked his ATV in the closed lane. Bradshaw passed him, turned around, and parked nearby.

Montalvo was hired by the GPD in September of 1992. He was promoted to Police Officer Senior, a rank now known as Police Officer II, in July of 2005. He was promoted to Police Officer Master, the rank below Corporal now known as Police Officer III, in August of 2012. This was his last promotion before he retired in April of 2020, seven months after Marcus Smith's death.

In his deposition conducted in December of 2020 by plaintiff attorney Flint Taylor, Montalvo described himself as 55 years old, 5 feet 9 inches and 178 pounds, with a Bachelor of Arts in criminal justice from Saint John's, an online university in Louisiana. He stated his reason for retiring as having turned 55, the age at which "you start losing your city supplement," meaning his pension.

Bradshaw was hired in January of 2004, promoted to Police Officer II in July of 2006, Police Officer III in April of 2013, Corporal in April of 2015, and Sergeant in April of 2016.

Although Sergeant Bradshaw was senior officer at the scene as well as ATV team leader, he did not give Montalvo or the others any orders. In his November 2020 deposition, he described himself as acting in tandem with the three junior members of the ATV team and the four who would shortly arrive in three patrol cars, rather than as their supervisor.

He gave his age as 39 in November of 2020 and stated he graduated from UNC Wilmington with a Bachelor of Arts in criminal justice. In September of 2018, Bradshaw had been a police officer for 16 years and a sergeant for five.

The body-worn camera (BWC) footage is timestamped at the upper right corner of the frame. Not all the times are in perfect sync. For instance, Marcus says "I'm Marcus, my is name Marcus" at 4:43:32 on Montalvo's video (the first number is four to denote the fourth hour of the shift), but 4:43:52 on Bradshaw's.

12:40:47 a.m.
Montalvo and Bradshaw encounter Marcus Smith.

Montalvo's video begins at 4:40:47, meaning he turned his camera on at approximately 12:40 a.m. after parking his ATV on the curb at 110 South Church Street. Due to buffering, there is no audio for the first 32 seconds, but Marcus is visible about ten feet in front of Montalvo, striding away from him and towards the open lanes on the other side of the orange-and-white-traffic cones and retractable black-and-yellow hazard belts.

Marcus walks towards the barrier, turns around, takes two steps, turns around again, and runs about ten yards south. He ducks under the barrier, does a wide loop, and stands in front of the Church Street entrance of the former Cadillac Service Garage at Church and Market. Moving to the curb, he waits for a white SUV to pass, then runs back across the street towards Montalvo. Montalvo's arm reaches out and lifts the hazard belt. Marcus ducks under it, dropping his bookbag in the process.

"Please sir!" says Marcus.

"C'mon, stay out of traffic," says Montalvo. "Just grab your bag."

"Please help me, sir!" says Marcus.

"Come on over here," replies Montalvo. "Sit down, sit down."

Instead, Marcus runs past him and then past Bradshaw, who has parked his ATV about 50 feet south. After passing Bradshaw, Marcus crosses to the other side of the street and yells "Please sir, gonna kill myself." It's hard to tell if he is addressing Bradshaw or the white car that drives past.

"He's gonna get run over," says Montalvo to Bradshaw.

Bradshaw speaks into his radio. "Did you copy about [inaudible] at Church and Market."

"In reference to a roadblock?" asks the dispatcher.

"In reference to 10-96," replies Bradshaw. 10-96 is code for "mental subject."

"I'm gonna kill myself, man!" shouts Marcus.

"You want an ambulance?" asks Bradshaw.

"Yes sir!" replies Marcus.

Montalvo is also on his radio. "To Lee, Warren, anybody else that's on." Lee is Lee Andrews, the third ATV Officer, who will arrive three

I AIN'T RESISTING

minutes later with his partner, Corporal Douglas Strader. The officer he addressed as Warren would remain some distance away, blocking off and redirecting traffic, and never appears on camera or engages with Marcus.

"Head down to Church and Market," continues Montalvo. "We've got an individual, ah, I'm not sure if he's high or what his deal is, but he's running in traffic. We're trying to contain him."

"No sir, no sir, no sir, no sir," says Marcus, pacing back and forth along the center line.

"C'mon, stay out of traffic, partner," says Montalvo.

"Hey man," says Bradshaw, "what's your name, what's your name, man?"

"Come on over here," says Montalvo to Marcus. "Get on this side."

"They're right here, sir!" shouts Marcus.

The Black male driver of a southbound white SUV pauses to let Marcus cross the street back towards the officers. "Hey man," says the driver, followed by something inaudible. It's unclear whether this is directed at Marcus or the officer.

Montalvo chuckles in response. "Just go slowly, don't run him over."

"Get that man some help," says the driver.

"We're trying," replies Montalvo.

"Slow down, slow down," says Montalvo to the driver of a black compact, as Marcus crosses the street again. While he crosses the street several times between cars, he appears to be somewhat aware of them, and does not pause in front of any.

Marcus ducks under the traffic barrier and approaches Bradshaw at the curb. "Please sir, please sir, they're gonna shoot me, man."

"Hey man, what's your name?" asks Bradshaw.

"Make that call, man!" pleads Marcus, again walking towards Montalvo, who stands on the center line of the street.

"What's your name?" repeats Bradshaw.

"I'm Marcus, my name is Marcus!"

The dispatcher is heard on Bradshaw's radio. "10-32. Can you respond to Church and Market?" 10-32 is code for "units needed". She repeats 10-96, the code for "mental subject," but the rest is garbled.

Marcus drops his backpack, goes down on one knee in front of Montalvo, then jumps back up. "Please sir, please help me, man. Call the ambulance!" He circles Montalvo, then follows him as Montalvo backs away. "We'll call an ambulance," says Montalvo. "We're calling one."

"He right there!" says Marcus.

"Start EMS at 10-40," says Bradshaw on his radio, code for "routine run—no lights, no siren."

Much of the dispatcher's reply is inaudible or drowned in static, but "EMS" and "traffic" can be heard.

"[inaudible] hallucinations," replies Bradshaw.

"I'm right there, man!" says Marcus, turning from Montalvo and crossing to the protected lane towards Bradshaw.

"Alright, man!" says Bradshaw.

"I wanna go, man," says Marcus. "Lock me up."

"Why don't you get out of the road, man?" says Bradshaw.

"Please sir," says Marcus, "please help me, man."

"Just stay there, go ahead and grab a seat," says Montalvo, motioning to the sidewalk. "Just grab it."

"Help me, man!" repeats Marcus, still walking in a circle.

"Stay out of the road, stay out of the road, stay out of the road," says Montalvo. "Stay out of the road, come over here."

"Okay, but y'all wanna get me a [inaudible]" says Marcus, then "Man, take me to jail!"

"We don't want to take you to jail," says Montalvo. "We'll have EMS respond. C'mon over here."

A woman driving a black SUV in the southbound lane slows her vehicle and shouts at Marcus. "Get on the damn sidewalk and go the hell on!"

Marcus runs north and crosses the intersection with Market Street to 100 block of North Church.

"Hey, don't forget his bookbag is right there," says Bradshaw to Montalvo.

"Head down there?" asks Montalvo, pointing at Marcus, now a block north.

"I guess," says Bradshaw. He chuckles, then says the following in a higher-pitched voice with an exaggerated sigh. "He says 'aaaaaaah!'"

"I don't know what's in here, but it's heavy," says Montalvo, carrying the bookbag as he and Bradshaw walk towards their ATVs on the southbound side of the street. Montalvo gets on his ATV, pulls a tight U-turn in the blocked-off lane and rides North.

12:45:03 a.m.
Officers Strader and Andrews arrive.

By this time Corporal Douglas Strader and Police Officer III Lee Andrews have parked their ATVs on the 100 block of North Church Street, across Market Street from where Montalvo and Bradshaw first encountered Marcus. Marcus is now walking in that direction.

Strader had been a GPD officer since January of 2004. He was promoted to Police Officer II in July of 2006, Police Officer III in May of 2013, and Corporal in November of 2016.

In his deposition, Strader described himself has having earned a Regents Bachelor of Arts degree from West Virginia University in Morgantown, where he studied to be an art teacher. He also stated that he left the West Virginia Police Training Academy after one week when he was "22 or 23," due to being homesick and "young and dumb," and that he moved to Greensboro after being hired by the GPD in 2004, when he was 29.

Along with Strader, who was fired in 2020 for an unrelated incident of deadly force described in the epilogue, and the retired Montalvo, Police Officer III Lee Andrews is one of the three officers involved in the death of Marcus Smith who is no longer employed by the City of Greensboro. He was hired January of 2009. He was promoted to Police Officer II in October of 2011 and to Police Officer III in October of 2016, and resigned in December of 2019, a year and three months after his encounter with Marcus Smith.

In Andrews' deposition, given in January of 2021, he stated that he resigned because "my business had started doing extremely well, and financially, it made better sense for me to go that route."

Earlier in the deposition, Andrews said he started that business, a pond management company, in 2012, and that he was 51 at the time of his deposition. He joined the GPD in 2009 and had been an officer for nine years at the time of his resignation. He told plaintiff attorney Taylor that he will receive a partial retirement pension when he turns 55.

Strader's body-worn camera video begins at 12:45:03 a.m., as he rides his ATV south on North Church Street, crossing Market Street and stopping at about 140 feet north of that intersection, at the curb in the cordoned-off far-right lane, beside the parking lot for Battleground Automotive and across the street from Lincoln Financial Group.

As Strader switches off his four-wheeler, Marcus becomes visible running south towards him down the cordoned-off lane. The first 25 seconds of their encounter have no audio, due to buffering.

As Marcus runs, he reaches into his left-side pants pocket with his left hand and pulls out his phone. He will continue to hold the phone and wave it around for the first minute of his encounter with Strader and Andrews.

Marcus stops in front of the ATV, then comes around to the left side and says something to Strader. He puts his hands on the ATV and leans on it, then twists around and momentarily sits in the street with his back to Strader, before standing and waving his arms while speaking to the officer in an agitated manner.

Strader's hands come into view on both sides of the frame as he appears to point or motion to Marcus. The audio comes on as he says "…look, I'm here to protect you."

"Man, take me to the hospital" says Marcus. "They're right there, I can see them, they're going to kill me!"

"Who is?" asks Strader.

"I'm high," says Marcus.

Andrews, who has parked and dismounted a few yards away, walks into view. Marcus turns to face him, circles Andrews, and paces back and forth between the two officers.

Then Marcus either sits or falls, but immediately gets up and resumes his pacing. Several times, he walks away from the two officers for about ten paces, turns on his heel, and walks back to them.

Andrews' camera is not on yet, but the following interaction between him and Marcus can be seen and heard on Strader's video.

"Man, stop, stop, stop," says Andrews.

Marcus walks towards Strader, says, "Man, please, please," then turns and directs a third "please!" to Andrews.

"Tell me what's going on," says Strader to Marcus.

"You've got to talk to us first," says Andrews. Marcus sits in the street and out of the bottom frame of Strader's camera. "What are you on right now?" asks Andrews. This is the first and only time any of the officers will ask him what drugs he is on.

Marcus bounces to his feet, no longer holding his phone. Saying something inaudible, he walks a few yards south, away from the officers. While the entire encounter begins in the 100 block of South Church Street and moves north across Market Street to the 100 block of North Church, Marcus will make multiple short runs south. Sometimes, the officers follow. At other times, they stand and wait for him to come back to them. That happens now.

"Is he on something?" asks Andrews of Strader.

"Yeah, he said he's high on something," replies Strader, as he bends down to pick up Marcus' phone.

Marcus runs to Strader. "My phone, man, you gotta give me my phone!"

"No man," says Strader, "you gotta sit down. Sit down, sit down. Relax."

"No," says Marcus, pacing back and forth in the road a couple of yards from the officers. Then he says either "Man, please take me," or "Man, please help me."

"We will if you'll come over here," says Andrews. "You gotta come over here."

Marcus walks past him towards Strader. "Sit down," repeats Strader.

"Can't sit down," says Marcus, turning away.

By this point, Andrews' camera is on, but there is no audio for the first 35 seconds.

"Relax, sit down. I got you. I'll make sure nobody hurts you," says Strader.

Andrews' audio comes on. He says, "Tell me where you want to go, first." Then, to Strader, "I'm on, by the way."

At this point, Bradshaw and Montalvo catch up to Marcus. Bradshaw pulls onto the sidewalk in front of the auto shop and parks his ATV. Montalvo parks in the cordoned-off curb lane beside him. Marcus runs up to him.

As Marcus approaches Montalvo, he waves his arms over his head and shouts "Help, help!"

"Strader, do you know him?" shouts Bradshaw. "Is he a regular?"

"I got his phone," says Strader, although it's not clear which officer he's addressing.

"Do you know him?" repeats Bradshaw.

Strader shakes his head.

"I didn't know if he was like a regular downtown," says Bradshaw. "We got a patrol coming."

Marcus has been pacing quickly back and forth between the two pairs of officers, which becomes a cluster of four as Bradshaw and Montalvo close the distance between themselves and the other pair.

Andrews reaches out and touches Marcus' shoulder. "Boss man, we'll help, but you got to chill out." Marcus continues pacing and circling.

Andrews turns to Strader with a sigh of frustration. "Let's just 10-26 him." That's the code for "detain." "Otherwise, he's gonna be in the middle of the street."

A grin is visible on Strader's face as he watches Marcus loop around and between the officers.

"He's going to be in the middle of the street," repeats Andrews.

"At this point, he's not hurting himself," replies Strader.

"But he's out in the middle of the street," says Andrews.

"We've got traffic stopped," says Strader.

"Hey boss man, you need to chill out," says Andrews again as Marcus circles back to him.

"He has been literally…" says Montalvo as Marcus walks between Strader and Andrews and continues a few yards south.

"All right, man, hold on," shouts Bradshaw at Marcus. "We got an ambulance coming!"

Marcus turns around and walks towards Montalvo, who holds out Marcus' bookbag. Marcus takes it and paces south, back towards the Market Street intersection.

"Hey, buddy, you want your phone?" asks Strader. Marcus doesn't seem to hear him.

"Is there a contact in there or anything?" asks Montalvo.

"Man, I don't know," says Strader with a chuckle as he watches Marcus run towards the approaching car of Police Officer I Robert Duncan.

12:46:40 a.m.
Officer Duncan arrives.

Duncan, alone in his patrol car, is driving north from South Church Street. He crosses the Market Street intersection and parks in front of the white concrete Lincoln Financial Group building across the street from the auto shop parking lot where the four ATV officers are conferring.

By this time, the GPD is diverting traffic away from the scene, and civilian cars no longer have access to this section of Church Street.

Police Officer I Robert Duncan is the youngest of the eight officers who interacted with Marcus that evening. As indicated by his rank, he is also the least experienced. Yet he would be the officer to make the decision that, according to the Office of the State Medical Examiner, cost Marcus Smith his life.

Duncan was hired in February of 2016 and finished his training in November of that year, a year and months before Marcus' death. In his deposition by Flint Taylor, conducted in February of 2021, Duncan describes himself as 29 years old and born in Ramseur, North Carolina.

He earned a bachelor's degree in English from UNC Greensboro and he did not work in law enforcement prior to being hired by the GPD in 2014. He said he first applied to the GPD in 2014 but did not complete his background testing. "I didn't finish that part of the exam because I had ongoing schoolwork and was in the process of completing my senior year at college."

In 2015, he reapplied and was accepted. He finished his field training in November of 2016, was assigned a patrol car, and began routine patrol on fourth shift, working 8 p.m. to 7 a.m. At the time he met Marcus

Smith, he was 26 years old and had been a Police Officer I for two years and seven months.

When Duncan arrives with his blue light flashing, Marcus runs towards him, waves as if to hail him down, moves aside to let the patrol car pass, and runs after him, yelling "Hey, wait up!" Duncan pulls over in front of Lincoln Financial Group. Marcus runs back to Andrews and Strader.

"Hey, you've got to chill out and we'll work with you," says Andrews. "Okay? Just chill out, chill out!"

Marcus runs back to Duncan's car. "They're fixing to kill me, fixing to kill me!"

Duncan steps out of the car.

"He's just bugging out on something," says Andrews.

12:46:29 a.m.
Officers Lewis and Payne arrive.

Approximately 30 seconds after Duncan parks his vehicle, partners Police Officer II Alfred Lewis and Police Officer II Justin Payne arrive from the opposite direction. Lewis, who is driving, pulls from the southbound into the northbound traffic lane, and parks diagonally opposite Duncan, whose car is parked in the northbound lane in front of Lincoln Financial Group.

Lewis and Payne were hired in July of 2010. Lewis was promoted to Police Officer II in January 2014; Payne, in July of that year. Both were promoted to Police Officer III in January of 2019, four months after Marcus' death.

In his November 2020 deposition, Lewis gave his height and weight as 6 feet 2 inches and his weight as 265 pounds. He stated he applied to the GPD in 2009 but was not selected. Within a few days of his initial rejection, he reapplied and was conditionally accepted upon completion of follow-up testing. He was admitted to the academy in July of 2010, at age of 30, making him 38 when he encountered Marcus Smith.

Lewis told Taylor he earned a Bachelor of Arts in trombone performance from UNC Greensboro, has no law enforcement officers in his family, and has been a friend of Justin Payne, his partner in the Center City Resource Team downtown, since the two went through the academy together. He was assigned to the Center City Resource Team in 2015, which is when he was first assigned a partner. He applied for the rank of Corporal, was not promoted, and has not applied for that promotion since.

In the deposition of Justin Payne conducted in March of 2021, Payne states he is 34 years old and currently a detective assigned to the Street Crimes Unit. He gives his height as 5 feet 9 inches and weight as 170 pounds and states that he joined the GPD at "around 23 or 24 years old." From 2005 to 2009, he attended Greensboro College, where he received a bachelor's degree in history. Greensboro College is a small private institution located just west of downtown Greensboro in College Hill, the same area that contains UNC Greensboro.

The three patrol officers all wear uniform short-sleeved shirts and no headgear. Duncan and Lewis wear long pants, while Payne wears shorts. Duncan, who appears shorter than the others, is stocky, with sandy hair, glasses, and a youthful face. Lewis is taller, with broad shoulders and dark hair. In Lewis' deposition, attorney Taylor repeatedly asked him if he lifts weights, and Lewis responded that he has not done so in a decade, but he is the most powerful looking of the officers. Payne appears slightly shorter, with a lean build and dark hair.

The three patrol car officers (and the fourth one who will arrive in the video described in Chapter 11) are easily distinguished from the four ATV officers standing on the other side of the street, as the latter all wear yellow safety vests and helmets.

Duncan's BWC footage begins with Marcus running towards him as Duncan emerges from his patrol car. "What's going on, boss man," asks Duncan. "What's going on?"

"Please," says Marcus, "they're trying to kill me, gonna kill me." As Duncan responds, "Who?" Marcus runs towards where Lewis and Payne are emerging from their car less than a dozen yards away.

The first 27 seconds of Lewis' footage have no sound and Payne's has none until 36 seconds after that, but on Duncan's video, Marcus can be distantly heard saying, "Please help me, [inaudible] gonna kill me."

Either Lewis or Payne responds, "Whoa, whoa, whoa!" and the other says, "Sit down!"

Marcus strides quickly back to the approaching Duncan and says, "They're trying to kill me! They said they'd kill me!"

"Ain't nobody killed you yet," replies Duncan.

"They're killing me!" repeats Marcus. "I want to go to the hospital. Man, please!"

"You want to go to the hospital," says Duncan. "Okay!"

Bradshaw chuckles as he walks across the street to Lewis and Payne's car. Strader follows. "Relax," he says to Marcus.

"Let us just check you real quick and we can put you in the seat, okay?" says Andrews to Marcus.

Marcus walks towards Lewis and then to the rear left door of Lewis and Payne's car. "Check me on the inside, bro!"

"Come here," says Andrews, "come right here and you can get in."

"Right there in the car," says Payne.

"He's buggin' out on something," says Andrews.

As Marcus paces past Payne, that officer attempts to push him towards the car, but Marcus shakes him off.

Strader approaches Lewis, who is standing inside the open driver's door. "Hey, let him in your back seat."

"Get me in the car, man," says Marcus, pacing around and between the officers.

The back left door of the car is shut, and as Marcus walks towards it, Lewis blocks the way, although this does not appear intentional. This is one of several moments when one officer will tell Marcus to get in the car, but the door isn't open, and another officer is in the way.

Bradshaw walks to the left rear of Lewis' car, and points at the driver's side and tells Marcus, "They're gonna help you right there."

"Let's see if we can get him into a car," says Strader.

Andrews grimaces after Marcus' careening path causes him to bump against the officer. "He's all nasty."

"Let's get him in over there," says Lewis. "We have club dumps coming up." While "club dump" is a slang term for having a bowel movement in

I AIN'T RESISTING

the usually nasty toilet of a crowded night club, in cop speak, it means the time in the early morning when large groups of patrons will be leaving such establishments. It's also the time when fights are most likely to occur.

Andrews points Marcus at the rear door of Lewis' car. "Right here."

Lewis examines his arm where Marcus bumped against him. "Aw, man."

"Has he got blood on him?" asks Andrews.

"Sweat and blood, apparently," says Lewis with a sigh. He reaches into his car for a bottle of hand sanitizer.

"I got EMS coming," says Bradshaw.

Marcus approaches the car door, but now Payne, Strader, and Lewis, distracted by Lewis' distress at having been in contact with Marcus' body fluids, inadvertently block his way. He starts circling them again.

"I just touched him, too" sighs Payne. "I got sweat all over me."

"Oh, my goodness," says Strader.

Marcus stands next to Lewis' car. "Get me in the car, man?"

Lewis points at Duncan's vehicle.

"Let's just see if we can get him into a car," says Strader to Lewis and Duncan, "and get EMS started."

Apparently not having noticed (or ignoring) Lewis' gesture at Duncan's car, Duncan points at Lewis and then at Marcus. "C'mon, man we're just trying to get you in the car right."

"We got a club dump coming up," says Payne to Bradshaw.

"Oh, I know," replies Bradshaw.

Strader waves at Marcus, "C'mon here buddy."

"Wanna go to the hospital?" says Bradshaw.

"Nobody's helping me man," says Marcus, as he runs a few yards south of the officers, then back towards them.

"We're trying to get you to the hospital, man," says Andrews.

"We're just trying to get him somewhere," says Bradshaw.

"We're trying to get you in the car so we can go," shouts Duncan at Marcus. "You're running around in circles, let's go!"

"Is the door unlocked?" says Duncan, pointing at Lewis' car.

"Do you mind taking him?" asks Lewis.

"That's awesome," says Duncan in apparent exasperation at being asked to transport Marcus. "That's great, y'all, thanks." He walks to his car, drives it north about 20 feet past Lewis' vehicle, and parks.

Marcus, still running loops in the street, slips and falls, but quickly gets back up. Watching him, Payne chuckles.

"He down, or stay down?" says Bradshaw.

Duncan gets out of his car and motions to Marcus. "Come on, my man, my door's open and unlocked."

Marcus moves towards Lewis' car.

"No, they ain't gonna take you," says Duncan. "They don't want you. This way."

Marcus reaches for the handle of the passenger side rear door of Lewis' car, but Lewis waves him towards Duncan's.

"Over here, over here, over here," says Lewis, pointing towards Duncan's car.

"Let's go," says Bradshaw.

"Here ya go, here ya go, here ya go," says Payne, clapping his hands.

Bradshaw points at Duncan's car. "You wanna go to the hospital?"

"Right in there, man," says Duncan. "C'mon, let's go." He opens the rear driver's side door for Marcus.

"Let's get you to the hospital," says Strader.

Marcus slips inside. He pleads, "Shut the door."

Andrews leans inside to frisk him. "I'm just making sure nothing's on you, boss man."

"Please shut the door," says Marcus. "Shut the door, shut the door."

"Watch your feet," says Andrews, as Marcus pulls the door shut.

Payne has been listening to the radio in Andrews' car. "Wesley Long is a crime scene right now; they just had two gunshot victims show up there, from Lucky 7."

The city's two general hospitals are Wesley Long and Moses Cone, and Lucky 7 is a club. Payne is indicating that Duncan should take Marcus to Moses Cone, due to Wesley Long being a crime scene after two persons who were shot at the club drove themselves to that hospital.

"No kidding," says Montalvo.

"Whose car is this?" asks Andrews, peering in at Marcus.

"Mine," says Duncan.

"I couldn't check him full," says Andrews, "I checked his legs."

"And his bag," says Montalvo. "We don't know what's in the bag. Somebody had his cell phone. Dude, he was literally jumping in front of cars."

Repeated viewing of the video makes certain this description is inaccurate, though it's understandable Montalvo has that impression. Marcus' distracted mental state clearly put him at risk, and on several occasions before traffic was diverted from the area, he let oncoming cars get close before he moved out of the way, sometimes by only a few feet, but at no point could he be seen jumping in front of them.

"I believed he was gonna tackle us," says Montalvo with a laugh.

"I did, too," said Bradshaw.

Duncan picks up Marcus' bookbag, which has been sitting on the hood of his car and puts in the trunk. The only officer appearing to watch Marcus in the car is Strader.

It is now 49 minutes and 50 seconds after midnight on the morning of September 8, 2018.

4   "THE SUBJECT PASSED AWAY."

When Michelle Kennedy first watched the video of Marcus getting into Duncan's car, she breathed an involuntary sigh of relief.

"I knew how it was going to end, but for just a second there, watching the video, I forgot that, and found myself thinking, *They'll get him to the hospital now, he's going to be okay.* But that's not what happened."

Why the car did not depart for the hospital, how Marcus came out of it again, and what happened to him on the pavement after he emerged, will be described later. But until attorney Graham Holt and Marcus' father George Smith watched the bodycam videos a month after his death, no one other than the eight officers (the last of whom would arrive two minutes after the events described in the previous chapter), two EMTs, and their various superiors would know what happened that morning.

For everyone else, there was only the initial press release and its subsequent updates. All versions of it left out how Marcus died. The first didn't include his name.

Marcus was pronounced dead at Moses Cone Hospital just before 2 a.m. on the morning of September 8, 2018. But to many who have watched the YouTube footage, including George Smith and Graham Holt, he appears to die on the pavement of Church Street at approximately 12:50 a.m., minutes before his unresponsive body is loaded onto the ambulance.

It would be another month before the public knew that, or the real reason he stopped breathing.

"WE ARE TRANSPARENT UP UNTO
5   WHAT THE LAW ALLOWS."

The death of Marcus Smith was not the Greensboro Police Department's first or only racial controversy during the four years and eight months Wayne Scott was chief, nor was it the first covered in the national press.

"I have a difficult decision to make," Greensboro City Manager Jim Westmoreland is quoted as saying in a May 9, 2015, *News & Record* article.[1] Westmoreland called Wayne Scott and Danielle Outlaw "exceptionally qualified" candidates for the position of police chief. Both were deputy chiefs of their respective departments, but one was a locally born white man who had spent over two decades as a Greensboro officer, and the other was a Black woman from California. All 22 previous GPD chiefs were men, most were promoted from within the department, and only three were Black.

In January of 1944, Samuel A. Penn and John L. Montgomery became Greensboro's first Black police officers but were not allowed to arrest white suspects. Defending their hiring, the City Council released a statement that "negro citizens and taxpayers are entitled to the services of negro officers." Greensboro would not have a female police officer until 1972, when Anne Garcia requested a transfer from meter maid to the uniformed patrol division.

Sylvester Daughtry was hired as the city's first Black police chief in 1987, after 17 years on the force. When Daughtry retired 11 years later, he was the last GPD chief to serve more than five years.

In 1998, Robert White became the city's second Black chief. He was also the first chosen via a nationwide search, having previously served 26 years on the Metropolitan Police Department of the District of Columbia.

White was succeeded in 2003 by David Wray, a white GPD veteran who had served 22 years since graduating from the city's Southeast High School and UNC Greensboro. Wray would be chief for only three years and would spend his last seven months defending himself against allegations of racial profiling within his own department.

The "History of the Greensboro Police Department" on the City of Greensboro web page is as brief and uninformative about his departure as it is about the Greensboro Massacre, stating "Wray became embroiled in departmental/city politics regarding his duties and responsibilities, and he resigned in January 2006." In truth, he "resigned" after being locked out of his office by City Manager Mitchell Johnson in what was effectively a termination.

The controversy began when GPD Lieutenant James Hinson discovered a tracking device on his car. Hinson, a veteran Black officer who later served as deputy chief under Wayne Scott, was himself a controversial figure, and he resigned in 2019 after being accused of covering up a sexual assault in a group home he owned, which sheltered at-risk teenagers.

The GPS tracker on then-Lieutenant Hinson's car was placed there by the GPD's Special Intelligence Section, or SIS, a covert unit investigating officers suspected of using their vehicles for personal business. An external investigation would find that SIS took repetitive and "somewhat extraordinary" measures investigating infractions already ruled groundless by Internal Affairs. Soon afterwards, City officials received complaints about a "black book" which white SIS investigators allegedly used to implicate Black officers in various crimes.

City Manager Johnson ordered an investigation of Wray and the SIS unit by outside consultants. Two high-ranking white officers retired immediately. After Chief Wray's resignation, Johnson told the *News & Record* that the five-man SIS unit had pursued "unproven, previously investigated, and unsubstantiated charges against certain African

American officers" and that, "if I was a Black officer, I would certainly feel targeted." Before his resignation, Wray allegedly attempted to hide the "black book" from both investigators and the city manager.

Wray was succeeded by Tim Bellamy, a native of the tiny unincorporated North Carolina community of Hallsboro, who served on the GPD for 26 years before becoming its third Black chief, first on an interim basis following Wray's 2006 resignation, then with "interim" dropped from his title the following year.

Bellamy and his white successor, Ken Miller, each served for four years. Miller's white successor, Wayne Scott, would serve for four years and seven months. In August of 2019, when announcing his upcoming retirement, Scott denied the decision had anything to do with the death of Marcus Smith, but rumors would persist that he, like his controversial (for very different reasons) Deputy Chief Hinson, was forced out. No City official would confirm this, but several stated or implied that Scott's relationship with the City's mayor, city manager and city council had become very hostile in his final months.

The Black ministers and activists who in 2015 unsuccessfully urged City Manager Jim Westmoreland to hire Danielle Outlaw over Scott were glad to see Scott go, but disappointed when former Deputy Chief Brian James was hired to replace him. James is Black, but like his former boss, had spent his entire career in the Greensboro Police Department.

One of the Black ministers who opposed Scott's hiring was Reverend Wesley Morris, senior pastor at Greensboro's Faith Community Church, and later one of the first Greensboro clergy to reach out to the family of Marcus Smith. When asked what he thought when James was chosen to replace Scott, Morris responded by citing one of his favorite texts, Reinhold Niebuhr's *Moral Man and Immoral Society.*

"'You can try to be a good person, but if you're in a culture that's not good, it's hard for you to achieve that goal of goodness.' What we saw with Brian James was the same thing we saw when the city manager ignored those of us who opposed Wayne Scott. Brian James can try to be a good chief of Police, he can have a good heart and make certain strides, but this is a systemic problem. And if you continue to hire from within without changing the structure of the police culture, you'll never solve the problem."

The other Black minister and community leader who reached out to the Smith family at around the same time as Morris was his friend and colleague Reverend Nelson Johnson, co-founder and executive co-director of the Beloved Community Center, of which Morris is the youth and student initiatives coordinator. Morris couldn't remember whether Johnson had been the one who told him about Marcus Smith, or if Morris had been the one who told Johnson. "Back then, we saw each other every day."

In 2015, the same year Greensboro City Council voted 7–2 to install a historical marker calling the Klan-Nazi attack Nelson Johnson had survived a massacre, the city manager hired by that council chose Wayne Scott over Danielle Outlaw as Greensboro's new police chief. Outlaw was later hired in Portland as the first Black woman to head that city's police force, and in 2020, was appointed police commissioner for the city of Philadelphia.

An hour before Scott's formal introduction, the Beloved Community Center held a rally on the City Hall steps condemning his selection. Greensboro City councilwoman Sharon Hightower spoke at the rally. Of the three Black women and two Black men who would serve on council during the controversy over Marcus Smith's death, Hightower was the most outspoken and critical of the GPD.

"It is with a dismayed heart that I stand here," Hightower said at the rally in opposition to Scott's hiring. "I am worried about the process because I was not included. When we are left out, we are counted out."

At the same rally, Nelson Johnson said his opposition to Scott was not personal, but that he was deeply concerned an insider was selected. He cited previous controversies involving the department, including discrimination lawsuits tied to the administration of former Chief David Wray. "It's about the culture, a way of acting in the department."

Seven months after Scott was hired, "The Disproportionate Risks of Driving While Black" was published on the front page of the October 24 *New York Times*, with the subheading "An examination of traffic stops and arrests in Greensboro, N.C." It uncovered wide racial differences in measure after measure of police conduct.[2]

In it, Sharon LaFraniere and Andrew W. Lehren wrote of Greensboro: "Here in North Carolina's third-largest city, officers pulled over African American drivers for traffic violations at a rate far out of proportion with their share of the local driving population. They used their discretion to search black drivers or their cars more than twice as often as white motorists—even though they found drugs and weapons significantly more often when the driver was white. Officers were more likely to stop black drivers for no discernible reason. And they were more likely to use force if the driver was black, even when they did not encounter physical resistance."

Noting that Greensboro's police chief was white, LaFraniere and Lehren quoted Scott as saying, "The way we accomplish our job is through contact, and one of the more common tools we have is stopping cars."

They also quoted elected officials less sanguine about the issue than their new chief: "Some Greensboro officials are indeed worried. In private meetings with Black community leaders, Mayor Nancy Vaughan, who is white, has asked: 'Are we the next Ferguson?' At a recent gathering of hundreds of citizens, she told them, 'We need to have this conversation before it's too late.'"

After citing the Siege of A&T and the Greensboro Massacre, the article quoted the man who may be the most prominent surviving witness to both events.

"The Reverend Nelson Johnson, a civil rights leader here since the 1960s, contends that like Greensboro as a whole, the Police Department 'has a liberal veneer but a reactionary underbelly.'" Johnson is also quoted criticizing the department's "deeply saturated culture that reflects itself in double standards."

It quoted Scott as stating his hope that, one day, the GPD would be allowed to release footage from the cameras all officers had been required to wear since 2013, something prohibited by North Carolina law at the time.

"Chief Scott said he believed that if the state allowed the police to share them, at least with the citizens involved in the encounters, it would help dispel suspicions of racial profiling. 'I am in favor of more transparency,' he said. 'Numbers don't say it all.'" Ironically, three years and three months later, the release of BWC footage of Marcus Smith's death would turn suspicion into outrage.

On November 10, 2015, eight months after the new chief was sworn in and a little less than seven after the *Times* article was published, Scott told City Council that his department would no longer stop drivers for minor infractions like broken headlights, stating "we must make the necessary changes to ensure that the issues created by statistics and perceptions are addressed."

Scott had previously implied that "statistics" might not be the most reliable measure of discrimination. In a profile by Jordan Green in *Triad City Beat*[3] two weeks after Scott took office, Green asked the new chief about racial disparity in policing. Scott called the issue "extremely complex" and "not as simple as comparing statistical data."

"We can say that 'X amount of the population in the city of Greensboro is Caucasian, X amount is African American', and then we say that 'X amount of the arrests are this or this.' And you can look at those numbers and say, 'There's a problem.' And there may be. But reality doesn't play into the socioeconomics; it really doesn't play into who are our suspects in crimes. When you look at simply arrests versus population, you have to look at who are our suspected criminals?"

In 2016, Scott was instrumental in three landmark releases of BWC footage in North Carolina. In May of that year, the City released graphic videos of the killing of Chieu Di Thi Vo, a mentally ill 49-year-old Vietnamese woman, who was shot by GPD officer Timothy Bloch after a 911 caller reported Chieu had been chasing her mother with a knife. As he would later with the Marcus Smith compilation video, Scott preemptively explained the footage, in this case attributing a portion of the video in which only the sky was visible, leaving the most disputed actions obscured, to Bloch pushing up his glasses, on which the camera was mounted.

In September of that year, the City released footage of GPD officer Travis Cole violently beating Dejuan Yourse, a Black man sitting on the

48   I AIN'T RESISTING

front porch of his mother's house, after Yourse told the friend he was talking to on his cellphone that Cole was "harassing me". The footage made the *Washington Post* and Cole resigned from the GPD while under departmental investigation. In 2017, the City released footage of 15-year-old Jose Charles being beaten by Greensboro police during the previous year's Fun Fourth Festival.

These were not the only controversies to occur under Scott's leadership of the department, either before or after the death of Marcus Smith.

In August of 2018, Scott sent the GPD's little-known Civil Emergency Unit, formed in 2012 to help provide security for the Democratic National Convention in Charlotte, to a nighttime rally at UNC Chapel Hill, where anti-racist activists demanding the removal of the "Silent Sam" Confederate monument were met by neo-Confederate counter-protesters from Alamance County's Taking Back Alamance County (ACTBAC NC).

In the resulting confrontation, the visiting GPD officers formed a cordon with their bicycles to allow ACTBAC members and their supporters to reach the toppled monument, and then extracted the neo-Confederates while pushing back against student activists. The Greensboro unit was under the command of GPD Captain Jonathan Franks.

Jordan Green[4] described the Greensboro unit ramming bicycles into anti-racist protesters and freely deploying pepper spray, paraphrasing an unnamed freelance journalist as stating the GPD unit escalated the situation. "I also watched an officer in the unit shove his bike against my colleague, Daniel Hosterman, before ACTBAC even arrived," wrote Green, who continued "Cpt. Franks also pepper-sprayed counterprotesters and journalists as ACTBAC reached the parking lot at the Morehead Planetarium."

In a later article,[5] Green reported that, at the previous evening's meeting of Greensboro City Council, activist Mitch Fryer read aloud from 2015 reporting by Nate Thayer, which described GPD officers Steven Kory Flowers and Robert Finch as control agents for KKK Imperial Wizard Christopher Barker, who became an FBI informant after being implicated in a domestic terrorism plot in 2012.

Fryer reminded Council of the crucial role that Edward Dawson, a Klansman turned informant to the GPD and FBI, played in the Greensboro Massacre, and that Dawson's GPD handlers failed to intervene when he informed them of the planned attack.

"Greensboro already has a dark history with GPD's relationship with the KKK," said Fryer. "We worry that as GPD protects the KKK they are simultaneously tagging people who oppose the KKK with illegal surveillance and creating a chilling effect on people's First Amendment's rights. And we are further concerned that the relationship with Barker has gone past mere protection, enabling the KKK's activity."

Expressing grave concern about the allegation, District 2 representative Goldie Wells, who is Black but typically less prone to criticize the GPD than District 1's Sharon Hightower, called Chief Scott to the podium, where Scott acknowledged that Flowers and Finch were GPD officers but would not confirm that they were control agents for Barker.

"I assure you that our officers—all of our officers—are acting well within the law and to the best outcome of the city of Greensboro," said Scott. "We are a model agency in this state related to our criminal intelligence. And we are transparent up unto what the law allows. We have to maintain certain relationships to keep the people of this city safe."

Background of Chief Wayne Scott

In his deposition, Scott stated he was born in Burlington, North Carolina. The town, 22 miles east of Greensboro, is partially in Guilford County, where Greensboro is the county seat, but mostly in Alamance, the county many anti-racist activists consider ground zero for white supremacy in the North Carolina Piedmont.

Scott was hired as a GPD patrol officer in 1991, when he was 20 years old. At the time, he had a two-year degree in commercial communications from Randolph Community College in Asheboro, North Carolina. After he joined the force, he earned a Bachelor of Arts from John Wesley

University, a small private interdenominational Christian college in High Point, North Carolina, and a Bachelor of Science in management from Liberty University, the private evangelical institution founded in Lynchburg, Virginia, by Jerry Falwell.

In 2007, he was promoted to lieutenant; in 2009, to captain; and in 2012, to assistant police chief. When he was sworn in as chief in March of 2015, he had been a Greensboro police officer for 24 years. He was one of two final candidates for the job, but many Black ministers and anti-racist activists, as well as one city council member, called him the wrong choice.

Wayne Scott's tenure as chief was marked by criticism from his first day in office. At the rally condemning his appointment,[6] Irving Allen, an activist with Black Lives Matter, called the selection of Scott a betrayal of the community.

Nelson Johnson, who had taken part in the selection process as part of a group that interviewed both Scott and Outlaw, also denounced the decision to hire Scott instead of the woman he called the most qualified candidate. "I had hoped that the occasion of selecting a new police chief would have been a fresh start," the *News & Record* quoted Johnson as saying. "This is wrong. There is no point in starting with division."

In his 2019 retrospective on Wayne Scott's five years as GPD Chief,[7] *Triad City Beat* co-publisher Brian Clarey expressed qualified praise for the departing chief.

"A police chief often gets judged by his worst failures," wrote Clarey. "But this much is true: Scott has been the longest-serving chief this century. And compared to his predecessors in that timeframe, he's the best of the lot."

⑥   A DEATH IN CUSTODY

Being in custody is not the same thing as being under arrest. In police terms, a person in custody is under the control of one or more officers, but this can be a temporary condition imposed on that person for their own safety or that of others, whereas arrest indicates that someone has been detained on suspicion or allegations of a crime.

Marcus Smith was never arrested by any of the officers who were in control of him at the time of his death.

In the March 2, 2021, deposition of Wayne Scott, taken one year and three months after his retirement from the Greensboro Police Department, the former chief stated he could not remember who called to inform him a subject had died in custody. When pressed on this subject by plaintiff attorney Flint Taylor, Scott said it was either Lieutenant Dan Knott, the watch commander, or Captain Nathaniel "Trey" Davis, commander of the investigative unit.

"November 30, 2018, Video 18" on the City of Greensboro's YouTube channel is from the dashboard camera of Lieutenant Knott. It begins at 1:46 a.m. with Knott's vehicle facing north and parked outside the crime scene tape on the west side of the 100 block of North Church Street. For most of its 42 minutes, no one is in the car and the loudest audio is the occasional burst of "incoming message" alerts from the dashboard computer. Led Zeppelin's "Black Dog" can be faintly heard on the audio system, as well as garbled scraps of conversation from persons near the vehicle.

At 2:18, Knott is still off-camera, but can be heard getting in the car saying, "You would need to put something in the 24-hour summary," followed by the sound of his door being closed. At 2:20, Knott says, "We got a club dump coming." A few seconds later, he received a phone call and says the following:

"Yes, sir.... Yeah, it would be kind of nice for them to answer their phone. [Chuckles] I mean, there ain't nothing but asphalt out here right now. Yeah, obviously there's a crime scene, but there's not anything, you know, I mean, it's just something that needs to be photographed, I mean, what-have-you, but there's not like evidence out here. I guess that's what I was looking for. But it is what it is, man, unfortunate, but that's the way it goes sometimes. All right, man, all right, bye."

The repeated "man" suggests he was not talking to his chief.

Someone outside the car asks if the camera is on. Knott states he isn't sure and doesn't know how to turn it off. Someone gets in the front passenger seat. A third party outside the car asks, "Is he good to leave?"

"Who's that?" asks Knott.

"Bradshaw," says the person outside the car.

"He needs to stay," replies Knott. "He's a witness."

The video ends at 2:28 a.m.

In Scott's deposition, he stated, "I really don't have a recollection" of when he received the phone call about the custody death. "Were you living in Greensboro?" asked Taylor.

"I lived in Guilford County, just outside the city limits."

Scott living outside the city limits of the municipality he served is typical of white officers, not only in Greensboro and North Carolina, but across the nation. At *FiveThirtyEight*, Nate Silver reported that, based on data from the US Employment and Equal Opportunity Commission and the Census Bureau, in 75 US cities surveyed, "49 percent of black police officers and 47 percent of Hispanic officers live within the city limits. But just 35 percent of white police officers do."

Taylor then asked Scott, "What were you told when you were reached by whomever it was that told you that there had been a death in custody?"

I AIN'T RESISTING

"Just very few details, typically," replied Scott. "The fact that we had a—someone who had passed away at the hospital after being placed in custody by us. The fact that the officers were not injured. And they were in the process of locking down the scene, and our detective division was coming out."

Scott then stated he got dressed and drove into town in his police vehicle to "assess the situation for myself."

He also called Police Attorney Polly Sizemore and Deputy Chief Brian James, who would replace Scott as GPD chief after Scott's retirement at the beginning of 2020, to "make sure we have our investigative folks on the scene."

Taylor asked Scott if, when he called Deputy Chief James, he was aware that the officers involved in the custody death were part of the patrol division, which meant they were under the command of Deputy Chief James.

Scott replied, "I may have misunderstood you," as he could not recall calling Deputy Chief James, but had instead called another deputy chief, James Hinson, who was not in command of the patrol division (four months before this deposition, Hinson, who had been predicted to succeed Scott as chief, retired following allegations that an employee at a group home owned by him sexually assaulted a teenager there).

"I don't recall if I called Chief James or any of the other deputy chiefs. My mistake. Sometimes, with his [James Hinson's] first name being James, and his [Brian James'] last name being James, it could be confusing, so my apologies."

Taylor then asked Scott when he first talked about the death of Marcus Smith with Deputy Chief Brian James.

"I can't recall exactly. It would have been before Monday. Probably the following—sometime on Sunday or Sunday morning, just to notify him that I was placing some of his officers on administrative duty."

While he could not recall the exact order of events on the early morning of September 8, he said, "I went by the scene and spoke to the watch commander and the Criminal Investigation Department (CID) commander. I went to the hospital and spoke with the officers at some point, and, of course, I went by the police department before I went home for the day."

Scott also said he watched "some small segments" of the BWC footage with Captain Teresa Biffle, who was then the head of the Professional Standards Division, and who in June of 2022, became interim chief, replacing Brian James, who retired in April of 2022.

Scott told Taylor that what he and Biffle watched "was a single camera view," and he could not recall which officer's camera it was from.

"What is your best recollection of it?" asked Taylor.

"I can't say with any certainty," said Scott. "I wouldn't want to testify to that."

He watched more of the videos when he arrived at the police station "in the wee hours of the morning," with Captain Biffle and a third officer whose name he could not recall.

The public information officer whose name would be included on the press release announcing the death of an initially unnamed man in custody was Ron Glenn, a civilian employee of the department. Scott said Glenn was not available that morning.

"He had went out of town and made me aware he was going to be out of town, and Captain Biffle was filling in for him."

Biffle then prepared a press release under Scott's direction, released early that morning with the absent Ron Glenn listed as the departmental contact, and with the name of the man who died in custody not listed at all.

Nowhere in Scott's deposition does the former chief mention Michelle Kennedy, the city council member and executive director of the Interactive Resource Center. According to Kennedy, she was the one who told Scott the name of the man who died that morning.

"During the overnight hours, I got a phone call from Wayne Scott, then the Greensboro chief of police," said Kennedy. "I was a [Council] member at the time. Chief Scott called and said there had been an incident and he believed the person was someone experiencing homelessness, who didn't seem to have an ID that matched their identity. I don't know what made him think it was someone experiencing homelessness, and we didn't talk about that, but it was probably what he had on him, a bus pass and an ID that didn't match [each other]."

Kennedy could not recall what name was on the city bus pass, but it was not the same name that was on the ID that listed his address as that of the IRC. Like many of the Center's homeless clients, he had an ID listing it as his mailing address.

"I asked if he could give me some description. He started describing the person, and that was who I thought it was. It would be a couple more hours before I received confirmation that it was Marcus and that he had died."

In her first conversation with Chief Scott that morning, it wasn't clear to Kennedy that the man involved in an "incident" with the GPD was dead. "I don't remember the exact language, just that something serious was going on and they needed to make an identification."

Then she was awakened by a second call from the chief, who said the subject in custody had died, but didn't offer any further information. Kennedy has never made any secret of her distrust of Scott and dissatisfaction with his job performance, even when he was still chief. In her deposition, she stated she had on multiple occasions unsuccessfully advocated that he be fired for withholding information about Marcus' death.

"I wasn't in any state to go back to sleep. As Council members, we get press releases by phone, and I looked at mine and saw the one about his death. Sometime in the early morning hours, not long after it was made clear that he died, the press release came through. The mayor was the first person I spoke to about it, sometime on Saturday morning. I can't remember which came first, but there was both a text and a phone conversation."

"I remember talking to Chief Scott that Sunday morning, but on a totally different matter," Nancy Vaughan said. "He didn't mention anything about a death in custody. And then a while later, either Michelle called me, or I called her. There were certain Council members I talked to on an almost daily basis, and Michelle was one. I was speaking to her that day and mentioned that I had been on the phone with the chief and she said, 'I assume he told you,' and I said, 'No, he didn't.' She said, 'We're not sure who it was,' as he'd been carrying someone else's bus pass."

According to Vaughan, Kennedy called her back shortly after that initial conversation, and said the person who died in police custody had been identified as Marcus Smith.

"That name meant nothing to me, but it did to her. She told me he had been a frequent guest for the IRC and cut hair there, and that he was due to start at Prestige Barber College, where he intended to get his barbering certification. I don't know if we knew how he died. I believe that I called [City Manager] David Parrish either that day or the next, because I knew he was going to watch the video, and his impression to me was that he thought the police did all they could to help him. After seeing the video, it's hard to understand that statement."

While the city manager saw one or more of the police bodycam videos that weekend, neither Vaughan nor Kennedy would see the footage until almost three months later, when they watched it with District 1 representative Sharon Hightower and several other members of Greensboro City Council.

A couple of days after viewing it, all three women would call the press release stating that Marcus Smith had been "combative" and "collapsed in police custody" a lie. But unlike Kennedy and Hightower, Nancy Vaughan would later walk back her use of that word.

Background of Mayor Nancy Vaughan

Guilford County voting records show that in the 1988 through 2006 elections, Nancy Vaughan was registered as Republican, but switched parties to vote in the May 2008 Democratic Primary.

Vaughan had been a Republican when she served on Greensboro City Council from 1997 until 2001. During those two terms, she represented District 4, currently the seat of Nancy Hoffman, who with at-large representative Marikay Abuzuaiter is arguably one of the two least progressive Democrats on Council. (In 2020, Hoffman and Abuzuaiter voted against apologizing for the Greensboro Massacre; in 2013, *YES! Weekly's* Eric Ginsburg reported that the tirelessly pro-police Abuzuaiter was a confidential informant for the GPD). But when Vaughan ran and won as representative at-large in 2008, she was a Democrat, and has remained one to this day.

Born Nancy Barakat in New Jersey, Vaughan is the daughter of basketball coach Fred Barakat, a former assistant commissioner of the Atlantic Coast Conference.

"My dad, who is not my birth father, was from Damascus. I claim it. He raised me. I'm a little regretful that his family did not keep up the language or the dress. They were Syrian Christians who, when they got here, assimilated with reasonable ease, and I've always been disappointed they didn't preserve more of their Syrian heritage. It's a tough language. My grandmother would say a couple of words, and I could never get the pronunciation right. They only spoke it when they didn't want us to know what they were saying."

In the "About Nancy Vaughan" section of mayornancyvaughan.com, she describes herself as having "always been a political wonk," and writes that some of her earliest memories were of when she was seven years old and polled her schoolmates on whether they supported Humphrey or Nixon in the 1968 election. She also describes how, after her father got a job with ACC, he and her mother moved to Greensboro in 1981 while she was still attending Fairfield University in Connecticut. She did not relocate to the city of which she is now mayor until the early 1990s.

In 1999, two years after she was first elected to City Council, she married Greensboro attorney Don Vaughan, who had served on council from 1991 to 2005. The couple separated in 2017 and are now divorced. In the bio on her website, she explains her hiatus from City Council between 2001 and 2008 as a decision to take time off to raise her daughter.

She was first elected mayor in November of 2013, defeating one-term incumbent Robbie Perkins with a 10-point margin of victory. She was reelected with 87.6 percent of the vote in 2015. For the next two years, she spearheaded the ultimately successful resistance to attempts by the Republican-controlled North Carolina General Assembly to make Greensboro more conservative.

7   A BUBBLE OF BLUE

"It seems like we're always at odds with the state legislature," said Greensboro Mayor Vaughan in a July 2022 interview. "I would say that Greensboro is a bubble of blue in North Carolina. We have a couple of bubbles, but this is definitely one."

Although Greensboro's municipal elections are nonpartisan, conservatives on local social media, who use "Democrat" as a pejorative, put that word in front of her name when they aren't calling her a socialist. In recent years, members of the public speaking at town halls have accused Vaughan and the majority of Council of being shills for wealthy developers, a criticism made not only by many progressives, but libertarians and some conservatives. In the lead-up to the lawsuit over Marcus Smith's death, and even more so during that litigation, Vaughan was condemned by anti-racist activists as a police apologist, particularly after she walked back her statement that the initial press release was a lie. On social media, Vaughan was often mocked for "kowtowing to" or "coddling" those critics. Conservative alt-weekly *The Rhino Times* (now owned by developer Roy Carroll, for whom editor and former publisher John Hammer continues to work) criticized her for having "lost control" of City Council meetings after her critics shouted from the audience, while *The Rhino*'s readers accused her of being either covertly or openly part of "the radical left."

In May of 2020, following the death of George Floyd, a spontaneous protest began in downtown Greensboro and then shut down a section of

Interstate 85. Patrol cars and officers on bicycles observed the event and cleared streets ahead of the march but did not interfere. When it ended on the bridge over the highway, the city sent buses to bring marchers back downtown rather than leaving tired stragglers trudging back along a major thoroughfare after dark.

Conservatives criticized Vaughan for this, especially after a second protest that evening ended in a confrontation with police. While GPD officers in riot gear literally turned their backs on the south side of Elm Street to pepper-spray and tear gas the marchers, vandals broke windows and looted several stores just two blocks behind the police line.

After Vaughan imposed a city-wide curfew, she was criticized by the ACLU of North Carolina, which called the order unconstitutional and overly broad, and expressed concern it would "likely lead to selective law enforcement against communities of color." The GPD arrested and charged several Black protesters who carried firearms, while ignoring members of a white supremacist militia who traveled 50 miles from Stokes County to "guard" Greensboro's businesses, and who commandeered the parking lot of a motorcycle shop on the other end of downtown from the protests, where they were photographed wearing paramilitary gear and brandishing semi-automatic weapons.

Over the next two months, protesters shut down city thoroughfares and marched through several shopping centers with the stated intent of disrupting access to corporate and white-owned businesses beyond the downtown Greensboro area where marches usually occurred. Conservatives called for the GPD to shut down the marches and arrest organizers and blamed both Mayor Vaughan and Police Chief Brian James for not doing so. Some of the most hyperbolic comments came from residents of Alamance County, who wrote that their beloved Sheriff Terry Johnson would not have allowed the "mob" to march through Graham, his county seat.

Twenty-two miles from Greensboro, Graham is ground zero for white supremacy in the 21st century Piedmont, with Sheriff Johnson publicly supporting rallies to "protect" the Confederate monument erected where the Ku Klux Klan lynched Black town constable Wyatt Outlaw in 1870. While Greensboro conservatives have in recent years accused Vaughan of being anti-police their more reactionary Alamance brethren use her city as a cautionary tale of what their county seat might become if Johnson stops arresting "the Black Lives Matter agitators who infest Greensboro and want to infect Graham with the communist plague."

That phrase was used by a Graham resident commenting on the Greensboro marches. Later, he wrote "Greensboro's Black police chief is politically and perhaps literally in bed with its socialist mayor."

Vaughan and James were not friends, and it need hardly be said that she's never been a socialist. She wasn't even always a Democrat, and some of her more progressive critics have in recent years called her a Democrat in name only. Conservatives disagree. Vaughan offered the following anecdote about one incident in which she and the City were at odds with the Republican state legislature.

"One of the most well-known ones was when former City Council member Trudy Wade, later a state senator, decided to come in and redistrict us. She came up with a couple of different plans, both partisan and non-partisan, mayor who could vote vs. non-voting mayor. We went at it pretty hard with the state legislature, and ultimately, we sued, and won. People wanted us to stay with our 3/5/4/1 form of government, meaning nine candidates and you can vote for five—the mayor, three at-large ones, and the one for your district. That was really the biggest thing we went up against."

Vaughan was referring to how, after Republicans won a majority in the North Carolina General Assembly, they attempted to redistrict the state's larger cities hoping to gerrymander power at the local level. At that time, 55 percent of the city's voters were Democrats and approximately 20 percent were Republicans, which meant Council was dominated by moderate and progressive Democrats and moderate Republicans, while state government was highly conservative. A law passed by the General Assembly in 2015 was co-written by Trudy Wade, who previously had often been the odd woman out on Greensboro's Democrat-dominated City Council. That legislation modified the structure of government in Greensboro to give that city's Republicans a much better chance at consolidating and controlling municipal power.

"No matter what they did with the maps, they couldn't really engineer something that would guarantee a Republican majority," Vaughan said, "So, Republicans did what they could to reduce the influence of Democrats who were elected by the whole city and make it easier for conservative candidates."

The 2015 law was passed after that year's election and would have greatly changed the next one if it had survived Greensboro's legal challenge, as it did away with the three at-large council seats in favor of eight district ones, making the mayoral election the only one in which the whole city could vote. It also changed district boundaries, lengthened council terms from two years to four, and limited the mayor's ability to cast tie-breaking votes. Eight rather than five district races meant that more conservative candidates could run, with no electoral pressure from parts of the city outside of those districts.

It also meant the structure of Greensboro's City Council would be imposed from the state capitol in Raleigh, with the new law stating that no city-wide referendum could alter its provisions. This was one reason why US District Court Judge Catherine C. Eagles ruled it unconstitutional in April of 2017. If Eagles had not struck down the law, that year's elections would have been very different. One result would have been that Michelle Kennedy, the first openly gay councilmember and at the time considered the most progressive ever, would have been unable to run at-large, as no such position would have existed. Instead, Kennedy could have only run in the district in which she lived, which was more conservative than the city as a whole.

"I think it was a very important decision for the state of North Carolina," Vaughan said. "It reaffirmed the ability of cities to determine their form of government. Importantly, it offered the citizens the ability to have a referendum, to have a voice in what their government looks like. That's something they were trying to do away with here—and if it had been successful, it's something a number of other towns and cities would have seen."

Ironically, a referendum would preserve the least controversial of the changes in Greensboro's electoral structure that had been struck down. In March of 2015, shortly after former council member turned state senator Trudy Wade introduced the bill to alter the city's elections, Greensboro City Council voted unanimously to hold a referendum on whether their terms should be extended from two to four years. That referendum passed, and was the reason why, when Mayor Vaughan was reelected in 2017, she did not have to run for reelection in 2019, the year after Marcus Smith's death.

How Marcus died and the allegations that his death was covered-up would likely have been major issues in a 2019 Greensboro election, and might still have been in November of 2021, when the next election would normally have occurred. However, a new redistricting issue arising from the 2020 census moved that election to the spring of 2022, resulting in the City's mayor and council members effectively serving a term of four years and seven months. By that time, a tentative settlement had been reached in the lawsuit over Marcus' death, and the average number of people speaking at council meetings who accused the City of covering up that death had dwindled from more than 30 to less than six.

A lot would happen before then. The controversy would reach its height in 2019 but did not find much traction in the first month after his death because few yet knew the first press releases describing that death were what Mayor Vaughan would briefly call a lie.

"MY BROTHER'S HEART WEIGHED 470 GRAMS."

During a brief phone conversation sometime between 3:00 and 5:00 a.m. on September 8, 2018, Michelle Kennedy told Chief Wayne Scott the person who died in custody was Marcus, but the identification was not official until that evening. At 8:14 p.m., Deputy Chief Trey Davis emailed Scott: "I have confirmed the ID of the victim through latent prints and photo, and the victim's family has just been notified with the assistance of Laurens, South Carolina Police Department."

Mary Smith recalls being informed about Marcus' death by two Laurens police officers who knocked on the evening of September 8, 2018, approximately 16 hours after her son yelled, "Please, I ain't resisting!" to the Greensboro police officers forcing him onto the pavement.

In a small mercy, she wasn't asked to look at photos of his body. The South Carolina officers were just there to tell Mary her son died that morning.

"Greensboro police had already identified him, and rather than telling us, they called our police department and told them to tell us. And the two Laurens officers who came to our door couldn't tell me and my husband anything but that our son was dead, because that's all GPD told them."

Four years later, Mary couldn't recall the names of the officers who came to her home that evening. "I do remember that one of them was very nice, and seemed upset that he didn't know anything more about it. In fact, he was so nice, I guess he called Greensboro and asked some questions, because he came back a week later, right after we buried

Marcus, and said the Greensboro police told him that my son OD'd. I don't blame him for that lie. He was just telling what he'd been told."

By the time Mary Smith was told Marcus overdosed in custody, at least five people had watched the videos depicting what happened: Captain Teresa Biffle, who wrote the press release stating only that a "suicidal" and "combative" man had "collapsed" in custody and died in the hospital; Chief Wayne Scott, who approved the press release; Deputy Chief Brian James; and City Manager David Parrish. Mayor Nancy Vaughan had not, but nothing in her deposition or public statements suggests she questioned the initial press releases and statements from Chief Scott.

Unlike Vaughan, whom Kim Smith vocally defended from shouted denunciations during a December 2018 press conference at Shiloh Baptist Church, Marcus' sister and mother never stopped calling the press release a lie. Within weeks of Kim telling those angry at Vaughan, "We're not going to attack Nancy; her conscience is going to tell her what to do," both mother and daughter were condemning Greensboro's mayor for being complicit in a cover-up.

And for her silence.

"Greensboro Police Chief Wayne Scott and Mayor Nancy Vaughan did not give us any information as to where his body was," said Mary Smith in 2020. "We had to call every morgue in Greensboro to find him. They told us he died at the hospital. From the bruises on his face in the morgue photo, I thought maybe they'd beaten him. Now I know it was worse than that. They said he stumbled and fell and died in the hospital. That was a complete lie. Being constantly lied to about how your son died is the ultimate betrayal."

On September 12, 2018, Marcus Smith's body was returned to his family by the state medical examiner's office in Raleigh. He was buried in Laurens, South Carolina, the next day. Thirteen months later and a year after Mary and George Smith found out how their son died, they moved from Laurens to the nearby but much larger Greenville.

Laurens had too many memories of their son.

"There was something worse than remembering him there when he was alive," said Mary. "That was the memory of those police ringing our doorbell, to tell us the lie that the Greensboro police told them. The lies that started then and never stopped were the worst thing. I mean, the worst thing besides how they killed him."

The first lie was the initial press release.

"Even Nancy Vaughan called it a lie, for about one day, before she said it wasn't. And before she said that and then changed her mind, she wouldn't tell us anything. Not in that month before we had an attorney, and in the two months afterwards. Here I was trying to find out how my son died, and she didn't even respond."

In her opening statement at the December 4, 2018, meeting of the City Council, Vaughan apologized for not answering those emails and letters. In her deposition, she acknowledged she had no contact with the Smith family in October or November of 2018. She defended this silence by stating that the letters "came from an attorney and should only be responded to by attorneys."

Before those letters, said Mary, there were the unreturned calls. "I kept phoning, trying to find out what happened," said Mary. "Chief Wayne Scott and Mayor Nancy Vaughan wouldn't even speak to me. Nobody could tell us nothing, not until a young man named Mitch Fryer, who worked for Michelle Kennedy at the Interactive Resource Center, told me to get in touch with an attorney named Graham Holt. Mr. Fryer was the one who represented us to Graham. If not for Graham, we might not have ever found out what really happened to my son."

Kim Smith agreed. "It wasn't until October that we found out. Not because Chief Wayne Scott was honest and truthful and called my parents to respect the dead and tell how he really died. We only found that out when we got an attorney who made the City show him and my Dad the bodycam videos, something which nearly killed my Dad. If that viewing wasn't established, it would have been longer. I can't say we would have never known, because later on, his death was ruled a homicide, and that's when everything became public."

"I buried my son with Chief Wayne Scott's lies," said Mary, on the first anniversary of Marcus' death. "I'm never going to forgive him that, and I'm never going to forgive the city government for letting him retire with a pension."

"My brother's heart weighed 470 grams."

Speaking at Shiloh Baptist Church three months after her brother's death and addressing a large group of her family's Greensboro supporters, Kim expressed her sincere gratitude to all those who had gathered to honor Marcus and learn how he died. Then, she spoke with angry irony.

"Thanks to the Greensboro Police Department, I now know that my brother's heart weighed 470 grams. I now know his stomach fat measured up to two centimeters in thickness. I now know his right lung was 1170 grams. I now know his left lung was 1010 grams. His liver weighed 2000 grams. His spleen weighted 120 grams. His right kidney was 210 grams. His left kidney was 210 grams. His brain weighed 1570 grams. So, thank you, Greensboro Police, for letting me know that."

"BEYOND ONE BAD APPLE, EVEN IF
⑨   IT'S IN CHARGE OF THE WHOLE ORCHARD."

The day before her brother's body arrived from the state medical examiner's office in Raleigh, Kim Smith posted on Facebook that his funeral would be held on Thursday, September 13, at Springfield Baptist Church in Laurens, South Carolina. A week later, Reverend Wesley Morris of the Beloved Community Center of Greensboro saw that post. Morris couldn't remember whether he or his mentor and colleague Reverend Nelson Johnson told the other about Marcus Smith. "I'm not sure who first mentioned the subject to who, but Nelson and I had been talking about it before I received a call from Marcus Hyde of the Homeless Union of Greensboro, expressing his concerns about that press release."

The two men named Marcus both spent a lot of time at the IRC in 2018, and Mary Smith would later refer to Marcus Hyde as part of "my Greensboro family," but they never met. According to Michelle Kennedy, when she told Marcus Hyde that the man whom the press release described as having "collapsed" on Church Street was Marcus Smith, Hyde didn't know who that was.

However, his friend and fellow Homeless Union organizer Mitch Fryer did. Fryer worked at the IRC as a member of its PATH (Projects for Assistance in Transition from Homelessness) outreach team for five years. He vividly remembered his boss Kennedy talking about Marcus Smith the Monday morning after Marcus died.

"She came into the office with the PATH team that I was on, the outreach team, which was my job. I'd just transitioned into being a case worker instead of preventive specialist. She came in, seemed enraged, and said she was going to fight her heart out to get justice for Marcus. We had to ask other people how to get contact info for the family, because as a representative of Greensboro, I don't think she was allowed to give that out."

Hyde learned of the death in the late morning or early afternoon after it happened. "On September 8th, I saw the *News & Record* report of the police news release and I posted something on Facebook to the effect of "Why are there so few details…seems suspicious."

Two days later, Michelle Kennedy phoned him while he was driving to the IRC and said she wanted to talk to him about something he had posted to Facebook.

"I get to the IRC and Michelle pulls me and Mitch Fryer aside and tells us that the person killed was Marcus Smith and that we should start asking questions because Michelle got a call from Chief Scott shortly after Marcus was killed and she couldn't tell us what she learned but something bad happened and we should find out what. She further said that she was going to fight to make sure that the truth comes out about what happened and when it comes out that she would fight to hold the police accountable."

The relationship between Kennedy and Hyde would grow increasingly hostile over the next year, and to this day, they remain extremely critical of each other when describing their interactions, although Kennedy, in keeping with her outspoken nature, has expressed her criticisms of Hyde much more bluntly than he has his criticisms of her.

After Hyde left the IRC that Monday, he called Greensboro attorney Graham Holt and retired Greensboro attorney Lewis Pitts to express his concerns about the unanswered questions in Smith's death. He informed both Holt and Pitts that the Homeless Union of Greensboro wanted to reach out to the Smith family.

"Michelle tells me the next day, I believe, that she has been in contact with the Smith family but that she would not give me or Mitch the contact information of the family. Then on Friday, September 14th, I reached out to Kim Smith via Facebook messenger. Over the next couple of days, we arranged a plan for them to speak to Graham and then plan a trip to come up to Greensboro."

"It was that really nice guy who worked at the IRC and knew my son," said Mary Smith when asked how she met Graham Holt. "I think his name was Mitch, and the reason my memory isn't clear on that is that he moved out of Greensboro not long after the autopsy report came in. But he'd worked at the IRC for years, and he knew Marcus well, and was the one who put us in touch with the attorney who watched the videos with my husband, those videos I've never been able to watch myself."

Wesley Morris said the Homeless Union of Greensboro had been trying to reach the Smith family. "I remember this part vividly, that no one had been able to be in touch with them."

Morris couldn't recall whether he learned the name of Marcus Smith's sister from Hyde, Fryer, or someone else at the Homeless Union, but said he found Kim's post about her brother's funeral after doing a Facebook search on her name. Shortly after reading it, Morris responded with the following comment:

"Peace, my name is Wesley Morris. I'm the Pastor of Faith Community Church here in Greensboro. A friend of mine at the IRC passed along your Facebook page so I could reach out. I pray for your family's comfort at what I expect is a difficult time with the loss of your brother. I read a news story about what happened and wanted to reach out if your family needed support to get answers or in any way just to be another place of support to you all at this time. Praying you all God's strength & peace."

Kim Smith replied to Morris via a Facebook message, in which she gave him her phone number. "I called and we talked and during one of the conversations, she put Mary on the line, but I actually got in touch with Kim first. I think it was probably a mixture of all of us getting together that eventually put the family in touch with Graham Holt."

Morris had been skeptical of statements in the City press release and the *News & Record* that the person initially identified only as "subject" in the former and "man" in the latter had either "collapsed in custody," as the press release claimed, or died in the hospital after he "collapsed in traffic," as the initial headline stated. Within a few minutes of talking first to Kim, and then to Mary, he became even more so.

"The first time I talked to the family, they kept saying this doesn't sound right about our son, this doesn't sound like Marcus. That was from the first phone call, in which they took issue with the claim he'd been combative and suicidal. But the first thing that got me was the headline, saying a man had collapsed and died. It was very quickly afterwards that I became aware of things in the City's account that were not true."

While his feelings were partially based on his empathy for the family, they were also fueled by his knowledge of GPD history.

"Talking with folks as a pastor, you listen as deeply as you can, and you try to be faithful to your call to provide the space to grieve, to be angry, to do all those things. But, after talking with them, my spirit just said, something's not right about this, and knowing the history of the Greensboro Police Department in the decades after sit-ins and the Greensboro Massacre; and then, more recently and personally, from the different engagements I've had with them through the Black/Brown Solidarity Project, and just the culture of the police department, which we really confronted through that solidarity work, I knew that the police or the City releasing something to the newspaper doesn't mean that it's the truth. So, I had those two competing things going on, from my having talked to the family and hearing them describe Marcus and his life, and their own feeling; and also knowing the history of Greensboro in matters like this, particularly when there is police engagement with, and violent force used on, people of color."

Morris spoke of Devin and Rufus Scales, Black siblings arrested in 2013 by GPD officer Travis Cole, who charged Rufus Scales with impeding traffic, being intoxicated and disruptive, and resisting a public officer, and cited Devin Scales for impeding traffic. The arrest went viral after a video of it was posted to Facebook.

The October 2015 *New York Times* article cited that arrest in its opening paragraphs, which described Rufus driving his younger brother Devin to a haircut appointment when they were stopped by Cole and Cole's Black partner for driving with an expired plate. When Rufus reached out to restrain Devin from getting out of the car, he was tased and yanked out of the vehicle by Cole, who dragged him face-down across the asphalt, chipping his tooth and splitting his lip, an injury which resulted in five stitches. The charges against the brothers were later dismissed.

Scales filed a civil suit, in which he was represented by Graham Holt. In a press conference at the Beloved Community Center, both Holt and retired civil rights attorney Lewis Pitts, who would later publicly speak many times on behalf of the Smith family, accused Cole of committing perjury by claiming the brothers' car had been blocking traffic.

The city settled with the brothers for $50,000 but admitted no fault. In 2016, Officer Cole made the *Washington Post* when a video of Cole assaulting Dejuan Yourse went viral. Yourse, who is Black, had been sitting on the stoop of his mother's house when Cole questioned what he was doing there. Not satisfied with Yourse's answer, Cole punched him in the face. An Internal Affairs investigation found Cole violated GPD regulations on use of force, courtesy toward the public, arrest, and search and seizure. Cole resigned from the force while the investigation was pending and was never charged with a criminal offense.

"I know Devin and Rufus Scales," said Morris. "I met the family. I was there when his brother was tased in front of a beauty shop. And then the City goes to lawyers and they settle and I just think that Greensboro has such an opportunity to break through and do something different. It could really be a lighthouse for so many other cities if we took the opportunity to do the right thing."

Morris also elaborated on his opposition to the hiring of Wayne Scott as chief.

"Wayne came on the heels of Chief Miller, and the hiring process was protested pretty strongly. There was then, and remains now, a desire on the part of the community to have a chief hired from outside of the culture of the Greensboro Police Department. There was another candidate who was from Ohio, a Black woman, who seemed to trend pretty high in terms of the options, and she wasn't chosen, which seemed a sham. The department had publicized this search, and then chose from within the ranks of the culture, hiring someone who seemed intent on upholding that culture at a great cost, not only to the city's bottom line, but also to the perception of equality and fair practice of the police department in the city. So, ministers such as Dr. Cardes Brown and Reverend Johnson and others took a pretty bold stand on that."

Well before Marcus' death, Morris had been one of many Black community members, organizers, and ministers pushing for the City to create an independent police review board with investigative and subpoena power, as well the authority to impose penalties on officers who violate departmental standards and regulations or are guilty of severe misconduct.

"We still don't have that, and it's very much something we still need."

He then referred to Brian James, the former deputy chief who was hired from within the department after Scott retired in 2020.

"We said we needed an independent police review board with subpoena power. Brian James is not a substitute for that community request. You can't substitute what the community is asking for with a single person." Morris contrasted the lack of community involvement in the City's process of hiring a new police chief with how statewide policies requiring officers to wear bodycams were formulated in Raleigh.

"There were state policies that were drafted around police cameras and who views the footage. That process was community led, it had professors, it had community leaders, it had attorneys, it had impacted people who joined together to review cases."

Before that, there was the 2009 case in which 39 Black officers, including future GPD Chief Brian James, sued the city of Greensboro, white former chief David Wray, and Wray's white second-in-command Randall Brady, for allegedly discriminating against them by directing subordinate officers to include their pictures in photo lineups and pursuing unsubstantiated charges against them because of their race.

"At that time, we were organizing with former police officers who were targeted by the department for termination. They began to serve the community that came with all these cases and started writing up these complaints. We were so effective because we were able to use the language of the department. We had folders of complaints from many community members, which we took to the Department of Justice. We took a busload of 37 folks up to the DOJ to sit around a table with various federal officials hearing all these cases that came out of Greensboro. We learned from back channels that the City was doing everything it could to undermine those efforts, but what we learned about that struggle made the City change what it was doing. That 2009 process helped spur the move for a review board that sat under the City of Greensboro's human relations department, rather than one controlled by the GPD, and 13 years later, we still don't have it."

Like former councilmember (and former IRC director) Michelle Kennedy and current councilmember Sharon Hightower (as well as the Smith family, their attorneys and multiple speakers at city council meetings), Morris believes the press releases inaccurately describing the death of Marcus Smith were part of an intentional cover-up. Like Hightower, and unlike Kennedy, he thinks that it extended beyond former Chief Wayne Scott.

"I really do not understand how it can be put on one person when there is supposed to be oversight of that person, there is supposed to be some level of transparency. When there is a community approaching the City Council every week for months, asking for answers, and to say it is just one chief, or even to say it is just one city manager or council member, that's an unconvincing excuse. As Reverend Johnson likes to say, this is literally a culture problem. So maybe we should define culture a little bit more strongly. It survives mayors, it survives city managers."

Morris said that the problem goes beyond the proverbial bad apple, even if that apple was in charge of the orchard.

"My perspective is that this is scapegoating by putting all the bad onto one person, as if that one bad actor excuses other parties. It doesn't make much sense to me that this could be one person's fault when, at every level, you lie, you make no attempt to correct that lie, and then, when the lie is exposed, there are no consequences for that lie. The chief got to retire with a pension. There was so much secretive movement that, in hindsight, it's unfair to say that all this boils down to the police chief. There's a lot of responsibility to go around. And I think our city will continue to struggle as long as scapegoating is the primary tool that folks take."

Morris repeated a phrase used by Mayor Vaughan in November of 2018, when she called the press release about Marcus' death "obviously a lie." Unlike Vaughan, he still calls it that.

"My take is that it was obviously a lie, and everything that comes after that. All the backtracking, what you say in the middle of a community meeting versus what you say when you're deposed, that's an example of the kind of legalistic confusion that seems to have dominated the City's communications with folks who are concerned about Marcus Smith's death, and it doesn't build trust, which is unfortunate. I would be very concerned about the judgment of anyone who would try to justify that newspaper headline and press release statement, that he simply collapsed in police custody."

Background of Graham Holt

"Had Graham Holt not been available, I don't know if the Smith family would have found representation," said retired civil rights attorney Lewis Pitts.

"There are very few, if any, attorneys in this town who I believe would take a case like this. There are a few who might take it on, but they would be going after a quick settlement rather than attempting to dig out all the facts through litigation. I can't think of anyone else in Greensboro who would have been willing to put out the time and cost it takes in discovery to find out what really went wrong. It was serendipitous not just for the Smith family, but for the larger revelations that came out of discovery."

When Holt was told that Lewis Pitts, Mary Smith, and Kim Smith all said the Smith family would have had serious difficulty finding out what happened to Marcus if he had not taken the case, he looked uncomfortable. When asked what he thought might have happened if he'd not been available, he refused to speculate. He looked even more uncomfortable when asked if he knew of other local attorneys as committed to social justice as he is.

I AIN'T RESISTING

"To me, this has always been the work," said Holt after some consideration. "It's what you're supposed to do if you're an attorney. I took an oath to uphold the Constitution and I'm an officer of the court, so I have first-hand knowledge of all the stuff that goes on. Given my status as an attorney, I think it's my duty under the oath I took to do this kind of work, to seek justice. Because that's what we do. I think I'm doing something very basic to lawyering, which is why I'm wary of this term 'social justice work.'"

When asked if there are other attorneys in Greensboro that do the type of work he does, he thought a while before answering.

"It depends on what kind of work you think I'm doing. There are attorneys who do civil rights litigations, and they do it in different ways. There's plenty of personal injury attorneys that would be willing to file a civil rights lawsuit on a good case, but they get handled differently, depending on who gets it."

Holt was born in Greensboro in 1976, three years before the Greensboro Massacre. Like many who lived here in the decades since, he knows the public narrative that began within days of the attack.

"As happens with all events like this," said Holt, "people's opinions about the massacre were formed before the event even happened, and were based on their own belief systems, personal narratives, the ties to their community, and the broken parts of those communities. They were all going to have a certain view of the event before it even occurred. As with the killing of Fred Hampton, it was doomed to be viewed the way it was."

At the time of the 1985 lawsuit, in which the discovery process revealed the GPD's complicity in the massacre, Holt was nine years old and attending Irving Park Elementary, "back when children from the other side of town were being bussed to my school." The controversy about cross-town busing as a way of desegregating public schools began in 1971 and would continue into the 1990s, when white parents, and many Black ones, pushed for the return to "neighborhood schools." Most of Greensboro's neighborhoods are still either majority-white or majority-Black.

Holt, who is white, attended UNC Greensboro and earned his law degree from North Carolina Central University, a state-supported historically Black university in Durham. At the time of Marcus Smith's death, he had been a practicing attorney for 12 years.

10 "WE COULD SEE HIM TAKE HIS LAST BREATH."

"I read the first press release in the paper and was suspicious about the veracity of it," said Graham Holt about how he first learned of Marcus' death. "It was really short and left out all the important points and seemed like an obvious lie. So, after thinking about that for a couple of days, I talked to Marcus Hyde of the Homeless Union, and discovered he had the same feeling about that press release, and the Homeless Community did, as well. He told me he talked to the family and asked me if I would talk to them. I said sure."

North Carolina enacted legislation in 2016 governing the disclosure and release of recordings from the body-worn cameras (BWCs) of law enforcement officers. The new law stated that such BWC footage could be shown only to a person whose image or voice is in the recording or to that person's personal representative. If the person whose image or voice was recorded died during, or subsequent to, the encounter with police, the videos could be viewed by their immediate family or their attorney following a written request. As is usual with such matters, having an attorney draft the request greatly facilitates the process.

In December of 2021, the law was amended in the cases of BWC footage depicting death or serious injury, so it requires a judge's approval before such footage could be disclosed, and states that the judge could impose any conditions on that disclosure they saw fit, including issuing a gag order against describing what the requesting parties saw on the disclosed footage.

If the 2021 amendment to that statute had been in effect in the fall of 2018, a judge could have theoretically forbidden Holt and George Smith to disclose what they saw on the BWC footage of Marcus Smith's death.

"At the time," said Holt, "I told the Smith family they could watch the video because then, under North Carolina law, family could still watch BWC footage without a judge's order. George Smith and I both had to sign a document stating we would not record what we were to watch in the viewing room of the police station, but nobody told us we couldn't talk about it afterwards. That wouldn't be the case today."

Holt said that, originally, he, George Smith, Mary Smith, Kim Smith, and Marcus' brother Len were all planning to watch it together, but Marcus' siblings were told it could only be viewed by Marcus' parents and attorney.

"I could have just watched it by myself, and I still have mixed feelings about George watching it with me. We all talked about it and George and I agreed that someone from the family should see it, as they had just met me. Mary was going to watch it with us, but at the last minute decided not to. I'm glad she did."

"I was going to watch it with Graham, but God told me not to," said Mary. "Then my husband George said he would and doing that almost killed him."

George Smith still can't speak about the video without getting emotional and stopping after a few words.

"My dad took the hardest hit," said Kim Smith. "He had to have stomach surgery. He had to have a Pacemaker put in. Up until my brother's passing, he'd been working 12-hour shifts, but he couldn't work at all after watching it."

Graham Holt recalled the conversation with the family as they stood in the public square outside the Greensboro police station.

"Mary said, 'I can't watch this,' and we all said 'yeah, you're not.' They took us in this little room with a TV screen and a remote control on a table. Officers came in and had us sign stuff, and we had to check our phones into a locker. There was a whole bunch of video files. I had my legal pad to take as many notes as I possibly could."

Holt said both he and George were overwhelmed by the number of video files. "I suggested to George we just start going through them, and that I might skip around during sections when Marcus wasn't on screen. I don't know how long it took till we got to one, but as soon as we saw Marcus, we just let it play. And then we saw them put him in the car, take him out of the car, and put him on the ground."

That video did not give a clear view of what the officers did next. George could see his son being handcuffed face down on the pavement, but what was the strap that one officer handed to another, and why was it being wrapped around Marcus' ankles attached to his handcuffs?

"That first angle wasn't that good," said Holt, "but I could tell they had his arms behind his back, and George goes 'what is that?' and paused it and rewound. We watched it again and could see that they tied him up, and I said, "It looks like they hog-tied him.' We could see his face when he died, and George said, 'He's dead.' We could see him take his last breath."

The two men didn't watch all the videos, but viewed parts of several more until they couldn't take it anymore.

"We needed to get out of there," said Holt. "We hadn't known what we were going to see, and this man beside me had just watched his son die."

They rejoined the rest of the family outside, with nobody speaking until they were well away from the police station. It was a while before the words came.

"I told the family that I wasn't sure what to do yet, because it looked like they killed him, but I wasn't sure how, wasn't sure what happened yet. I told them I just need this afternoon to figure out what happened, and said I'll call you later today and we'll go from there. They said thank you and went back to South Carolina."

The Community Responds

11 "THIS IS NOT GONNA TURN OUT GOOD."

12:50:15 a.m. to 12:50:41 a.m.
Marcus is in Duncan's patrol car.

At 12:50:15 a.m. on Andrews' camera, Marcus is visible in the back seat. Shifting his weight and fidgeting, he fumbles with the interior door handle and armrest, then tries to open the door in an apparent attempt to exit the car he entered two minutes earlier.

"Hey, boss man," says Andrews. "We're getting ready to take you. That door won't open."

The window is partially down. Marcus reaches through the gap and grips the glass.

"You said you wanted to go," says Andrews. "So, we're getting ready to take you. Watch your hands."

"Watch my window, man," says Duncan.

Strader shines his flashlight on Marcus. "EMS is coming?" he asks.

"Well, they're 10-40," says Bradshaw, using the code for a silent approach without siren or flashing lights.

"He's gonna break the window," says Strader.

"This is not gonna turn out good," says Montalvo.

Payne walks past Strader and peers at Marcus through the rear passenger-side window.

Payne's previous video ended at the timestamp of 12:49:38. His second one begins at 12:51:30, but with no audio until 30 seconds later. Bradshaw's first video ended at 12:49:37 and his second one does not start until 12:54:26, after Marcus has emerged from the car and is immediately taken to the pavement. While the actions of Bradshaw and Payne can mostly be seen on the videos of the other officers during that interval, they are often too far from the cameras to be heard.

Someone, apparently noticing the approaching ambulance, says, "There they are." As it's not said by any of the officers whose cameras were operating and recording sound, the speaker appears to be either Payne or Bradshaw.

"This is excited delirium right here," says either Payne or Bradshaw.

"I'm high, they're killing me!" the other off-camera officer says in a theatrically shrill voice, apparently mimicking Marcus. In his deposition, Montalvo identified Bradshaw as the speaker, but did not agree with attorney Flint Taylor's characterization of Bradshaw's tone as mocking Marcus' distress.

"Then he said he's gonna kill himself," says Montalvo.

There is a loud thump from inside the car.

"Whoa!" says Montalvo.

Marcus can be seen slapping the window with the flat of his hand. He appears to be trying to get the attention of the officers. His mouth is moving, but their cameras do not pick up whatever he might be saying.

"Oh, he's gonna go through it, watch your eyes!" shouts Montalvo.

Marcus can be seen staring at, then rattling, his door handle.

"He's flipping, dude," says Montalvo.

Marcus lies back in the seat. "There he goes," says Montalvo. "He's gonna start kicking now."

"He's gonna break it," says Andrews.

"Is he kicking it?" asks the officer who might be Bradshaw.

"He's hitting it with his hands," replies Andrews, who then turns to Duncan. "Notify the hospital you got one coming. 10-96 [mental subject]. Probably gonna need to be geodoned." Geodon is a brand name of Ziprasidone, an anti-psychotic used to treat schizophrenia.

Duncan speaks into his radio. "We've got one experiencing excited delirium, he's gonna need to go to the hospital, I'm gonna be 10-76 [Guilford County 10-code for "en route"]. I don't think EMS transport is gonna be appropriate."

"Excited delirium," sometimes called "agitated delirium," is a term often used by law enforcement officers but not recognized by the American Medical Association, the World Health Organization, or the American Academy of Emergency Medicine. A December 2020 policy document by the American Psychological Association's Council on Psychiatry and Law states that the concept "has been invoked in a number of cases to explain or justify injury or death to individuals in police custody, and the term excited delirium is disproportionately applied to Black men in police custody."

Raising his hand to shield his eyes from the flashing lights, Lewis steps up to the window to peer in at Marcus. Every officer who looks through the glass while Marcus is in the car either shades his own eyes in response to the strobing light or shines a flashlight directly into Marcus' face, as Strader did earlier, and Lewis does now. Leaning over the window, Lewis shines his light on Marcus for 50 seconds. Grimacing, Marcus squints, then flinches away.

"I know this is something cops regularly do when they have a subject in the back seat of a patrol car," said Graham Holt, "and it can definitely make the person in custody agitated even when they're not having a mental health crisis, but what I saw on that video seemed more like lack of training and perhaps casual indifference rather than malice."

On Andrews' video, Marcus can be seen trying to open the door.

"He's on something big time," says Andrews.

There is another thump from inside the car. "Do not kick it!" shouts Andrews. There is no camera view of Marcus at this moment, but the noise is more like a loud slap than someone kicking a window while wearing shoes.

EMS arrives and Marcus emerges from the patrol car

Paramedic Ashley Abbott and Emergency Medical Technician Dylan Alling emerge from the ambulance, which appears to be parked about 60 feet away.

Guilford County EMS do not wear video cameras. Paramedic Abbott (a paramedic can perform more complex procedures than an EMT) is a short woman with straight blonde shoulder-length hair parted slightly to the right. EMT Alling is slightly taller and has curly dark hair. Like the officers, the EMS responders are white.

Strader walks around the rear of Duncan's car and towards Abbott. "This guy's high on something," he says to her. "He was jumping out in front of traffic, he won't stay still, ah, right now we got him, he's scared somebody's trying to kill him, so we got him into the back of a car but he's wanting to get out of the car."

"He a Black guy?" asks Abbott.

Strader replies, "Yeah."

Abbott approaches the rear passenger window and glances briefly into the car. Alling talks to Lewis, but what he says is not audible. Abbott says something that seems to indicate previous familiarity with Marcus. The exchange is very muffled, but at one point she says what sounds like "I know this guy" and "He says the same thing every time, somebody is trying to kill him."

In his deposition, Montalvo said that Abbott described Marcus as a "frequent flyer," meaning a patient she had worked with on multiple occasions in the past. In Strader's deposition, plaintiff attorney Taylor asked him, "Did she tell you that she had dealings with him in the past?" to which Strader replied, "No, but I felt that was why she asked me [if he was Black]." Taylor then asked Strader to elaborate on why he thought Abbott was familiar with Marcus, but Strader's response is redacted.

"They're 10-23," says Duncan into his radio, meaning EMS has arrived on scene.

Duncan, who has turned off his radio, says, "Probably ought to RIPP hobble him" to the other officers. "So that he doesn't bust..."

I AIN'T RESISTING

Explanatory Interlude:
The RIPP Hobble

A RIPP Hobble is a device from RIPP Restraints International, Inc., a company created in 1987 to design, manufacture, and market restraints to law enforcement agencies. It consists of a strap that is placed around the ankles of a person in custody to bind their feet. The other end of the strap contains a hook that can be attached to the person's handcuffs once their wrists have been fastened together behind their back. When the person is restrained face down, the Hobble can be tightened to bring the person's feet off the ground and into close proximity with their wrists near the small of their back, elevating their calves, knees and shoulders, and concentrating their weight on their chest and stomach.

Restraining a person in this manner is colloquially known as "hog-tying."

The RIPP Hobble was issued to all GPD officers at the time it was used on Marcus but was discontinued during the controversy over his death. 21st-century law enforcement agencies typically refer to putting a subject in this position as "prone restraint" or "maximum/maximal restraint." In their depositions, Chief Wayne Scott and his Deputy Chief and successor Brian James claimed unfamiliarity with the term "hog-tying." The 2020 discovery conducted by attorneys for the Smith family found that "hog-tie" was used multiple times in a GPD training document regarding the RIPP Hobble.

There is also an established history of the term being used by both law enforcement officers and their supporters. A 2008 article from Americans for Effective Law Enforcement, an advocacy organization for "law-abiding citizens" and "professional law enforcement," defines "hogtying" as "placing the suspect in a prone position with his or her hands secured by handcuffs, and legs held together with restraints. The hand and leg restraints are then connected, resulting in the slight elevation of the suspect's upper and lower body."

The dangers of applying this restraint are described in a 1995 bulletin from the National Law Enforcement and Technology Center (NLETC), a program of the National Institute of Justice, which is part of the Office of Justice Programs (OJP) branch of the United States Department of Justice. The article defines "positional asphyxia" as "death as a result of body position that interferes with one's ability to breathe—as it occurs within a confrontational situation involving law enforcement officers." It offers this information "to help officers recognize factors contributing to this phenomenon and, therefore, enable them to respond in a way that will ensure the subject's safety and minimize risk of death," recommending that officers "avoid the use of maximally prone restraint techniques (e.g., hogtying)." It also states, "As soon as the suspect is handcuffed, get him off his stomach."

"RIPP Hobble Usage and Application," a PowerPoint slideshow instructing officers on how to safely use the device, created by the GPD in 2011 and used until 2019, stated that a subject's legs should be subjected to "no less than 90-degree bend." The accompanying graphic makes it clear that, when the prone subject's ankles and feet are pulled towards his or her hips by the tightened hobble or pushed in that direction by the officers applying it, their lower legs, ankles, and feet should come no closer to their hips, buttocks, and thighs than at right angles.

Chief Wayne Scott would later claim Marcus was restrained in this manner at the request of EMS. Actually, it was Robert Duncan, the youngest and least experienced officer on the scene, who proposed using it before he talked to Abbott or Alling. Duncan had been on the force for two years and seven months at the time he suggested hogtying Marcus. Neither Sergeant Bradshaw nor Corporal Strader voiced any objection.

12:51:31 a.m. to 12:51:59 a.m.
Marcus is released from the patrol car and taken to the pavement.

As Duncan suggests using the restraint, Marcus can be glimpsed sitting upright and trying to work the inside door handle, still grimacing at the bright light directed at his face from a few feet away.

"We definitely need to RIPP Hobble him, so he doesn't bust my window and fly out on the way to the hospital," says Duncan.

"Is anybody willing to help me do that?"

Marcus again flinches away from the light and scoots backwards in his seat. He lies on his back and places his feet on the window glass.

"Don't kick that window, boss man," warns Andrews.

"That's what I was afraid of," says Strader.

"If he's going with us, he'll have to be restrained," says Abbott to Lewis.

"No," replies Duncan, "I just told them that we're not taking him in your truck because..."

"Last time, they wouldn't send me an officer," says Abbott.

As they are saying this, Lewis opens the door of the car.

Marcus quickly emerges. The imposing Lewis, 40 pounds heavier and roughly three inches taller than Marcus, steps in as if intending to push him back, but then moves to the right and out of the way.

Duncan either steps forward to block Marcus, or Marcus bumps into Duncan. There's no good view of their impact on the other cameras and Duncan's turns off when they collide. It will not be turned on again until Duncan is in his patrol car following the ambulance.

In his February 2021 deposition of Robert Duncan, Flint Taylor asks the officer why he left Marcus in his car for several minutes rather than driving him to the hospital as soon as he got in the back seat.

"I was interrupted in the process," says Duncan.

"And that's because he started to thrash around and hit the window, among other things," says Taylor. "Is that right?"

"Yes, sir," says Duncan. There is then a 30-line redaction before Taylor asks, "Well, specifically in terms of his becoming paranoid and expecting that you would leave immediately, is that correct?"

"I think he was paranoid the whole time," replies Duncan. He also states that, while he was "fearful" that Marcus might break the glass with a kick, "by the time we opened the door, he had not kicked the window yet."

Duncan also tells Taylor he can't recall who opened the door. Taylor says, "And you and Officer Andrews escorted him to the ground, correct?"

"Yes, sir," replies Duncan.

In Montalvo's deposition, he states Marcus emerged from the car door and "stumbled on the ground, and Officer Duncan just sort of, like, braced him as he was falling to the ground."

At 12:51:52 of "November 30, 2018 video 1," which is from the body-worn camera of Officer Andrews, Duncan can be seen grabbing Marcus from behind and encircling Marcus' waist with his arms. The officer and the man he is clutching move to the right and down, and then are out of the frame. At 12:51:58, Marcus is visible on his knees, yelling, "I ain't resisting!" as multiple officers force him down on his back and then roll him over onto his stomach.

12:52:00 a.m. to 12:54:39 a.m.
Officer Jordan Bailey arrives and joins officers restraining Marcus.

At around 12:52 a.m., Jordan Bailey arrives at the scene in his patrol car. Like the other seven officers, Bailey is white. He was 28 in the fall of 2018, making him the second youngest. Although Bailey had joined the downtown patrol more recently than Police Officer I Duncan, he held the higher rank of Police Officer II.

In his December 2020 deposition, Bailey gave his height as 5 feet and 9 inches and his weight as 150 pounds. Plaintiff attorneys did not ask every defendant how tall and heavy they were, but Lewis was 6 feet 2 inches and 270 pounds, Montalvo was 5 feet 9 inches and 178; and Payne was 5 feet 9 inches and 170.

Like three of the other officers on scene, Bailey earned a university degree from a four-year program, having majored in biological sciences at North Carolina State University in Raleigh.

Since 2016, Bailey had patrolled downtown Greensboro as part of the Central Community Response Team, which Duncan, Andrews, Payne, and Lewis also belonged to. He had far more extensive medical training than the other seven officers on scene, having worked as an emergency medical technician for Guilford County EMS in 2013-14, where paramedic Ashley Abbott was a co-worker. Despite his training, he expressed no concern about the restraint applied to Marcus soon after Bailey got out of his car. Nor did paramedic Abbott or EMT Dylan Alling, who impassively looked on even when Marcus evidenced signs of respiratory distress.

In his deposition, Bailey stated that he parked about 30 feet away from Duncan's patrol car as Duncan took Marcus to the pavement. After getting out of his car, Bailey activated his body-worn camera, put on his search gloves, and joined the officers rolling Marcus over onto his stomach. As he did so, the distressed Black man being rolled face down by five white officers yelled, "I ain't resisting."

Sergeant Duncan attempts to push Marcus onto his stomach.

"Please don't do that!" cries Marcus. "I ain't resisting!"

Duncan, Andrews, and Montalvo attempt to roll Marcus onto his stomach, but are not immediately able to do so, due to Payne twisting Marcus' legs in the opposite direction, which causes Marcus to cry out in pain.

"Can you [inaudible] me?" moans Marcus.

"Watch yourself," says Strader. "Somebody's got blood on him."

"Roll him the other way," says Andrews to Payne. Payne does so.

"There you go," says Andrews, holding Marcus' left hand with both of his.

"Help!" cries Marcus.

Payne, Andrews, and Duncan are joined by Bailey. The four hold Marcus face down on the pavement. Standing next to them, Strader says "keep him on his stomach." Then, to Marcus, Strader says "put your other hand behind you."

"Give us your other hand behind your back," says Duncan. Marcus answers with a muffled groan. "Relax," says Strader, "we're trying to help you."

"Can you help me?" pleads Marcus.

"You got the cuffs?" asks Andrews.

"Well, I did," says Duncan.

"They're right there," says Andrews.

"This is not gonna turn out good."   95

For the next 35 seconds, Duncan, Andrews, Montalvo, Payne, and Bailey press Marcus to the pavement as they handcuff his hands behind his back. Marcus groans, cries out, and writhes. His movements appear to be spontaneous and sometimes involuntary reactions to pain and fear.

Marcus appears to have difficulty breathing. He starts wheezing and cries out in pain. The officers do not appear to notice and take no steps to determine if Marcus is in medical distress.

In one excerpt from her deposition, Paramedic Abbot tells attorney Flint Taylor she was not close enough to Marcus to hear him struggling for breath, but that, on the video, "it sounds like he's in respiratory distress." She then tells Taylor that it's only audible on the video "because it's right next to a bodycam," but if she had been able to hear it at the scene, "I would have sat him up and gotten oxygen on him and moved him to my unit" and "it's the first thing you do if somebody can't breathe, sit them up."

Montalvo holds Marcus' right shoulder and arm. Duncan holds Marcus' left arm and handcuffs his wrists together behind his back, then stands up.

"He's secure," says Duncan, looking down at his own bare hands.

"He's bleeding somewhere," says Andrews.

"Mostly sweat," says Strader, "but Al [Lewis] got some blood on him."

Duncan reaches into his own pocket and produces the RIPP Hobble.

"In the Hobble?" asks Strader.

"Let's just go ahead and do this and you guys can help me carry him to the truck," says Duncan. "I know you guys aren't trying to get all involved."

"Nah, we're good," says Andrews. "Bring him up."

"I'm [inaudible] here," moans Marcus.

"Do you want him restrained on my truck?" asks Abbott.

"I'll ride with you," says Duncan.

"That would be the best thing," says Strader.

Marcus emits a loud and protracted groan.

Duncan stands up and holds out the RIPP Hobble. Montalvo takes it and slips it over Marcus' feet and tightens it around his ankles.

Payne pushes Marcus' legs toward his buttocks. Marcus shakes and attempts to extend his legs. Payne straddles Marcus' legs and forcibly bends them back towards Marcus' buttocks over Payne's own leg. Marcus cries out, groans, and extends his legs again.

Possibly recognizing that Payne is bending Marcus' legs in an unnatural manner, Montalvo says "Get behind his feet the other way."

Payne grasps Marcus' right foot with both hands and shoves Marcus' legs and feet toward his buttocks with considerable force, bending Marcus' legs at an angle much less than 90 degrees from his body, a position a GPD training document warned against.

Meanwhile, Andrews forcibly presses his right knee down into the middle of Marcus' back and holds it there for 14 seconds while Marcus gasps and moans.

Payne forces Marcus' feet and legs toward his buttocks while Andrews pushes his knee into Marcus' back and Montalvo tightens the Hobble, attaching it to Marcus' handcuffed hands.

Lewis stands behind Payne and presses his foot against one of Marcus' shins. Payne pushes Marcus' feet down until they touch his handcuffed hands at the small of his back.

As Payne shoves Marcus' legs toward his buttocks, Marcus moans, groans, and gasps, something Abbott would also acknowledge in her deposition, in which she told Taylor that the reason she was not standing close enough to hear these sounds when Marcus was making them is that she did not want to put herself in danger from the man being restrained by multiple officers.

Saying, "I don't got it all the way tight," Montalvo wraps the Hobble around Marcus' ankles and tightens it so that Marcus' hands are touching his feet.

Andrews takes the Hobble and tightens it further, wraps it again around Marcus' ankles and feet, and attaches the clasp.

Four minutes and 52 seconds into "video 1," recorded by the body-worn camera of Lee Andrews, Marcus takes his last audible breath.

Standing nearby, Sergeant Bradshaw, the senior officer on duty and technically in charge, applies lip balm.

"Need the stretcher right up next to him?" asks Abbott's partner, Alling.

"Yeah," says Strader.

"This is not gonna turn out good."

"For medical reasons, I'd rather he go with y'all," says Duncan. "I don't want him running around trying to kick my window and flying out."

"What needs to happen at this point," says Strader, "is somebody needs to go take out papers, otherwise, you know what I'm saying? He needs to be in custody."

"It would be nice if someone who witnessed him running around in traffic would take out those papers," says Duncan. "I mean, he just said to me, 'I'm gonna kill myself.'"

"Oh, he was doing it in front of us," says Andrews. "We can take him. That's all you needed to hear."

After the RIPP Hobble is secured and tightened, binding Marcus' feet to his hands behind his back, all the officers except Bailey stand. Marcus lies limp and unresponsive, face down, and does not appear to be breathing.

12:54:40 a.m. to 12:56:51 a.m.
Officers notice that Marcus is not breathing

Roughly 24 seconds after the restraint procedure he initiated is completed, Duncan notices Marcus is not responsive. "My man, you okay? You still with us?"

Bailey, the only officer still squatting by the man they've just hog-tied, shakes Marcus' left shoulder.

Duncan bends over Marcus and feels for his carotid. "Hey, you okay? You good, man?"

Andrews grasps Marcus' limp left arm and pulls him over on his side.

Abbott approaches, bends down and briefly puts her hand on Marcus' head. "Hey!"

"Hey, hey, hey, hey," says Duncan, "I don't feel a thing!"

"Take it all off!" shouts Strader. "Take it all off!"

Lewis unsnaps the RIPP Hobble from the chain of the handcuffs. Marcus' feet drop limply to the ground. "Whose RIPP Hobble is this?" asks Lewis.

"I don't think he's breathing at all," says Bailey.

"Huh?" says Abbott.

"Doesn't look like he's breathing at all," says Bailey.

Strader rolls Marcus onto his back. In the officer's flashlights, his features are slack and grey, although some of that color is dust and grit from the asphalt into which his face has been ground. His autopsy will later report multiple bruises and abrasions, but the dust hides any discoloration or blood.

Abbott puts her right hand on Marcus' chest.

"Nah, he ain't breathing," says Bailey. "His chest is [inaudible]."

Abbott checks the pulse in Marcus' right wrist with her gloved hand. "Get him in the bed and get him in the truck," she says.

"Did you get a pulse?" asks Andrews.

"Yeah," says Abbott, "he's got a pulse. I just need to get him on the truck."

"Y'all help her," says Alling to the officers as he trots towards the ambulance. Bailey, Andrews, Payne, and Lewis lift Marcus onto the gurney. Duncan moves his car out of the middle of the street. Strader picks something up off the asphalt.

"You want the cuffs all the way off?" asks Bailey.

"Unless they want it on," says Montalvo.

Alling checks Marcus' neck for a pulse.

"You want the cuffs all the way off?" asks Bailey again.

"Is he breathing?" asks Montalvo.

"No," says Abbott as she fastens a strap over Marcus' thighs to secure him on the gurney. "That's why I need to get him on the truck."

"You want it off?" repeats Bailey.

The gurney is wheeled towards the ambulance. "I can do this walking," says Bailey, removing the cuffs, which he hands to Duncan.

"Probably gonna need to ride with him, right?" says Bailey.

12:56:52 a.m. to 1:04:37 a.m.
Marcus is loaded into the ambulance, where EMS does CPR.

The gurney is lifted into the ambulance. Alling places a bag valve device on Marcus' face. Three minutes and 15 seconds after being informed Marcus was not breathing, Abbott starts manual chest compressions.

"This is not gonna turn out good."

"Is that your [inaudible] right there?" asks Bailey.

Bailey unpacks the CPR machine and hands the backboard to Abbott. "You want me to slide this under?"

She takes it from him and slides it under Marcus. Bailey hands her the CPR machine, then holds Marcus' arm up and out of the way. Alling cuts open one leg of Marcus' pants.

While EMTs Abbott and Alling and Officer Bailey work on Marcus in the ambulance, Sergeant Bradshaw, still the senior officer at the scene, is approached by Montalvo. "Call a supervisor," says Montalvo to his superior.

Bradshaw turns on his radio. "ATV One, if you have a supervisor, can you start him?"

Meanwhile, Duncan, having moved his car, climbs into the back of the ambulance and hands an intravenous bag to Alling.

"I'll follow in my car," says Bailey to Duncan. "That way, we can shuttle us back or do you want me here? I'm good either way."

"Either way's fine with me," says Duncan.

"I used to be [EMS], I used to work with them," says Bailey.

"I don't know if Lee [Andrews] is taking out the charges," says Duncan.

"At this point it doesn't matter," says Bailey. "He's gonna be at the hospital."

Duncan has trouble opening a bag for Alling. "I got gorilla hands right now," he says, referring to his gloves.

Bailey opens the bag and holds it out to Alling.

There are drilling sounds from off-camera. "It's not going in there," says Alling, who removes the device from Marcus' face. There is an injury visible on Marcus' forehead.

Lewis cuts open Marcus' right pants leg. Alling attempts to insert a tube into Marcus' leg,

Bailey puts on sterile gloves. "I got free hands if y'all need me to do anything."

Alling attaches a bag to the intubation. Abbott drills into Marcus' right leg and attaches the tubing.

"I've never seen that before," says Andrews.

"You've never seen them do the bone drill?" asks Payne.

"I've seen stuff connected to it before," says Andrews, "but I've never seen them actually use the drill. What's it for?"

I AIN'T RESISTING

"I don't know," says Payne.

A bone drill is used to quickly insert a needle into the bone to dispense fluids or medications directly into the marrow.

A firefighter appears in the doorway of the ambulance. "What y'all need?"

"[inaudible] EPI and [inaudible]" says Abbott.

Andrews pokes his head in the side door. "He was jacked up on something major."

"I didn't see what happened," says Bailey.

"Running around like he was psycho, basically," says Andrews.

"We are being told that no officers will be going," says Strader from outside the ambulance. "Everybody that was here when it happened needs to stay."

The last significant recorded audio from any of the officers directly involved with Marcus' death can be heard on "video 9," from the body-worn camera of Sergeant Bradshaw. The final minutes of that video, beginning at 1:02:30 and ending at 1:04:37, record Bradshaw speaking on his phone.

"I know you're busy probably, I'm assuming... [listening to person on the other end] ...well...[listening]...no, no, we're not, we're working downtown at the Folk Festival. We had a gentleman extremely delirious, running around high. We called EMS, he started trying to kick out the window."

As previously noted, while Marcus can be seen and heard slapping the window, there is no video or audio of him kicking, although the officers state their belief that he intends to. He places his feet on the glass before Lewis opens the door, but it's unclear whether he's drawing back his legs to kick.

"EMS got here," continues Bradshaw. "We pulled him out, we RIPP Hobbled him, within about a minute he stopped breathing, they're doing CPR right now."

He listens to the person on the other end.

"No, he is not breathing or [has] a pulse."

He listens again.

"All we did was to try to get him in a car. We got him in a car, he started kicking the window, we took him out, we put him down, we RIPP-Hobbled him for not even, it's all on camera, but not even a few minutes."

"This is not gonna turn out good."

Handcuffing Marcus took one minute and 29 seconds. After the handcuffs were applied, it took the officers another minute and 12 seconds to apply, tighten, and fasten the RIPP Hobble. Forty-four seconds passed before it was removed.

"I wouldn't say, nobody was on top of him or anything," says Bradshaw.

While no officer sat on Marcus, four of them, at one time or another, pressed him against the pavement, and Andrews pressed a knee into the small of his back for 14 seconds.

"We RIPP Hobbled him and he stopped breathing," says Bradshaw, "as we were talking to EMS about getting him to the bed, fire is coming, they're still doing CPR. Suddenly, we realized he wasn't breathing, we un-RIPP Hobbled him, took everything off. EMS is doing CPR. Fire is pulling up now."

Bradshaw listens and chuckles.

"The entire ATV team, two CCRT and one patrol guy..."

He listens.

"Right, we're still here on the scene."

He listens.

"I'll call you back if they go to the hospital or whatever. They're still, fire just pulled up so I'm assuming they're getting them to drive."

Corporal S. A. Hairston, Bradshaw's on-duty supervisor for that shift, approaches. Hairston, who is Black, arrived at the scene while Marcus was in the ambulance and will not be named as a defendant in the lawsuit.

"I'm about to call Sigmon," says Hairston. Renae Sigmon, then a GPD sergeant, is now part of the department's command staff as a deputy chief.

"Hairston's here," says Bradshaw on his phone. "He's gonna call Sigmon. Do you want me to ..."

He listens, then speaks to Hairston.

"Sigmon's on the way to the hospital so he [the person Bradshaw is speaking to] says hold off."

Bradshaw listens, then speaks to Hairston.

"He's on the way to the homicide, but we gotta get somebody out here." By "homicide," Bradshaw is probably referring to the Lucky 7 shooting that occurred earlier that evening.

At that point, his video ends.

I AIN'T RESISTING

Here, again, is the version of these events described on the City of Greensboro's press releases:

At 12:45 AM Greensboro Police located a disoriented suicidal subject running in and out of traffic in the 100 block of North Church Street. Officers worked with the subject for several minutes in an effort to give him assistance. EMS arrived at the scene at 12:50 AM. While officers were attempting to transport him for mental evaluation, the subject became combative and collapsed. Both EMS and on scene officers began rendering aid. The subject was transported ty EMS to a local hospital for additional treatment. The subject passed away at approximately 1:50 AM.

There are multiple issues with these statements.

Montalvo and Bradshaw first encountered Marcus at approximately 12:40 a.m., not 12:45. EMS arrived at approximately 12:51. Marcus did not collapse but was taken to the pavement by Duncan. Montalvo joins him in holding Marcus down, as do Andrews, Payne, Lewis, and even Strader, the second-highest-ranked officer on the scene. Arriving, Bailey joins in. The seven hold Marcus face down and apply the handcuffs and Hobble while Bradshaw, the senior officer on the scene, looks on.

At no point prior to being taken to the pavement is Marcus "combative." In several motions filed during litigation, defense attorneys argued Marcus' thrashing constituted active resistance, while plaintiff attorneys responded that these were the involuntary actions of a man being suffocated. Even if one accepts the defense arguments and the statements by several officers in their depositions, that his movements while being pressed face down on concrete and having his feet shoved towards the small of his back, thus placing all his weight (and that of the officers pressing him down) on his diaphragm, constituted resistance and thus were an example of his being "combative," none of this happened prior to his being taken down by Duncan, the action that the press release describes as Marcus having "collapsed."

Even the claim that "the subject passed away at approximately 1:50 AM" is erroneous.

During Paramedic Abbott's deposition, Taylor asks, "when did you determine that he was no longer alive?" She replies that "the radial

"This is not gonna turn out good."   103

pulse started to feel weak when we were in the ambulance, and I got the monitor out, cut his shirt off, and applied the defibrillator pads, and that's when he was no longer in a perfusing rhythm and lost pulse, and we began CPR." Taylor then asks, "Does your report indicate when in the timeline that was when he basically had died?"

"CPR was initiated at 12:57," responds Abbott. "That's when I started doing chest compressions." Taylor asks her if Marcus was "clinically dead" shortly after being taken aboard the ambulance. Abbott responds that "his heart was not beating anymore" and "We were beating it for him."

Marcus Smith may have been declared dead at Moses Cone Hospital at "approximately 1:50 a.m.," but Abbott testified under oath that he died almost an hour before. The obfuscation lies less in the timeline of his death than where it occurred. The press release stated he "passed away" at the hospital. This implied something very different from what the Office of the Chief Medical Examiner would conclude, which is that he was killed by the Greensboro police officers pressing him face down onto the pavement of Church Street with his feet pulled towards the small of his back by the RIPP Hobble.

"Killed" is an appropriate term here. The Medical Examiner's determination of "Homicide" implies no criminal or malicious intent, nor that the men who committed it are guilty of murder, manslaughter, negligence, policy violation or bad manners, but it absolutely means they killed him. The term is derived from two Latin words, "homo" for "man" and "cidium" for "act of killing."

Misrepresenting the time and place of Marcus Smith's death creates both temporal and spacial distance between that death and the actions of the officers who caused it, but the biggest issue many would have with the initial press releases issued in September and October of 2018 is that none mention the use of the restraint that killed him.

The Greensboro Police Department would not acknowledge what was done to Marcus until 81 days after his death, when journalist Jordan Green asked Chief Scott to respond to attorney Graham Holt's public statement that Marcus was hog-tied. No City press release would reference how and why Marcus died until after the state medical examiner ruled that death a homicide on November 30, 2018.

Both the initial September 8, 2018, press release and the updated September 10 version that contained Marcus' name stated, "the officers involved will be placed on administrative duty, as according to the policy of the Greensboro Police Department."

An officer on administrative *duty* continues to work at headquarters but has no contact with the public. An officer on administrative *leave* turns in their badge and firearm and is sent home, typically with full pay, until an investigation concludes.

On September 10, officers Andrews, Duncan, Lewis, and Payne were placed on administrative duty pending the results of an investigation by Professional Standards, GPD's Internal Affairs. The investigation concluded five weeks later, on October 18, 40 days after Marcus died, 17 days before Graham Holt and the Smith family told the press that Marcus was hog-tied, and 43 days before the state medical examiner determined it was the hog-tying that killed him. As investigators concluded the officers had acted in accordance with department directives and did not violate professional standards, Chief Wayne Scott returned them to active duty on October 19.

Sergeant Bradshaw, officers Montalvo and Bailey, and Corporal Strader were never placed on administrative duty and were not the subjects of the investigation, even though Bradshaw was the senior officer on the scene, Bailey and Strader assisted in restraining Marcus, and Montalvo was the first to apply the RIPP Hobble handed to him by Duncan.

In Scott's deposition, Flint Taylor asks, "and you chose those four because they were more involved in the maximum restraining of Marcus Smith than the other four who were present, correct?"

"Not necessarily more involved," replies Scott. "It was more about their proximity to Mr. Smith."

Taylor points out that Payne was not just "in proximity" to Marcus, but grasped his feet and pushed them towards his buttocks.

"It's difficult for me to remember what was on the beginning video that I saw when I made that decision, particularly around names," replies Scott. At multiple times in his deposition, he claims not to know or recall the names of who was doing what at certain points in the BWC footage.

"This is not gonna turn out good."

"UNFORTUNATELY, WE NEVER GOT TO THE POINT WHERE WE WERE TRANSPORTING MR. SMITH."

After George and Mary Smith, their children Kim Smith and Len Butler, and the man who was now their attorney left the Greensboro police station on October 8, 2018, the family returned to South Carolina and Holt to his office.

"When I sat down at my computer and googled hog-tying prisoners," said Holt, "all these studies of how it's killed people popped up. I found images of compressed diaphragms and people on their bellies suffocating. I learned that you're particularly vulnerable to this if you've just undergone rigorous exercise and your blood is starved for oxygen. So, I thought, there it is: they killed him."

Holt's next thought was to wonder whether the Greensboro Police Department had a policy against restraining a person this way.

"I have a copy of the Department's directives manual. I looked up what it said about putting someone in this position. That's when I knew the Smith family definitely had grounds for a lawsuit."

Holt was referring to section 11.1 of what was at that time the most recent update of the Greensboro Police Departmental Directives, titled "Handling and Transportation of Persons in Custody." Paragraph Four, "Additional Restraints," stated "At no time shall the wrists and ankles of an arrestee be linked together using the RIPP HOBBLE restraining device, unless the arrestee can be seated in an upright position, or on their side."

In a November 29, 2018, *Triad City Beat* article,[1] Jordan Green wrote: "Greensboro Police Chief Wayne Scott has acknowledged that Marcus Smith was lying face-down when officers applied a controversial restraint known as 'hog-tying' shortly before he became unresponsive and died, corroborating a critical point in an account by the family's lawyer, who has reviewed police body-camera footage."

When asked about this by Green, Scott responded, "Those specific things you're indicating are designed for when we're transporting persons in custody. Unfortunately, we never got to the point where we were transporting Mr. Smith."

In Flint Taylor's deposition of Scott, Taylor asks: "And yet, in this press release, there is no mention of the subject being maximally restrained, correct?"

"That is correct," replies Scott.

"And that was a significant bit of information, in terms of the events that led to Marcus Smith's death, wasn't it?"

"I would not define it as significant," says Scott. "That's something, to my knowledge, we never put in a press release."

Taylor then asks Scott about instances in which an officer shoots someone. "You'd put that in [the press release], wouldn't you?"

"Possibly," replies Scott, after his attorney's objection to the form. "That would be considered a use of force. Mere restraint is not a use of force."

"So, it was just a—an insignificant detail, the fact that he had been maximally restrained, and while maximally restrained by eight Greensboro police officers, that he became unresponsive? That was not a significant enough detail to include in a press release that was supposed to be accurately informing the public about a person who died in your custody?"

After asking for the question to be repeated, Scott replies.

"It was a detail, but I didn't see it as a significant one for the press release. Our directives around press releases are fairly specific. We give a date, the fact that the incident occurred, the fact that an independent investigation was being run by the SBI was important to include. That was my decision."

Taylor presses Scott further.

"And as you sit here today, do you still think that the fact that Marcus Smith was maximally restrained was a detail not significant enough to include in a press release?"

"I don't think that I can answer that fairly," replied Scott, "because I didn't have the opportunity for hindsight at the time to know what the investigation would fully unfold. The purpose of the press release was what I knew at the time in the wee hours of the morning, and I think it was accurate, and I think the press release fits our criteria."

The restraint that killed Marcus was never described or even acknowledged in any subsequent press release or other statement to the public from the City of Greensboro until the state medical examiner ruled his death a homicide.

Earlier in the deposition, Taylor asks Scott, "Did you become familiar with hog-tying when you were at the training academy?"

"I am familiar with the term being used," says Scott, "that was not the term we used, and we did not identify it as hog-tying."

Taylor directs Scott's attention to an exhibit containing the transcript of his January 2019 interview with Alma McCarty of Greensboro TV station WFMY News 2, in which Scott said:

"We don't hog-tie. That was something abandoned by our Police Department a long, long time ago. We do something called maximum restraining. Sometimes people will perceive it that way, but there are slight differences."

Taylor asks Scott about those "slight" differences.

Scott defines "hog-tying" as "the connecting of the hands and feet together where they are touching one another. In the maximum restraining world, there is always a distance between the hands and the feet."

Taylor brings Scott's attention to the training document "RIPP Hobble Usage and Application" that includes in a list of "Dangerous Positions," one in which a subject is "face down and 'hog-tied' (knee bend greater than 90 degrees) in transit."

Scott says that the word "hog-tied" is "likely quoted there because it's part of [meaning it used to be included in] the state lesson plan [for police officers]." Scott also denies that this training document defines hog-tying as a position in which the knees are bent greater than 90 degrees.

Taylor asks Scott if, when observing the videos, he noted that Marcus' legs had been pushed to an angle of less than 90 degrees from his body as the RIPP Hobble was being applied.

"I couldn't tell you if I could ascertain the exact degree of his legs," replies Scott. "I watched the event unfold. And based off that, I felt it was necessary to issue the press release. I think we complied with the directive, and I stand behind the details that are included."

Taylor again asks Scott if, when he first watched the videos on his laptop in the hospital, and later that morning at the police station, he noticed "whether Marcus Smith's legs were at an angle of less than 90 degrees from his body at least part of the time that the RIPP Hobble was being applied?"

Scott replies, "I can tell you that I watched the video," but that he did not pay close attention to the angle of Marcus' legs. "I was looking for the basis of everything that occurred so I could complete the press release. So far as the specifics, that's something that would unfold in an investigation going forward."

Taylor asks Scott why, after viewing the videos that morning, he concluded that Smith was combative and had collapsed, "but you didn't take from it the fact that he had been maximally restrained by your officers and that he had become unresponsive before he was returned to a recovery position?"

"No," says Scott. "Obviously, I could tell that he had been maximally restrained. I could tell that the officers had begun the recovery position and that they noticed something, and that they had summoned EMS."

That is not what any of the videos show. In the same deposition, Scott defined the "recovery position" as when a "maximally restrained" subject was placed on their side so that officers can "monitor their breathing, watch the rise and fall of their chest, and adjust, you know, everything from the handcuffs to the RIPP Hobble, if necessary."

Marcus had not yet been placed on his side when Duncan notices he is unresponsive and has stopped breathing. He is still face down when

I AIN'T RESISTING

Duncan asks, "Hey, man, you OK?" It is only after Duncan asks and EMT Abbott says "Hey!" that Andrews grabs Marcus' limp arm and rolls him over on his side. Nor had anyone "summoned EMS," as the two EMTS are standing there watching, and Abbott kneels beside Marcus without any prompting from the officers.

"But again," says Scott, "I did not view it from an investigative standpoint. It was to glean the information that I wanted to push out in the press release."

Later in the deposition, Taylor asked Scott if, before approving the September 8 press release drafted by Captain Teresa Biffle, Scott observed the BWC footage of Marcus emerging from Duncan's car.

"I viewed one angle version of it, yes," says Scott.

"And in that angle," asks Taylor, "you saw that an officer who either at that time or was later identified as Officer Duncan, as well as another officer, Officer Montalvo, had their hands on Marcus Smith at the time he was taken to the ground, correct?"

"I don't remember the specific officers at this time," says Scott. "I have reviewed the video several times, but I couldn't name those two officers. There were officers in close proximity with him, yes."

"All right," says Taylor. "And Officer Duncan has characterized what he did as escorting Marcus Smith to the ground. Do you agree that the video showed that, the video that you watched?"

Scott replies after his attorney's objection to the form.

"The video I saw on the night in question, I remember seeing Mr. Smith go to the ground. I don't know that I would define it as escorting. Those would be his words, not mine."

After Scott says that "escorted to the ground" were Duncan's words rather than his own, Taylor asks whether "collapsed" was his word or Captain Biffle's.

"Quite honestly," says Scott, "I don't remember, but I approve all, so I take responsibility for the wording in the press release."

Taylor again asks Scott if he believes the description of Marcus as having "collapsed" is accurate.

"I believe it was an accurate description," says Scott.

Taylor then asks Scott about the use of the word "combative." "Is that your language, or is that Captain Biffle's language?"

Scott reiterates that he is responsible for everything in the press release. "I don't know who actually wrote the word initially."

Taylor then asks Scott about Marcus' behavior while being handcuffed and hog-tied.

"Focusing on being combative before, in your terminology, he collapsed, what was it that you saw that made you conclude that it was— to use the language 'combative' in your press release?"

"He was failing to comply with the officers' request," says Scott, "and he was physically pulling away from them, and more or less failing to—I don't know if I can find the right word for you. But in a combative way, he was flailing his arms around, pushing and pulling away from them. I would view that as combative and failing to answer or do what the officers request."

Taylor asks Scott if, in his view, this behavior was before or after Marcus was on the pavement.

"I think there was some both before and after," says Scott, "but I don't have that specific of recollection of when."

Scott uses "I don't recall" or such variants as "not to my recollection" 81 times in his deposition.

After some back and forth about Scott's description of Marcus' behavior, the wording of which Scott claims not to be able to recall less than minute after stating it, Scott says that Marcus was "failing to comply" with the officers.

"He was in somewhat an agitated state where he was flailing around, and that's being combative, in my opinion."

13   "IT'S NOT AN INVESTIGATION."

In February of 2021, Taylor deposed Wayne Scott's successor Brian James, who had been a deputy chief when Marcus Smith was killed, and who himself would retire the following May, after serving a year and three months as Chief.

In his deposition, James states he is 50 years old and that his promotion to chief took effect on February 1 of 2020. James, who is Black, was born and grew up in Greensboro and graduated in 1994 from North Carolina A&T State University with a bachelor's degree in business administration. He went to work for the Guilford County Sheriff's Office as a detention officer in the county jail, then joined the Greensboro police force in 1996. In 2007, he earned an MBA from Pfeiffer University and, in 2012, obtained a graduate certificate in criminal justice from the FBI National Academy through the University of Virginia.

In 2009, James was a plaintiff in a lawsuit brought by Black GPD officers alleging discriminatory treatment by then-Chief David Wray and white officers in the Special Intelligence Division. When asked by Taylor if this unit still exists, James says it does not, but "We do have an intelligence squad."

At the time of Marcus' death, James was deputy chief of patrol and all the officers involved in the death were under his command. He would later sign off on the investigation clearing them of any responsibility.

In his deposition, Taylor asks:

"And when you saw—watched the video, you realized that the characterization that the subject collapsed in police custody was not accurate, correct?"

"I don't agree with your statement," responds James.

"You didn't see him collapse, did you?" asks Taylor.

"I did see him go to the ground during the video," replies James.

Taylor then asks James if he agrees the press release left out an important fact, "that he was maximally restrained prior to his death."

"I would not agree with you," says James. "This is a press release, not a case report or an investigative report."

Taylor keeps pushing. "A press release is supposed to give accurate information to the public, isn't it?"

"Absolutely," says James.

"And this didn't, did it?"

"Yes, it did," responds James.

"It says that Marcus Smith collapsed in police custody and later died in the hospital," responds Taylor, "not mentioning that eight Greensboro police officers participated in maximally restraining him in a prone position before he died, correct?"

"This is a press release," repeats James, "not an investigative report, and that information would not have been included in a press release."

Taylor asked James if, as the current chief, "you would approve press releases similar to this one, in terms of describing a death in custody?"

"I would not give investigative information in a press release that was pertinent to an investigation," says James. "The press release is simply to make the public aware of an incident that has occurred. It is not a detailed investigative report."

Taylor then returns to the subject of what happened the night Marcus died.

"And you're telling me that, in your opinion, after watching the video, that Marcus Smith collapsed in police custody and later died in the hospital, and that's an accurate public statement to be given by the chief of the Greensboro Police Department?"

"I watched the video," says James. "I saw Marcus Smith fall down during the video, or collapse, so that information that he collapsed is correct."

"Didn't you see the part of the video where Officer Duncan escorted, in his view, Marcus Smith to the ground?"

After the expected objection to form, James asks Taylor, "At what part of the video are you speaking about?"

"I'm asking whether you saw that in the video," replies Taylor, "that Marcus Smith didn't collapse to the ground, but that he was, at the very least, guided by two Greensboro police officers to the ground before he was maximally restrained?"

James again asks Taylor, "At what point of the video are you talking about?"

"I'm asking you, sir," says Taylor, "about the time that Marcus came out of the car until he went to the ground. Obviously, he was escorted to the ground by Greensboro police officers, wasn't he?"

"Okay," says James. "Now you reference him getting out of the car, that's what I was asking—at what point in the video you were talking about. So, when he stepped out of the car, what I observed is Mr. Smith going to the ground and the officers placing hands on him that essentially broke his fall to the ground. So, when you say guided him to the ground, in my opinion, they broke his fall as he was going to the ground after he stepped out of the car."

"Well, I'm just using the terminology of the officers," says Taylor, "so pardon me."

"After watching that video and seeing Marcus Smith go to the ground and then being maximally restrained for two and a half minutes, being handcuffed and then being maximally restrained, it's your testimony that this press release is complete and accurate? Is that right?"

"It does not contain every nuance of this encounter," says James after defense attorney Alan Duncan's objection to the form. "The information that is in the press release is accurate."

"You—you—are you sitting here, as the Chief of Police—Chief of Police who now has presided over the banning of maximum restraint, sitting here and telling me that the two-and-a-half-minute maximum restraining of Marcus Smith was an insignificant investigative detail that didn't need to be told to the public on March, on February, on September 8, 2018, when this release was given to the public?"

"It's not an investigation."   115

"Sir," replies James after the expected interjection from attorney Duncan, "the information contained in this document is accurate."

Taylor asks James, "Have you heard the term 'hog-tie'?"

"I've heard it used," says James, "in terms of describing this case by individuals not affiliated with the department."

Taylor asks James to describe his "understanding of the term 'hog-tie' with regard to its use within the department."

"I'm not familiar with that term," says James. "Maximal restraint is what I've always referred to it and what I've seen it documented in our policies."

Taylor then quotes from page 11 of "RIPP Hobble Usage and Application." Taylor points out that "Arrestees face down and hog-tied" is on the list of "dangerous positions."

James replies that "the term is obviously used in this training aid, but it was not referred to in policy."

In their depositions, Scott and James repeatedly make the statement that a press release is not an investigative report and hence, a description of the device that was fatally used on Marcus did not belong in it. Scott calls a press release "a snapshot in time" and says, "it's simply a way to convey to the public something happened. So, you want to be as accurate as possible, but at the same time, it's not an investigation."

14 "REASONABLE AND WITHIN POLICY."

The Greensboro Police Department's internal investigation began on September 10, 2018, and ended on October 18, although the final report would not be issued until four months later.

In his deposition, Brian James acknowledged that the final report from Sergeant Matthew Stein of the Professional Standards Division was sent to him on February 7, 2019, and it stated that the actions of officers who killed Marcus were "within policy." James also stated that it's normal for the chain of command in an internal investigation to end with a deputy chief, and he was the highest-ranked officer to read the report and approve it.

Unlike Chief Wayne Scott, who read a preliminary version of the report on October 18, 2018, and returned the officers to active duty, Deputy Chief James read and approved the final version after Marcus' death had been ruled a homicide by the state medical examiner.

In his deposition by Flint Taylor, Sergeant Matthew Stein states he submitted the final version to Lieutenant Milford Harris on January 24, 2019, and that it went up the chain of command from Harris to Captain Ryan Walton before receiving final approval from Deputy Chief James.

Stein claimed not to remember exactly which officers' BWC footage he reviewed. "I know I looked at Strader's," he says, and "Bailey's, I believe," referring to two of the four officers who were not placed on administrative duty. "I believe there is at least one or two others, but I don't remember which ones."

When Taylor reminds Stein that several officers had multiple videos, Stein says he does not remember how many individual videos he watched. "I primarily focused on the incident leading up to Mr. Smith being on the ground."

Stein testifies that, when he joined the GPD in 2004, he was trained that "secured wrists and ankles of the arrestee may be linked together using flexicuffs or the hobble device," but that "once the arrestee can be seated in an upright position or on their side...the knees of the arrestee will not be bent more than 90 degrees," due to the danger of "a positional asphyxia situation." Unlike his superiors Chief Scott and Deputy Chief James, Stein does not claim the term "hog-tying" was never used by GPD officers, but instead says that "the general understanding" of the term was "wrists touching ankles, or within a few inches of it."

In the deposition, Taylor questions Stein not only about his investigation, but about a memo issued by Chief Wayne Scott to all GPD personnel on September 30, 2019, a year and 22 days after Marcus was killed. The directive was titled "Handling of Persons in Custody, Restraint, and Transport of Individuals."

This directive advised staff of the risk of restraining individuals suffering from "drug-induced psychosis, genetic psychosis or excited delirium," who may exhibit such symptoms as tremors, convulsions, seizures, delirium, hallucinations, and "superhuman strength."

While the concept of excited delirium is, in itself, highly controversial, the term "superhuman strength" is even more so, at least partially because many officers have attempted to justify excessive force by arguing that suspects were exhibiting it. The term became popular in police departments during the 1990s due to hyperbolic claims about the allegedly increased strength and ferocity of PCP users. The Los Angeles police officers who beat Rodney King in 1991 wrongly assumed that King was high on "angel dust" and LAPD Sergeant Stacey Koon told investigators that, after having heard so many stories of PCP giving its user "superhuman strength," Koon feared King could "turn into the Hulk" and put officers in a "death grip."

In the 2021 trial of former Minneapolis police officer Derek Chauvin for murdering George Floyd, Chauvin's attorneys argued that their client had a reasonable fear of Floyd's "superhuman strength," and defense use-of-force expert Barry Brodd testified that drug-influenced suspects "don't feel pain" and "may have superhuman strength."

This echoes an old canard described in "PCP Hallucinations in Ferguson," by Jacob Sullum,[1] who points out that marijuana was once regarded as a "killer drug" that made Black people superhumanly dangerous. Sullum cites a 1917 report from the US Department of Agriculture which quotes an El Paso police captain who said that Black marijuana users "become very violent" and "seem to have no fear," are "insensible to pain," and display such "abnormal strength" that "it will take several men to handle one man."

In his deposition, Stein acknowledges he interviewed Officer Payne for 16 minutes, Officer Andrews for 14 minutes, and Officer Lewis for 11. He also conducted a six-minute interview with Sergeant Bradshaw, even though Bradshaw was not a subject of the investigation. He did not interview Duncan, who made the decision to hog-tie Marcus.

Stein states that the draft of his report he completed on November 28, 2018, was 35 pages long and did not include the state medical examiner's report. This draft was sent to Captain Teresa Biffle, who on December 6, 2018, forwarded it to City Manager David Parrish.

Stein stated that no version of the report included any mention of Chief Scott's November memorandum that the RIPP Hobble would no longer be used in the manner it had been applied to Marcus, and acknowledged finishing the first draft of his report before the conclusions of the state medical examiner were released. He said he found the medical examiner's report "significant," and discussed it with Captains Teresa Biffle and Trey Davis, but could not recall being asked by Davis or Biffle "whether the officer's actions were appropriate pursuant to department policy and training."

"Reasonable and within policy."   119

When asked by Taylor for his opinion on the actions that killed Marcus, Stein replies, "They were within their training and legal right to take custody of Mr. Smith and acted as how they were trained."

Stein also says that the Professional Standards Division had no way of cataloging or reviewing the GPD's uses of maximum restraint. He acknowledges that the police departments of North Carolina cities Durham, Raleigh, and Winston-Salem, as well as the police department of New Orleans, Louisiana, all "prohibit connecting ankle restraints to handcuffs," as do the Guilford County Sheriff's department; the NYPD; the Tucson Police Department; the Tampa Police Department; and the Saint Paul Police Department.

Stein acknowledges that Captain Ryan Walton sent a February 4, 2019, email to Deputy Chief James stating that "the facts of this investigation reveal that all officers' actions were within policy" and that Walton made this decision based on Stein's report. James replied with a statement to the Professional Standards division that "the officers involved in this action were reasonable and within policy."

The purpose of the internal investigation conducted by the Professional Standards division of the Greensboro Police Department was not to determine if the officers who killed Marcus Smith committed any crimes, but whether their actions violated departmental directives or standards of conduct. Whether the officers would face criminal charges was a matter for the North Carolina State Bureau of Investigation and the Guilford County District Attorney.

As Mary Smith's federal civil rights lawsuit was against the City of Greensboro, the eight police officers employed by the City, and the paramedic and EMT employed by the County, there were no direct statements by SBI officials or agents produced in discovery. However, there is the letter written on October 15, 2018, by Assistant District Attorney Stephen Cole to Chief Wayne Scott, in which Cole told Scott that the SBI's preliminary findings indicated Scott's officers had acted within the scope of both their duties and the law.

The SBI investigation concluded two months later would find what Cole indicated they would in the letter Chief Scott read before returning the officers to active duty: that the officers had committed no crime when they fatally hog-tied Marcus Smith.

From the date of the initial press release stating that an unidentified man had "collapsed" in GPD custody until the medical examiner's report labeled his death a homicide, neither the Smith family nor the public knew that the GPD, the DA's office, and the SBI were in the process of absolving those officers of any criminal or procedural misconduct. The Smith family had learned what happened within a month of Marcus' death. Weeks before their attorney Graham Holt described to the press and City Council what he and George Smith saw on the bodycam footage, suspicions were growing among those members of the public with questions about just how and why Marcus had died.

"WHAT I SAW ON THE VIDEOS WERE
15   HORRIBLE INSTANCES OF PURE ESCALATION."

Since he had read the initial press release, IRC staff member and Homeless Union of Greensboro co-founder Mitch Fryer had been troubled by the word "combative."

"It just didn't fit my own experience with Marcus," Fryer said.

"That was my last year at the IRC, and I had dealt with Marcus at that point for five years. Even when he was in his throes of a mental health crisis, whether drug-induced or whatever, it never turned into combativeness. The immediate impression that I got was that, if he had become combative at all, it would have to do with the handling by GPD, as we had successfully de-escalated him on several occasions and never once felt threatened or that we were going to enter into some kind of involuntary combat with him. In my experience in de-escalation with him, combativeness wasn't really a thing. And as you can see on the video, he never threatens anyone."

It also didn't fit with what several members of the homeless community told Fryer the Monday after Marcus' death.

"I talked to the people who knew him, and one of his lady friends, who was with him an hour or two before his death, described him as being normal and certainly not in a fit of rage or anything like that."

Like his boss Michelle Kennedy, Fryer said the situation could have been avoided if Officer Duncan had driven Marcus to the hospital sooner, rather than leaving him alone for several minutes in the parked car. He was deeply troubled by how other officers kept shining their flashlights in Marcus' face.

"I was on our de-escalation team and certified in non-violent crisis intervention and therapeutic crisis intervention, via the NC Crisis Prevention Institute, and at that point had been doing de-escalation stuff for eight years. What I saw on the videos were horrible instances of pure escalation. They were never going to, with that approach, get him into a lowered state. When you're forcing compliance on somebody who is not a threat, you really are taking it to a level that it doesn't need to be."

Fryer said successful de-escalation takes listening and attentive patience.

"If they had just taken time with him, and paid more attention to what he was saying, he would have been fine. I think the GPD was more concerned about the fact that he was blocking traffic, and that they wanted to open the road back up again, and that's why they ended up being so hands-on with him."

Fryer said that, rather than surrounding Marcus, it would have been better if the officers moved out of the road, which was already blocked so traffic was not an immediate issue, and let Marcus come to them.

"They should have invited him to the sidewalk or gone to a field or patch of grass and let him come to that position voluntarily and let him be as incoherent and emotional as he wanted. I know the idea of just sitting down on the grass with him would have been completely alien to them and their training, but that's how you work these situations."

Long before Fryer saw the video, he wasn't buying the City's narrative. "And neither was anyone else in the HUG [Homeless Union of Greensboro]. We all thought it just didn't add up."

Fryer and Marcus Hyde talked a lot about that in September and early October of 2018. "Marcus [Hyde] was a Homeless Advocate from the anarchist collective Denver Out Loud and had moved to Greensboro the previous year to attend UNCG. I myself am an anarchist and had done a lot of activism around the John Brown Gun Club and militant anti-fascism."

Fryer said this was one reason why Michelle Kennedy, Mayor Vaughan, and other members of City Council may have been suspicious of both him and Hyde, although his own relationship with Kennedy never became as overtly adversarial as Hyde's.

"He and I were seen as too much, and I think Michelle was trying to angle behind the scenes to not let the HUG set the pace of everything, so she could get other people on board. But without the Homeless Union's involvement, I don't believe the Smith family would have been connected to their attorneys."

Fryer alleged that, by the time the Smith family met Graham Holt on October 8, 2018, to view the videos of Marcus Smith's death, Michelle Kennedy had become less supportive of Hyde's attempts to publicize the Marcus Smith case.

"Initially, Michelle really encouraged both Marcus and myself, and made multiple statements urging us to keep pressing the City on the matter, and telling us she would be fighting with us. But that changed after the HUG started organizing around the issue of Marcus' death."

He said one reason for the change may have been Kennedy's deteriorating relationship with HUG co-founder Hyde.

"Michelle had been allowing the HUG to meet in and organize out of the Worker's Center in the back of the IRC, and things had seemed fine all year, but once people started organizing about Marcus Smith's death, it became much more of an adversarial relationship. I don't believe that she appreciated how hard we were pressing. I know for a fact Michelle, along with Mayor Vaughan and most of the other Council members, were trying to watch Marcus Hyde very closely, and really put him under the microscope. There were multiple comments made by Michelle about how Marcus had been voluntarily homeless, ignoring his rough homelife, and accusing him of choosing homelessness in an attempt to delegitimize him." Fryer was referring to Hyde's life in Denver before he moved to Greensboro.

"Michelle was saying that he was the face of the Homeless Union, and kind of steering the ship himself, and it wasn't really organic, so despite the fact that we had 15–20 participants weekly at that point, you could tell that her attitude towards the Homeless Union changed as things progressed, and that really became evident through that period of October through December."

"What I saw on the videos were horrible instances of pure escalation." 125

From the end of 2017, when Kennedy became arguably the most progressive white representative in the history of City Council as well as the first openly gay one, until August of 2021, when she resigned a month after angrily reading aloud a statement prepared for her by the city attorney, Kennedy was known for being outspoken. While she couched her statements in the language of a policy wonk, she could also be blunt to a degree that John Hammer, editor of the conservative weekly *The Rhino Times*, described as "rude" in several columns (a term that he never applied to board members like Republican Zack Matheny or the conservative, very pro-police Marikay Abuzuaiter, both of whom have been contentious and abrasive).

Kennedy's deposition, conducted by Flint Taylor in June of 2021, is so often critical of police and City officials that Taylor repeatedly asks her to consider being represented by attorneys other than the City's, whose instructions not to answer certain questions she ignores. In that deposition, she made no secret of her dislike and distrust for Chief Wayne Scott and for Chuck Watts, who was hired as city attorney in May of 2019. Watts later made scathing descriptions of activists and supporters of the Smith family even while criticizing them for attempting to "try the case in the court of public opinion."

Just as she had regarding Scott and Watts, she made no secret of her distaste for Hyde, whom she accused of being untruthful and of acting like a white gatekeeper of Black homeless people. When questioned on this subject by Taylor, Kennedy said:

"To be a white, non-homeless man who has decided to speak on behalf of people experiencing homelessness and decide that it is your role to be their so-called voice is problematic to me on a number of levels." When asked about the reasons for her dislike of Hyde, she replied "I don't think I had a personal or political dispute with Marcus. I just simply don't have any respect for the way in which he engages people experiencing poverty."

Tensions between Kennedy and Hyde escalated after December of 2018, when Fryer resigned from the IRC and moved to Lexington, North Carolina, a smaller city 40 minutes from Greensboro.

"While I was there [at the IRC], I did a good deal of talking to Michelle to try to serve as a buffer in their relationship. She and I had locked horns on a couple of things, and I had almost gotten fired from the IRC on a couple of occasions. It was quite a dance for me."

Yet, in the week after Marcus Smith's death, Fryer insisted that he, Kennedy, and Hyde all appeared to be on the same page.

"That first morning, Goldie Wells came, and I overheard a conversation between her and Michelle about it, where she [Wells] said, 'the police didn't do nothing but kill that boy.'"

Wells, who represents District 2, is one of four Black members of City Council. Like District 1's Sharon Hightower, Wells is a longtime community leader in economically depressed northeast Greensboro. Unlike Hightower, Wells never publicly criticized either the police or the City over Marcus Smith's death, and defended the officers involved after watching their bodycam videos, resulting in enmity between her and multiple A&T students speaking about the case to City Council. During those often-heated exchanges in late 2018 and early 2019, Wells, who was 75 at the time of Smith's death, rebuked Black students and young Black activists for not respecting elders such as herself.

Fryer described an informal meeting that Kennedy and Mayor Vaughan held on December 2, 2018, to which Kennedy invited a selected group of community leaders, and then expressed dismay when some uninvited ones attended.

"Shortly thereafter was the meeting that was supposed to happen at the IRC, where Michelle was there, Goldie was there, and I can't remember what the critiques were from the folks from the community that showed up. I think Michelle was really fishing behind the scenes to get Goldie on board for an independent investigation. At that meeting, people lobbed hard criticisms at them for not doing more quicker."

According to Fryer, that meeting, which will be described in more detail later, was when the tensions between Michelle Kennedy and the Homeless Union became apparent to anyone outside the IRC. Several community leaders present, including Reverend Brandon Wrencher and

Reverend Wesley Morris, said this was the first time they were aware of hostility between Kennedy and Hyde.

"At some point after that, Michelle stopped allowing the Homeless Union to meet at the building," said Fryer. "I think she saw where they were going with it as politically untenable, as she needed five votes on Council to get an Independent Investigation. Not only Marcus Hyde and the Homeless Union, but Nelson Johnson and Wesley Morris of the Beloved Community Center, whom Marcus had invited to that meeting over Michelle's objections, were seen as too radical and delegitimized. She was trying to get some moderate and milquetoast organizations on board. 'Those are the people things will happen with, and can get the ball rolling,' she said to me, or words to that effect."

Although that informal and hastily organized meeting at the IRC would not be held until December 2, two days after Marcus Smith's death was declared a homicide and the videos of his hog-tying made public, it was a belated response to a letter the Homeless Union of Greensboro sent to Chief Scott, Mayor Vaughan, City Manager David Parrish and the eight members of City Council on September 18.

"WE URGE YOU TO PROMPTLY RELEASE ALL RELEVANT INFORMATION."

On September 18, 2018, ten days after Marcus Smith died, the Homeless Union of Greensboro sent the following email to the Greensboro police chief and thirteen City officials. The additional recipients were Mayor Vaughan, the eight members of Council, City Attorney Tom Carruthers, Police Attorney Polly Sizemore, and City Manager David Parrish.

> *To:*   Scott, Wayne
> *Subject:*   Marcus Deon Smith
>
> Dear Police Chief, Mayor Vaughan, Mr. City Manager and Members of Council,
>
> Please see the Attached Letter Regarding the death of Mr. Marcus Deon Smith. We appreciate your prompt response regarding this matter.
>
> Sincerely,
> MITCH FRYER
> For the Homeless Union of Greensboro

The attached PDF was a longer letter that was also physically mailed to City Manager David Parrish.

Dear Mr. City Manager, Police Chief, Mayor and Members of Council,

On Saturday September 8th, Greensboro lost a beloved member of the community, Marcus Deon Smith. We are concerned about his death and the lack of information from the Greensboro Police Department regarding the circumstances of his passing. We urge you to promptly release all relevant information regarding this incident so that the community that knew and loved Marcus may properly process and mourn his passing.

This death hits hard in one community in Greensboro in particular— the homeless community. Marcus was a stalwart figure at the Interactive Resource Center, a place designed to care for and connect people experiencing homelessness to their needs and offer services. Often seen cutting people's hair at the IRC, speaking and motivating people to get their life on track as he worked to do so himself, and giving out his own few possessions to help others in need, Marcus had an amazing ability to both receive help and pour life into others.

News of his death has prompted questions from our community as well as in the broader community in Greensboro. All people seek closure at the loss of loved ones, and we seek clarity as to how his death unfolded so that we can fully honor his character, his memory, and come to understand how such a beautiful life can come to such an abrupt end.

The press release offered by the Greensboro Police Department is quite brief and it lacks context and detail. It is difficult to understand how this event progressed so quickly from Marcus's initial contact with police to his death. Statements about him being "combative" and then "collapsing" leave too much room for interpretation and beg for further explanation. Because of the way this information was presented, there is a lot of speculation among his friends and others who are interested in finding out what actually happened. People who knew Marcus intimately are adamant that he was not suicidal and are understandably confused by his untimely death.

We believe it is within the interest of safety and community trust to release all the pertinent facts concerning this situation. We ask that whatever body camera footage is available be released to the public so that we can understand what happened, along with any pertinent information regarding his condition at the time of arrest, transport and at the time he arrived at the hospital.

Chief Wayne Scott, we need answers. Waiting for the SBI investigation to come to completion, a process that could take several months—if not

I AIN'T RESISTING

years—is unacceptable. No family should bear the death of their child without being given a full understanding of the circumstances. No community should mourn a valued and loved member of that community while questions loom as to how and why that person died.

We look forward to your prompt response regarding this matter.

Sincerely,
MITCH FRYER
For the Homeless Union of Greensboro

"That letter in particular was on behalf of the Homeless Union," said Fryer. "It was composed collectively—I certainly didn't author the entire thing. But the immediate questions we had, pertaining to their description of him collapsing and becoming combative, just did not fit with my experience with Marcus."

In his deposition of Chief Scott, attorney Flint Taylor asked Scott if City Manager David Parrish indicated it was appropriate for the chief to respond to Fryer. "Yes," replied Scott.

TAYLOR	And within your discussion with Mr. Parrish, the chief city manager, did you inform him that Marcus Smith had been maximally restrained with a RIPP Hobble?
SCOTT	Mr. Parrish was aware of that.
TAYLOR	When did he become aware of it?
SCOTT	I had a discussion with Mr. Parrish Monday following the incident.
TAYLOR	And did you show him some of the body camera footage?
SCOTT	I did.
TAYLOR	And he saw the same footage that you saw a couple of days earlier?
SCOTT	I will say approximately the same footage, yes.
TAYLOR	And did he also read the updated press release that went out? Did you discuss with him whether further details should have been included in it?
SCOTT	No.

TAYLOR   Did you discuss whether further detail should be publicly released at that time?

SCOTT   My conversation was the fact that I could not release any further details and the fact that the SBI was now the lead investigation, and it would be inappropriate for us to discuss any details. It's up to the SBI to handle the investigation. But I did intend to reply and try to answer Mr. Fryer's questions or help alleviate some of the obvious stress that he indicated from his writings.

TAYLOR   Are you saying that you could not publicly reveal that Marcus Smith was maximally restrained because there was an SBI investigation?

SCOTT   I am saying it was not proper for me, as an agency not within the SBI, to release any more of the facts of the investigation. It's their investigation once I ask them to come in and begin, and I didn't want anything that I would release to interfere with that investigation.

TAYLOR   Well, how would it interfere with the investigation if you gave a more complete picture of what happened to Marcus Smith to the public?

SCOTT   The SBI did multiple interviews, and they need to be able to interview people from their perspective, not something they heard in the media.

TAYLOR   It was a video, right, that the SBI had?

SCOTT   They had access to all the videos; that's correct.

TAYLOR   Well, you felt that you weren't precluded from releasing publicly that Marcus Smith was supposedly suicidal, that he was combative, to use the language in the press release, that he collapsed, that officers worked with him for several minutes in an effort to give him assistance, and that he was disoriented and running in and out of traffic. You felt that was okay to release all of that information, but you could not release the information that he had been maximally restrained; is that right?

SCOTT	Yes.
TAYLOR	And did Parrish go along with you on that, that you should not and could not release the fact that Marcus Smith was maximally restrained just prior to his death?
SCOTT	Again, I made him aware of my stance on it, and he didn't direct me otherwise.

Taylor also questioned City Manager David Parrish about the letter from Fryer and the Homeless Union.

TAYLOR	That letter was asking you for more detail specifically about how—the circumstances surrounding Marcus Smith's death, correct?
PARRISH	That's not the way I read it. I believe it makes statements. I don't see a question.
TAYLOR	And whose decision was it to not release any information, either by press release, press conference or by any other means?
PARRISH	I don't recall any decision about what to do or not to do. It wasn't release any information or withhold any information. I don't recall any contemplation around that.

On September 19, Chief Scott sent the following reply to Mitch Fryer and the Homeless Union of Greensboro:

Please allow me to offer my condolences for the passing of your friend. Any loss of life in our community touches all of us and is concerning for me personally.

I can tell you that being transparent around this incident is the goal of the Greensboro Police Department. While I also think it's important for the community to have confidence that the investigation is done independently of the GPD, and that's why I requested the SBI to lead the investigation into the matter. While the SBI investigation is still ongoing and I cannot speak for the SBI, I can tell you I have personally reviewed much of the information available from that evening (body-camera recordings, radio traffic, initial

"We urge you to promptly release all relevant information."   133

autopsy reports) and it is my belief that the Greensboro police officers on scene acted appropriately and with great compassion while trying to help a citizen in need.

Unfortunately, because of our state personnel laws, I cannot share this information with you directly. However, as your Chief of Police, I will work with the SBI to bring closure to this investigation and update the community of their finding as soon as it's legally possible.

In his deposition of Chief Scott, Taylor says "you were not being transparent concerning the maximum restraining of Marcus Smith, were you?"

Scott replies that "I believe we were being as transparent as I felt was proper, given the fact the independent investigation by the SBI was underway."

Taylor asks if Scott is "invoking the body-camera footage, which was not public; invoking initial autopsy reports, not final ones; and invoking radio traffic to give the Chief's imprimatur, or stamp, on the statement that the Greensboro police officers acted appropriately and with great compassion while trying to help a citizen in need."

"That is correct," says Scott.

Taylor presses Scott on this claim.

"So, you weren't telling them that he was maximally restrained, because that was—that was gonna improperly get in the way of an SBI investigation, but you were telling the public, and telling all the Council people, and other public officials that, according to the chief of police, having looked at all this stuff that isn't public, that everything was above board and done with compassion and appropriately, right?"

Scott replies, "That was my opinion, yes."

Taylor asks Scott if "in your view, it did not run afoul of the ongoing SBI investigation to tell the public that, based on your review, it was your belief that the officers on the scene acted appropriately and with great compassion while trying to help a citizen in need?"

"Correct," says Scott.

When Taylor asks if it was "legally possible" for Scott to have told the Homeless Union and the public that Marcus died while being "maximally restrained," Scott concedes that it was.

I AIN'T RESISTING

On September 27, City Manager Parrish sent an email to the mayor and City Council that included the following brief update on the Marcus Smith case: "Early indications from these investigations are that nothing out of the ordinary took place." In Flint Taylor's deposition of City Manager Parrish, Taylor asks him if he had watched the videos before making that statement.

"I don't recall when I viewed the body-worn camera footage," replies Parrish, "so I can't say that it was by this date or any other date."

Taylor reminds Parrish that he sent that email about three weeks after Marcus' death. "By this time, you knew Marcus Smith had been maximally restrained, did you not?"

"I knew that Marcus had been restrained by the police department," says Parrish, becoming the only witness other than Kennedy to call the homicide victim by the GPD by his first name.

Taylor asks if it was Parrish's conclusion that "nothing out of the ordinary took place, or was this the statement of the chief?"

Parrish states that he can't recall. "The email came from me, but this information and the general information, I would have gathered from conversations or information from the Police Chief."

Taylor asks if Parrish agreed with Chief Scott's opinion "that nothing out of the ordinary had happened with regard to Marcus Smith?"

"The nature of the commentary would have been related to the actions of the officers," says Parrish. "So, again, this information, I would have gathered from the police chief."

Taylor asks if Scott told Parrish that the GPD routinely hog-tied people experiencing a mental health crisis.

"I don't recall," says Parrish. He repeats that claim when Taylor asks if he had any conversations with Michelle Kennedy about Marcus' death.

Taylor is incredulous. "You don't recall having conversations with her at any time about the Marcus Smith case?"

"I do recall having conversations," replies Parrish, "but I don't recall the timing or the content."

In Taylor's deposition of Kennedy, she states she agreed with most of the statements Mitch Fryer made in that letter. The only one she disputes is Fryer's description of Marcus Smith as having "an amazing ability to both receive help and pour life into others," to which she replies "unfortunately, he did not have an amazing ability to receive help," and that "he was struggling with the issues that he was struggling with."

But when Taylor quotes each statement from Fryer about the need for greater transparency, Kennedy expresses complete agreement. She also agrees that the GPD's descriptions of Marcus as being combative and collapsing "leave too much room for interpretation and beg for further explanation."

Kennedy then states: "There were multiple conversations happening at that time as it related to the letter. I know I had spoken to City Manager Parrish about it, I spoke to the mayor about it, and other members of Council."

"Did you tell them you agreed with the letter in the ways that we have gone through just previously?"

Citing legislative privilege, attorney Alan Duncan instructs Kennedy not to answer. On this occasion, she complies, although on others, she ignores similar instructions.

In his deposition of Mayor Vaughan, Taylor asks about the letter from Mitch Fryer.

TAYLOR   Did it occur to you that it would be significant and important to let the public know that Marcus had been maximally retrained, or hog-tied as it was commonly known, at the time of his death?

VAUGHAN   We had not seen the videos and were not in a position to talk about what happened that evening. I believe this email was responded to by Chief Scott.

TAYLOR   So, you were not in a position to respond and let the community know that Marcus Smith had been maximally restrained?

VAUGHAN   As I said, we did not see the body-worn camera videos, and we did not have a deep knowledge of what happened that day.

TAYLOR	You knew, from talking to the chief and the city manager, that Marcus had been maximally restrained, right?
VAUGHAN	I also knew that it was under investigation by Internal Affairs and the SBI and felt it was important that those investigations run their course.
TAYLOR	Well, the investigations could have run their course at the same time, you could have amended the press release to say he had been maximally restrained while in police custody, couldn't you?
VAUGHAN	I believe the only way we could have responded, as Council, to this request was after seeing the body-worn camera video.
TAYLOR	Why?
VAUGHAN	Because we have no firsthand knowledge of what occurred that evening.
TAYLOR	You were told, were you not, by the city manager and the chief of police, that Marcus Smith had been maximally restrained, or hog-tied as it's commonly known, while in police custody, correct?
VAUGHAN	If I am going to put out a statement, I'm gonna want to see it firsthand, and I believe that the chief of police did respond.

Taylor then questions Vaughan about Scott's response to Fryer. "Did you make any effort to supplement what he said to the Homeless Union?" Vaughan replies, "No."

She then retracts an earlier statement, denying that she spoke to Scott about the email, stating, "I am not sure" Council knew how Marcus was restrained.

"But you knew from the first couple of days," says Taylor.

"No, I don't know that is correct," replies Vaughan.

Taylor reminds her of her previous statement that Chief Scott and City Manager Parrish told her that Marcus was maximally restrained, meaning hog-tied.

"We urge you to promptly release all relevant information."   137

"I knew that he had been restrained," says Vaughan, "but I wouldn't necessarily know what that restraint was."

Taylor asks Vaughan if "you're saying now that you didn't know that he was maximally restrained when this email went out form the chief in September of 2018?"

"I am saying that is possible," replies Vaughan.

17 "A CONCERTED EFFORT TO COVER UP."

On November 12, 2018, Smith family attorney Graham Holt sent the following letter to Greensboro's mayor and City Council:

Re: Marcus Smith

Dear Mayor Vaughan and City Council Members,

I represent the family of Marcus Deon Smith. On the night of September 8, 2018, Marcus Deon Smith died in the custody of the Greensboro Police Department. On October 8, 2018, I watched the body worn camera footage captured by officers at the scene.

Officers encountered Marcus on N. Church St. near the Folk Festival that was going on downtown. Marcus was pacing back and forth in the street and in and out of slow-moving traffic. He appeared exasperated and was waving his arms in the air. He would walk out into the street and then walk back again to the officers standing on the sidewalk and say things like, "please help me! I need help!" Marcus was clearly having a mental health crisis.

Officers continued to arrive until they were 10 officers on the scene. They called an ambulance to come take Marcus to the hospital. The officers were relaxed and not in the defensive posture. While waiting for the ambulance to arrive, the officers put Marcus at the back of a police car. Marcus complied at first, but as soon as he was in the back of the car, he wanted out. He was not under arrest.

In an attempt to get out of the car, he slammed his hand against the window and then he leaned back and kicked it. Worried Marcus might break the glass, the officers open the door and he quickly got out and resumed the same erratic but non-threatening behavior he exhibited before he was put in the police car. Officers grabbed Marcus and forced him down to the ground, facedown. Once on the ground, Marcus began to try to get back up. He didn't want to be held down. He began to flail legs. Not trying to kick the officers, but just kicking the air. Then something inexplicable and deeply disturbing and tragic happened.

While multiple officers held him down, one officer cuffed Marcus his hands behind his back. Another officer then grabbed Marcus's ankles and pushed up on his feet, forcing Marcus to bend his knees. The officer pushed his feet all the way to the point that Marcus's feet were touching his handcuffed hands at the small of his back. Then they hogtied it. Using a strap of some kind, they bound his hands to his feet behind his back. He was still face down. The officers tightened the straps so tight that Marcus's shoulders and his knees were suspended above the ground. Marcus's breathing quickly became strained and under a minute later he stopped breathing altogether. The officers were talking to each other over his body while he stopped breathing. A few moments after Marcus stopped breathing, one of the officers looked down and saw that Marcus's eyes were closed and ascertained that Marcus was unresponsive. Knowing that the hogtie was the problem, one of the officers exclaimed "Untie him now!" But it was too late. EMS tried to resuscitate him in the ambulance, and it looked to me like he had already passed or else he passed a short time later.

A concerted effort to cover up the cause of Marcus's death began immediately. Here is the City's press release following Marcus's death; the lies begin in the title which is almost completely devoid of truth, "Subject that collapsed in police custody later dies at hospital": [Whereupon Holt quotes the press release before continuing]

Marcus Smith did not collapse. He was taken to the ground by police and hogtied. He died as a result.

The family of Marcus Deon Smith wants the Greensboro Police Department to watch the police body worn camera footage and take appropriate action to ensure this doesn't happen to anyone else. Please contact me to schedule a time that I can meet with each of you to discuss what's on the footage and steps to be taken.

Sincerely,
GRAHAM HOLT

Attached to Holt's letter was a statement by the League of Women Voters and a coalition statement signed by the Homeless Union of Greensboro; Reverend Julie Peeples of Congregational United Church of Christ Greensboro; Reverend Brandon Wrencher for the Pulpit Forum of Greensboro; Reverend Wesley Morris of Faith Community Church; Reverend Nelson Johnson for the Beloved Community Center; Reverend Sadie Lansdale of the Unitarian Universalist Church of Greensboro; Reverend Randall Keeney of St. Barnabas Episcopal Church; Reverend Carter Ellis of St. Timothy's United Methodist Church; Reggie Weaver and Karen Archia for the Good Neighbor Movement Church; Irving Allen of the Greensboro Human Relations Commission and the Criminal Justice Advisory Commission (GCJAC); Greensboro Police Community Review Board Commissioner Lindy Garnette for the YWCA of Greensboro; Hester Petty for Democracy Greensboro; retired civil rights attorney Lewis Pitts; Dr. Spoma Jovanovic for the faculty of Reclaiming Democracy; Tiera Moore for Community Play!/All Stars Alliance; Thomas Burwell for Greensboro Food Not Bombs; Nikki Marín Baena for Siembra NC; Andrew Willis Garcés for American Friends Service Committee of the Carolinas; Holden Cession for Ignite NC; Afrique Kilimanjaro for the *Carolina Peacemaker*; and President Vicki White-Lawrence, Vice President Anna Fesmire, and Board Member Gary Kenton for the League of Women Voters of the Piedmont Triad.

In Mayor Vaughan's deposition, Flint Taylor questions Vaughan about her memories of November 12, 2018, and asks if she received a letter from Graham Holt on that date.

"That's possible," replies Vaughan.

Taylor then asks whether she knew the Smith family had seen the videos and was aware Marcus died from being hog-tied.

"That's possible," says Vaughan, a phrase she repeats almost as often in her deposition as variants of "I don't recall."

Taylor rephrases the question. "You knew that Marcus Smith's father and his lawyer had viewed the video, right?"

"I knew that they had viewed the video, yes," replies Vaughan. She then acknowledges she received Holt's letter but says, "I don't know how this letter was delivered, whether it was in person, by email or through the mail."

Taylor asks Vaughan if the letter caused her and other Council members to be concerned about what happened on the night of Marcus' death.

"I'm sure we discussed it," says Vaughan.

Taylor calls Vaughan's attention to the section of the letter where Holt accused the City of a cover-up that began with the initial press release. "And was it your belief that press release did not mention the fact that Marcus Smith had been either maximally restrained or hog-tied, that that didn't amount to a cover-up?"

"It did not," replies Vaughan.

Taylor presses the matter, pointing out the omission of any mention of the hog-tying and that the press release simply described Marcus as having "collapsed."

"I don't believe there was a cover-up," says Vaughan.

"And so, you didn't believe it then and you don't believe it now, is that your testimony?"

"Yes, it is," says Vaughan. She then explains she did not believe it was appropriate to respond to the letter from Holt because the SBI reports had not yet been finalized. She also states that she would not use the term "hog-tied" for what happened to Marcus. "He was maximally restrained."

Taylor asks her what that term means to her.

"It meant that, when they were having trouble transporting an individual, that it was a method of restraint. And that it was the maximum position."

Taylor asks her to be more specific.

"It meant immobilizing somebody so they could transport them for treatment. By using the RIPP Hobble device."

"Immobilize how?" asks Taylor.

"I'm not trained on how to apply it," says Vaughan. "I don't know that I could verbalize that."

Taylor asks if she spoke to Chief Scott after reading the letter, and if she spoke to City Manager Parrish. To both questions, she responds, "I don't recall." She also says, "I don't recall a specific conversation" with City Council members.

On November 14, 2018, Graham Holt held a press conference at which he quoted from his letter to the mayor and City Council and handed out copies. Later that afternoon, the City of Greensboro issued its third press release related to the death of Marcus Smith. The first, on September 8, stated an unidentified man had collapsed in custody and died at the hospital after being "suicidal" and "combative" during an encounter with GPD officers. The update on September 10 identified that man as Marcus Smith.

The press release, signed by City of Greensboro Communications and Marketing Director Carla Banks, read:

City's Response to Press Conference Regarding Marcus Smith

Greensboro, NC (November 14, 2018)—In response to today's news conference regarding the in-custody death of Marcus Smith the city's response is as follows:

- Per Greensboro Police Department policy, the State Bureau of Investigation was contacted to conduct an independent investigation.
- The Guilford County District Attorney's Office forwarded a letter to the Greensboro Police Department (GPD) indicating, based on the information collected by the State Bureau of Investigations (SBI), pending the final report, there was no criminal liability with the police actions concerning this incident. The District Attorney's Office states the officers acted at all times within the scope of their duties and with justification under all applicable laws.
- The SBI final report is not complete, but the position of the District Attorney's Office is there is sufficient evidence to support his decision related to the officers' actions.
- A GPD internal review was completed and no violations of policy were found.

The loss of any member of the community is unfortunate. The City of Greensboro has a process for residents to bring concerns to the Greensboro Criminal Justice Advisory Commission. The commission is tasked with reviewing criminal justice issues and working closely with Greensboro Police Department.

When the Greensboro Criminal Justice Advisory Board (GCJAC) was formed in 2018, the previously existing Police Community Review Board (PCRB) was revamped and folded into it as a subcommittee. From the time of its creation, it's been heavily criticized by community leaders and activists as being essentially toothless, with no subpoena power or administrative authority, and muzzled not only but its inability to take punitive measures, but by the fact that any member who discloses details of a complaint or an investigation is potentially subject to 20 days in jail and a $500 fine.

"The PRCB only gets what the police department decides to hand them," said retired civil rights attorney Lewis Pitts. "Everybody paying attention knows it's a sham."

In her deposition, Michelle Kennedy also expressed skepticism about the PCRB's ability to bring any truth or transparency to the controversy. "But North Carolina law has so many restrictions on their ability that I don't know to what extent any satisfactory resolution would've come from that."

At the December 4, 2018, meeting of Greensboro City Council, two Black PCRB members described the board to which they'd been appointed in terms that, if not as harsh as Pitts', were more blunt than Kennedy's. At that same meeting, 35 members of the public expressed their concerns about Marcus' death to Council members. His name had already been spoken at Council meetings in October and November.

At the October 2, 2018, meeting, UNC Greensboro professor emeritus, author, and Democracy Greensboro member Mary K. Wakeman became the first member of the public to speak to Council about the death of Marcus Smith.

"I would like to know whether you have found out anything about the death of Marcus Smith early on September 9th [sic], a homeless man who cut people's hair and was much beloved in the IRC community. People who know him say he was not suicidal and not by nature combative, as was reported in a press release from the Greensboro Police Department. A friend at the IRC reported he once had witnessed Mr. Smith being accosted by a belligerent man. He responded by refusing to fight. What really happened? Mr. Smith was fine on the afternoon of September 8, dead that night. His family deserves an explanation. A paragraph is not enough."

Mayor pro tem Yvonne Johnson then became the first Council member to publicly address the issue of Marcus' death. Johnson had become the city's first Black mayor in 2007 but lost the 2009 election to Bill Knight.

Prior to Johnson's term as mayor, she had been a member of Council for 14 years and Mayor pro tem for six. Short for "pro tempore," that designation means she exercises the mayor's authority in the case of absence, disability, or vacancy in office. In Greensboro's municipal elections, the three candidates for City Council At-Large who receive the most votes all become Council members, with the one receiving the highest number of votes also becoming Mayor pro tem. In 2011, Johnson again ran for City Council At-Large and received the most votes of any candidate in that municipal primary. She has won the majority of at-large votes in every election since. Johnson was 76 in 2018. Her current term ends in 2026.

In 2019 and 2021, Johnson attended vigils and press conferences for Marcus Smith, and spoke privately to his mother and sister. At these events, Reverend Nelson Johnson of the Beloved Community Center, who is not related to the mayor pro tem, acknowledged her from the podium, thanked her for her respectful presence, and asked activists and supporters of the Smith family to respect her in turn. She and Sharon Hightower are the two Black Council members not personally criticized by public speakers during meetings between 2018 and 2022, whereas district representative Justin Outling was regularly condemned for his silence and his lack of support for an independent investigation into Marcus Smith's death, and District 2's Goldie Wells would be excoriated for her remarks stating that the officers had not been cruel to Marcus and that "maybe it was just his time to die."

"I'd like a report on this from the police department," said Johnson to City Manager David Parrish after Wakeman spoke. "And whatever else we can get on what happened and what's being done."

"The SBI is investigating," said Parrish. "They have done interviews with those that knew him that were involved with the incident, and they are conducting their final report."

Then, at-large representative Michelle Kennedy spoke about Marcus.

"Obviously, Marcus was somebody that I knew very well, and [District 2 representative] Dr. [Goldie] Wells knew Marcus well. His mother is someone who called every day just to see how he was doing and has continued that practice. So, she reached out a week ago and had questions about the process. I spoke with her on the phone and relayed that message to the city manager and the city attorney, and explained to her what was going on. It's a difficult situation when you lose a child. I know that all too well, and no matter what, the family deserved a clear explanation of the sequence of events, no matter what the outcome of that explanation."

The subject of Marcus Smith would not come up again at Council until the November 20 meeting, eight days after Graham Holt wrote Council and six after his press conference.

"I want to throw this out, and will probably make everybody nervous," said District 1's Sharon Hightower at the end of that meeting. "But I want to make a request to see the body-worn camera footage of Marcus D. Smith. I've had several requests, so I do want to be able to see that."

"I spoke with the chief this evening and I'm going to speak to him again," said Yvonne Johnson. "I'm going to speak to him and offer you his response in December."

"Obviously, to ask to see it, we have to go before a judge to get permission," interjected Mayor Vaughan, "but we also have a policy and I think we need to encourage the family to follow that policy, which is to file a complaint and bring it before the PCRB. We just spent a year developing the new PCRB and coming up with the GCJAC, and this is the first case that will follow that new policy, and if we abandon the policy now, there will be no PCRB, everyone will come to City Council from here on forward."

While criticism of the mayor's response would be eclipsed when she called the City's initial press release a lie on December 4 and then walked back that statement shortly thereafter, this would be the most controversial public statement she made about the Marcus Smith case until then. Lewis Pitts called Vaughan's response to Hightower "an effort to delay and suck any investigation into a system that's completely confidential. You've had so many PCRB members resign for just that reason. That 20 days in jail and $500 fine is a huge threat."

At the next City Council meeting, held on December 4, 2018, six days after the Medical Examiner's report and the City's public release of the bodycam videos, two Black members of the PCRB would state that taking the matter to that board would be useless.

"This is not that," said Hightower. "This is a request for me to want to see the video."

"And I want to see the video," said Vaughan, "but I don't know that we can intervene in the policy. What I believe what is wanted is to watch the video and make the determination of what happened. I am all for watching the video, but I believe we need to follow the policy that we developed."

"So, are you saying we cannot watch the video unless there is a complaint?" asked Hightower.

"I think we can watch the video," said Vaughan, "but I think we also need to stress that this family should file a complaint."

"Well, I think you just said it," replied Hightower, "so hopefully they heard it."

"I believe that their attorney as of last week claimed to be unaware that there was a review board, and seemed to be unaware that we even have to get permission to watch the videos."

Graham Holt would later say that he was aware of the new review board, but like several of its own members, he considered it muzzled and ineffective. Both he and Lewis Pitts would criticize Mayor Vaughan and much of Council for accepting the claim from the city attorney that they could not watch the videos without permission from a judge, an issue that became moot when the videos went public ten days later.

"We do have a review board," said Hightower, "and we do seem to have a problem keeping folk on it, because this is the second or third time we've had to replace somebody."

"We've just spent a year revamping this process and we put new people on the review board with the help of community advocates," replied Vaughan. "I think it would be really unfair to short-circuit the review process."

"How does watching the video short-circuit this process?" protested Hightower. "Help me with that."

"I think saying that we've had problems with the review board in the past when we've just spent a year revamping, it short-circuits the process," said Vaughan with apparent irritation. "We've spent a year working on this and I think we should encourage the family to follow the process. We can petition the judge to watch the video, but I don't think we should intervene in the process."

Hightower's reply also expressed frustration. "How is that intervening? Help me out. I'm saying I want to see the video, not that I want to file a complaint."

"That's fine," replied Vaughan, "but I'm gonna say what I say before. Watch the video, but we're not going to make the determination. We need to encourage the family to file the complaint."

"But I'm not making the determination," said Hightower, "so I still don't know…"

"But I think you need to make that clear," said Vaughan before Hightower had finished her sentence, "that we still want the family to follow the process."

At that point, District 3 representative Justin Outling, who would later clash with two of his fellow Council members over several issues related to the Smith case, spoke over Hightower, calling for the meeting to be adjourned. He and Hightower shouted over each other for some seconds, with Hightower accusing Outling of rudeness, before Outling's motion was seconded, and Council voted to adjourn.

18 THE HOG-TYING OFFICIALLY BECOMES A HOMICIDE

"I don't know that they will ever determine a cause of death," said Scott Williams, the special agent in charge for the State Bureau of Investigation's Northern Piedmont District, who oversaw his agency's investigation into the death of Marcus Smith.

In a November 29 interview[1] with Jordan Green, Chief Wayne Scott acknowledged Marcus had been hog-tied but refused to use the word. When responding to Green's observation that GPD directives appeared to prohibit putting a subject in that position, he made his soon-to-be-infamous defense of what happened by arguing that the prohibition only applied to transporting persons in custody, and "unfortunately, we never got to the point where we were transporting Mr. Smith."

Special Agent in Charge Williams told Green the district attorney's determination that the officers who restrained Marcus bore no criminal liability in Marcus' death was consistent with his agency's forthcoming report. Williams added that the pending toxicology report "will explain why the person was acting the way they were."

Earlier that month, Mayor Vaughan attempted to speed the release of the toxicology report.

"This email will confirm the voicemail I left this morning," wrote Vaughan on November 21 to North Carolina Chief Medical Examiner Dr. Deborah Radisch. Vaughan described the Marcus Smith case as "becoming a flash point in our community" and asked about the possibility of expediting the report.

"I am sure that you are asked this often. Please know that I understand you have a tremendous workload. I would not make this request if it wasn't very important to maintain police-community relationships."

"I cannot expedite the toxicology testing," wrote Radisch in a response later that morning. "I will speak with the single reviewing toxicologist to see if the results are ready for review and finalizing, and ask him to review them if they are. I will also make the pathologist who performed the autopsy aware of your inquiry. This case may need additional discussion, but everyone involved will be made aware of your request."

Eight days later, and one day before the report was released, Associate Chief Medical Examiner Dr. Craig Nelson emailed Vaughan that Dr. Radisch had forwarded him the mayor's comments. "I hope by this afternoon to have a better idea of when we are able to finalize Mr. Smith's report and will update you. In the meantime, thank you for your patience as we work on this. As you know, being accurate and correct in our reports is what is most important, even if that means longer times to completion."

The final report issued by the Office of the Chief Medical Examiner, released on November 30, 2018, listed the decedent as "Marcus Dion Smith," although his middle name is spelled correctly in the body of the report. It bore the joint digital signatures of pathologist Dr. Cori Breslauer, and Assistant Chief Medical Examiner Dr. Craig Nelson, but the determination of homicide was made by Breslauer.

The causes of death were listed as "SUDDEN CARDIOPULMONARY ARREST" [capitalization in original] due to: "PRONE RESTRAINT; N-ETHYLPENTALONE, COCAINE, and ALCOHOL USE; and HYPERTENSIVE AND ATHEROSCLEROTIC CARDIOVASCULAR DISEASE." The listing of prone restraint before the others means it was considered the primary cause, with the drugs in his system the secondary cause, and his blood pressure and cardiovascular disease tertiary.

The report went on to state that "this 38-year-old man had a history of hypertension, smoking, and alcoholism. It was also reported that he was known to use cocaine and 'molly', a term that typically refers to MDMA, or 'ecstasy.'"

It concluded:

"The manner of death is classified as homicide."

As Mayor Vaughan and several members of City Council would repeatedly state over the following weeks, the word "homicide" is not a synonym for murder and used in this sense, the word implies no criminality. It did mean, however, that the primary cause of Marcus' death was his being placed in prone restraint. This may not have been the finding that City officials, the police department, the SBI, or the district attorney's office were anticipating.

"We knew that, when the autopsy report came out, the finding would be sensational," said Mayor Vaughan in her deposition. "So, we thought we needed to have a video released along with that." When asked what she meant by "sensational," Vaughan responds, "Well, you know, when you look at the certification and cause of death, we knew that would raise more concerns."

Taylor reminded the mayor that, ten days prior to the decision to release the videos, she told Sharon Hightower that "we need to respect the process," meaning that Mary Smith needed to file a complaint with the Police Community Review Board. He then asked her why she had changed her mind.

"We changed position because we felt it was in the public good. In order to maintain confidence, you can release a video. We have to have certain reasons to release a video when we go before a judge. We cannot unilaterally release videos without a judge's authorization."

"And the fact that the community was asking that the video be released was not sufficient for you to go in front of the judge until the results of the autopsy came back?" asked Taylor.

"No," said Vaughan, "we wanted to see the results of the SBI investigation completed and we were hopeful the Smith family would file with the PCRB. But when the autopsy report came out, we decided to go ahead and petition the judge. It was obvious the Smith family was not interested in filing a complaint with the Police Community Review Board."

As described later in this book, two members of that board told City Council that any investigation by the Police Community Review Board would have been both useless and censored.

When deposing City Manager David Parrish, Taylor asked Parrish if the City's decision to petition the judge was a response to the medical examiner's report.

"On November 30th, we decided at that time it was necessary to pursue the release of the court order of the body-worn camera footage," replied Parrish.

Taylor asked who the "we" in that statement was.

"The City of Greensboro," replied Parrish. "I can't recall the specifics around that afternoon, but it would have been a consensus of the City to pursue that release."

In Wayne Scott's deposition, he stated that the decision was his. "I chose to file a request for the petition, and in North Carolina it's got to be a single individual. The City could not file a petition."

On November 30, GPD Detective Antuan Hinson emailed Scott and the GPD deputy chiefs: "Attached is the completed autopsy report in the death of Marcus Deon Smith." According to Scott's deposition, minutes after reading the report, he decided to petition Superior Court Judge Susan Bray for permission to release.

In Scott's deposition, he told Flint Taylor he found "the fact that prone restraint was listed amongst the 'due to' clause disturbing."

"Which was the maximum restraining, correct?" asked Taylor.

"There is some discussion about clarification of it being the maximum restraining or the positioning" replied Scott. "Regardless, it was something that caused concern to me, as a chief, and I wanted to learn more about it."

Taylor then brought to Scott's attention a press release issued November 30 by City of Greensboro Communication Manager Jake Keys, which stated:

> Due to the multitude of factors that led to the tragic circumstances for Mr. Smith, detailed in the North Carolina Department of Health and Human

Services Medical Examiner report, the City of Greensboro believes there is a compelling public interest to share the videos. The City continues to review the initial findings of the Medical Examiner's report. Chief Scott has elected to modify the application of the RIPP Hobble used to restrain individuals while police continue to review the use of this method of restraint.

The compilation of the body-worn camera footage with narration from Chief Scott is available on the City of Greensboro's website. The remaining body-worn camera footage from all involved officers will be added to the website as it's available. Greensboro City Council members have viewed the footage in small groups.

When Taylor pointed out that the report released by the medical examiner's office was not "initial," but the final version, Scott replied, "I didn't write the press release. That's not my wording."

The evening of November 30, Scott issued Special Order 2018-17 to all GPD personnel, stating, effective immediately, "neither the RIPP Hobble nor flexicuffs will be linked to the wrists/handcuffs of a combative prisoner or individual during their use."

In Scott's deposition, Taylor asked whether this policy, if in effect at the time of Marcus' death, would have prevented him from being maximally restrained.

"I'd have to speculate," replied Scott, "but you could still maximally restrain, it's just that you cannot connect the hands and feet together. So therefore, we were kind of redefining what maximum restraint is."

Taylor asked Scott if he changed the policy because of Marcus' death.

"I changed the policy because of many factors, one being the incident Mr. Smith was involved in."

"What were the other factors?" asked Taylor.

"As chief, I have to be very aware of the fact of certain individuals in our community making accusations which can undermine the trust in our community, those kind of things. While I believe we had quite a bit of trust and community goodwill, we did have a small group of individuals in the community that were making accusations around the use of this device. It was not productive for the department to continue down that road until we understood what best practices would be."

Taylor then asked Scott about the compilation video posted to the City's website that evening. Scott told Taylor he recorded his five-minute introduction to the video earlier that day, before the judge ruled the footage could be released, and that he did not write it out beforehand. Taylor asked him who created the compilation.

"My Professional Standards division has control of all of our body cameras and editing, and they did it at my direction."

Taylor then asked if the compilation was created that afternoon, or if the Professional Standards department had been working on it for a while.

"They had been working on it, but it wasn't completed until that day, if I remember correctly."

When Taylor asked how long Professional Standards had been working on it, Scott replied "I couldn't tell you. Sometime before then. That was a standard practice for us in an incident."

Taylor expressed skepticism. "So, they just miraculously finished with this video on the very afternoon that you decided to seek release of the videos publicly and to put the compilation on the website?"

"I made them aware that I was seeking the court order, and I wanted it finished up," replied Scott. "It was pretty close to being finished, but they went through it to polish it, if you will, to make sure, as best as possible, the frames come together and those kind of things." He also said he watched the compilation video directly before recording his introduction to it.

When interviewed in November of 2022, Taylor addressed the question of just when the video compilation and the narrative with which Scott introduced it were created.

"I never could get a definitive answer. It seemed like they were resisting the release of the videos, first after Graham [Smith Family co-counsel] revealed that Marcus had been hog-tied on November 14, and then when Vaughan kept insisting 'we must respect the process' of their useless review board, an argument she stopped making after the homicide declaration. Then, they do a 180 and go to court and get an order to release the videos. And in a couple of hours, they have this compilation video."

Taylor implied that Scott's five-minute introduction was scripted. "Scott isn't improvising. And I asked him about that, and he was so vague. The question remains, why were they working on it if they were fighting against it being released? Were they hedging their bets? I suppose the best explanation for it might be that after Graham had the press conference on the 14th, they decided they needed a counter-narrative, so they put together a compilation video and scripted out a statement for the chief to make before people watched it, then released it on their own terms. And then when all Hell broke loose around the homicide ruling, they no longer could pick the spot to drop this video, but they knew the public and many on the Council would watch the compilation and might not bother with all the individual videos."

Speaking to Greensboro City Council on May 17, 2019, eight months and nine days after Marcus' death, Democracy Greensboro activist Hester Petty detailed what she described as "three false statements" in the framing narrative with which Chief Scott introduced the compilation video.

Petty said Scott's "first false statement" was when he described Marcus Smith as "turning on his back and kicking the window" of the patrol car the police asked him to enter while waiting for EMS to arrive. She acknowledged that his feet were pressed briefly against the glass and that "he might have kicked the window if the car door had not been opened, but that would be speculation, not truth."

Scott's "second false statement," she said, was:

"We made the decision very quickly that we had to transport him [Marcus] for further medical examination, and connecting with EMS personnel, the decision was made at their request that he had to be restrained."

While it may be a matter of opinion and interpretation as to whether Marcus was preparing to kick the car window, the claim that the decision to restrain Marcus was made at the request of EMS is demonstrably false. As Petty noted:

"EMS had not yet arrived on the scene when Officer Duncan told the dispatcher that he would take Marcus to the hospital. Officer Duncan then told the officers standing near him 'probably ought to RIPP Hobble him.' It is clear, watching the unedited body cam videos, that the decision to restrain Marcus was made by Officer Duncan before the EMTs walked up to the patrol car and it was not made at the request of EMS."

It was around this point that Chief Scott, who had been present at the Council meeting to deliver a commemoration speech, left the room as Petty said, "Chief Scott's third false statement" was this:

"The application of the RIPP Hobble takes a little less than a minute. You'll see the officers following our procedures, immediately rolling him on his side where they could adjust the RIPP Hobble and check his condition."

Petty adamantly disputed Scott's description. "In fact, once the RIPP Hobble was fastened, the officers did not immediately roll Marcus over on his side. Instead, they stood up and looked down at him as he lay lifeless face down on the pavement. Only then did they roll him over, and that was to take the RIPP Hobble off so EMS could do something, which of course, they could not because he was dead."

As was the case every time between 2018 and 2022 Petty made detailed statements about the Marcus Smith case which she supported with evidence, and which conflicted with the official narrative put out by the Greensboro Police Department, neither the mayor nor any City Council member asked any questions or requested copies of the supporting materials she brought with her.

After the meeting was adjourned, Mayor Vaughan stated: "The one thing I would say about the City releasing all of these videos is that it gives everybody the opportunity to watch every video and the compilation video and to make their own determination. And I think that's very important that the City was transparent in releasing everything that we have available, unlike other cities that we've seen. I think that by releasing all the videos at the scene by every officer that was there was extremely transparent and let people draw their own conclusions."

In May of 2021, Flint Taylor asked Chief Scott about Petty's assertions.

"Did you agree or disagree with her statement that the video did not show him kicking the window, but rather putting his feet by the window?"

"I disagree," replied Scott. "If you watch other videos and listen to the sound of striking on the inside of the videos, I draw a conclusion that he was kicking the window or the window frame."

I AIN'T RESISTING

Taylor then asked about Petty's allegation that it was "absolutely clear that the decision to restrain Marcus was made by Officer Duncan before EMTs had walked up to the patrol car." Scott acknowledged that Duncan made those statements about the RIPP Hobble before paramedic Abbott said, "He'll have to be restrained," but then said:

"It is my belief that he made those statements concerning transporting him in a patrol car, which was no longer the case. I think once EMS arrived on the scene and the decision was made that he was going in an ambulance, then the EMT or EMS worker said, 'He'll have to be restrained.' I think that's when the decision was made that he ought to be restrained in the ambulance."

Taylor replied that, in Ashley Abbott's deposition, she stated she did not know what a RIPP Hobble was, and she never meant to request one be used on Marcus Smith.

Scott replied that the term restraint "could be defined in multiple ways, yes."

Taylor pointed out that Hester Petty had accurately stated that Officer Duncan not only made the decision to hog-tie Marcus but did so before telling Abbott that Marcus would not be transported in the ambulance. After Scott replied, "I don't believe that was accurate at all," Taylor asked Scott to elaborate.

"I believe that the words that the officer uttered were his evaluation while Mr. Smith was in the car and that the actions immediately after he got out [sic]. It's logical and fair to bring that up. But equally, I think, had Mr. Smith ceased his agitation and complied, that he would have went and sat in the ambulance. So, I believe the fact that when the EMT said, 'we have to restrain him,' the officers were really left with no other option, except to use what they had been trained do, which is the Hobble, to secure him in a way that he could be transported."

Taylor then asked Scott if "you didn't see anything inaccurate about trying to put the decision to maximally restrain Marcus" on the EMTs who arrived on the scene after Duncan had twice said "we are going to have to RIPP Hobble him."

Scott replied that "given the context of the introduction, I believe it's accurate."

"And it's your testimony that you made no inaccurate statements concerning the video in your introduction?"

"It's my statement or my testimony that the purpose of the video was to highlight areas to allow people to understand what they were watching," replied Scott.

When Flint Taylor questioned Michelle Kennedy about this in her deposition, he asked her if she believed that Chief Scott "attempted to put the decision to hog-tie unfairly on the EMTs."

"I can't speak to whether it was fairly," replied Kennedy, "but he did put that decision on the EMTs."

Kennedy said that it was "my understanding at the time" that Marcus was in EMS custody, and that, due to her shock at what she saw on the videos, she did not initially question the claim that it was "a protocol issue, in terms of who made the determination for restraints" and that EMS made the decision to restrain Marcus, but that after watching the videos several more times, "I don't believe that it was true."

She made it clear throughout her deposition that she had always been skeptical of every claim made about the incident by Chief Scott, and of Scott's character and truthfulness. When Flint Taylor asked her if the reason she'd never asked Scott about what was depicted on the videos prior to the time she watched them herself was that "you didn't trust what he would tell you," she replied she did not.

Her concerns were not allayed when, the day after she watched the videos, she and Mayor Vaughan talked to Scott in his office.

"I was concerned that his representation of the events of that night were inconsistent with what I had seen on the video," said Kennedy. When Taylor asked her if Vaughan appeared to share her concerns, Kennedy said, "I don't remember."

Taylor then asked if, in that discussion, Scott had given "what you consider to be clarity?"

"No," said Kennedy. "It was more reiteration of the things he had said prior, and I just couldn't reconcile that with what I had seen."

Taylor asks Kennedy if watching the videos reinforced her opinion that Scott should've been fired.

"That opinion for me has been consistent throughout," replied Kennedy. "So, it didn't change any of that."

Taylor then asked if she believed there had been a cover-up.

"I don't believe that I'd ever used the language that he engineered a cover-up," replied Kennedy. "I think it's more appropriate to say that he did not provide full information as it relates to that. And I have to acknowledge, as I've said before, he is not someone that I had a high degree of confidence in to begin with."

Taylor asked if Kennedy shared her concerns about Scott with other Council members or the city manager.

"Yes," she replied. "I made it clear that I believed that, while it was not our decision to make, it was my opinion he should be relieved of his duties. I don't think there was anybody that was unclear that was my opinion. However, the chief of police is not an employee of the City Council. It is the city manager's right and responsibility to make employment decisions as it relates to the chief. So, I don't know at what point I said to City Manager Parrish how I felt about that, but I'm sure I did at some point."

When Taylor asked Kennedy if other Council members agreed that Scott should be fired, defense attorney Alan Duncan cautioned her not to describe anything said by other Council members unless it was in a public session. "Never had a Council meeting where termination of the chief of police was discussed," said Kennedy.

Taylor then asked Kennedy if she'd ever discussed the matter with District 1's Sharon Hightower. Duncan repeated his instruction not to answer if the conversation wasn't held during a public session.

"Not in any open setting that I recall," said Kennedy.

Taylor pressed the matter by asking, "Did she share a personal opinion as to whether she agreed or disagreed with your position that Scott should be removed?"

After considerable back and forth between Taylor and Duncan as to whether Kennedy could answer the question, Kennedy said, "It is my understanding that she shares the same view as me." Taylor then asked about the opinions of Mayor pro tem Yvonne Johnson and District 5 representative Tammi Thurm. Duncan again told Kennedy she could only describe what was said in a public meeting.

"The easiest way to answer this is," said Kennedy, "is I would have liked to have a Council meeting where we publicly discussed this issue, but that never happened. So, a lot of conversations around this never transpired."

19 "POLITICIANS GON' POLITICIAN."

On the evening of November 30, 2018, the Greensboro Police Officers Association (GPOA) released a statement responding to the controversy around Marcus Smith's death to WFMY News 2, the local CBS affiliate.

Despite regularly being described as a union in the local press, the Association is not one; it is a political action committee made up of members of the Greensboro Police Department. On its website, it promises members 24/7 legal representation through Amiel Rossabi of Rossabi Law Partners to "provide advice and consultation with GPOA members who have been involved in an officer-involved use of deadly force, a critical incident, a situation of grave importance or other serious job-related incident."

Rossabi is a longtime bulldog advocate for the GPD who has defended, either in the media or the courtroom, multiple officers accused of misconduct and excessive force.

The statement of the GPOA reads:

The Greensboro Police Officer's Association expresses its unwavering support and appreciation for its officers involved in the tragic death of Marcus Dion [sic] Smith earlier this fall. The officers acted with compassion, respect, and concern for the safety of Mr. Smith and others affected by Mr. Smith's actions. We are confident that a review of the body camera footage released this evening will convince all of our citizens that the officers did everything possible to correctly and safely perform their duties.

The same broadcast included a statement from City Council at-large representative Marikay Abuzuaiter who, in the Marcus Smith case as in almost every incident of alleged police misconduct before and after it, was a tireless defender of the GPD.

In 2013, journalist Eric Ginsburg obtained over 20 emails revealing council member Abuzuaiter served as a confidential informant for the Greensboro Police Department.[1]

At the October 2, 2018, City Council meeting, the same one where Mitch Fryer criticized the actions of the GPD's Civil Emergency Unit in Chapel Hill and revealed two of Wayne Scott's officers were handlers for a former KKK Imperial Wizard,[2] Abuzuaiter responded to speakers from the floor who accused her of being a "police snitch."

"You can call me anything you want to. But I want to say that I was at a rally, and I was at a rally where children were there. And there was a car that drove by—a van that drove by and stopped. And when that van drove and stopped and started throwing beer bottles at the children, I called the police. I dialed 911. I did it several times. Even when I was at rallies after—I had people telling me: 'Are the police around in case that happens again?' So yes, I developed a relationship with the police. But I was not the things that were called and that you've called out. I don't think I'd be here if that were true."

However, as *Triad City Beat* editor-in-chief Brian Clarey wrote about that meeting,[3] "the term 'confidential informant,' or 'CI,' used to describe Abuzuaiter comes straight from the police. A November 2009 email from Lieutenant Mike Richey to police employees Teresa Biffle, John D. Slone, and Steven Kory Flowers begins with a phone number, and then Richey writes, 'The number above is Marikay Abuzaiter [sic]. She was a frequent CI during the Palestinian protests. She called a few minutes ago to advise us that Tim Hopkins is planning a protest for 1530 ours [sic] at Market and Elm the day after Obama announces a troop buildup in Afghanistan." Hopkins is a longtime Greensboro activist who in January of 2007 had organized protests against George W. Bush's build-up of U.S. troops in Iraq.

"His surge protest in 2006 [sic] was the time we ended up arresting 11 when they tried to take over the street." Richey continued. "You should have the intel report on your computer. Marikay said you can call her, just keep her involvement among us."

The November 30, 2018, broadcast that included the Police Officers Association statement also included the following from Abuzuaiter: "Council viewed the body-worn camera video in small groups this evening in the Marcus Smith incident. We are still waiting for the SBI & DA determinations. The public can view the video on the City website. If you watch it in its entirety, it is my personal opinion that the officers were doing their utmost to assist Mr. Smith and called EMS. EMS asked the officers to restrain him before they could transport him. My sympathies go out to Mr. Smith's family."

On Sunday, December 2, 2018, two days after Abuzuaiter gave that statement to News 2, Nancy Vaughan, Michelle Kennedy, Sharon Hightower, and Goldie Wells held a meeting at the IRC that was meant, at least on the part of the mayor and the IRC director, to be a small and private meeting with some of the community leaders who had signed the November 14 letter from Graham Holt.

The meeting is captured on video recorded on a cellphone and uploaded to YouTube in three parts.[4] The angle at which the phone is held suggested that the recording may have been made surreptitiously. It was shared to Facebook by Greensboro Criminal Justice Advisory Commission executive member Cherizar Crippen, who posted:

> So, we crashed a meeting where our elected officials did not deem it necessary to invite the family of the victim or the orgs working so hard to see justice JUST ONCE in this corrupt system.
>
> Major takeaways:
>
> We can play all day with the word homicide but as Rev Nelson so eloquently stated by definition, medical or Webster's, it means other people (not drugs or health) is responsible for the death of Marcus Smith. Those other people work for GPD.
>
> We can back and forth about when and where a rule was put in place to gag the police accountability review board I serve** on from talking about cases but the rule remains and will result in us serving jail time and paying fines if we speak out.

"Politicians gon' politician." 163

We can talk all day long in these meetings the community at large are not invited to or know about, but until THE PEOPLE become part of the process, we will be doomed to repeat a cycle of forgetfulness and this fake ass progressive veneer Greensboro calls home.

GPD been racist. Government been secretive. The people been tired. Join us at Shiloh Baptist Church tomorrow 6:30pm so we can get #justiceformarcussmith

** Correction, I serve as an executive member of the Greensboro Criminal Justice Advisory Commission not the Police Accountability Review Board although my job is to talk about police accountability and attend the police accountability review board meetings. If anybody knows the difference, I'm all ears since my job seems to live in the same grey area where police make all their bad decisions. Still gagged if I signed the non-disclosure agreement as it is currently worded which was the ACTUAL point of bringing this up. But politicians gon' politician.

"At this point, everybody in this room has seen this video, right?" says Michelle Kennedy at the beginning of the first of the three Facebook videos. By "this video," she clearly means the BWC footage of the death of Marcus Smith, which at that point had been on the City of Greensboro website and YouTube approximately 48 hours.

Kennedy then makes it clear that there are a lot more people in the IRC workroom than she and Mayor Vaughan had intended or invited.

"[inaudible] have opinions and beliefs and all those things, and there will be space tomorrow night and Tuesday night to have that conversation, but that's not what this conversation is about. This is a conversation about mentally treating a thousand people who live in the city and how do we step from this into something that makes us better and not the same-old same-old that keeps us [inaudible] in this place. So, with all the respect that I can muster, we are going to have a small group meeting with the people that we asked to come to this meeting, and I'll take responsibility for being the one who said this is who we asked and that's what we intend to do."

A good portion of the audio on all three videos is difficult to decipher, partially because the person recording it seems to be sitting in the back of the room and possibly trying to keep the phone out of Kennedy's view, and definitely because the phone, in the first video, is repeatedly dragged or scraped across what appears to be a table top, creating a sound which drowns out the speakers they are trying to record.

Kennedy's next statements indicate she intended to take some but not all the people in attendance into another room for a private conversation, something that ultimately did not happen.

"The meeting that we asked to have is going to happen. Everybody is welcome to stay out here, and we'll come back out and have a conversation with you after that, but this was never intended to be community meeting. I'm very sorry it was put out that way."

When asked how she decided who to invite, Kennedy says "it was from looking at the folks who signed on to the initial communication," apparently referring to the November 14 letter from Graham Holt.

The audio is garbled, but Kennedy then pointed to several people in the room "who have been involved in social justice work and the faith community" as having been invited, as well as a representative from the League of Women voters. She explained that "we obviously couldn't invite everybody" who signed the letter, and that this "was never intended to be a large meeting."

Someone points out that the Homeless Union of Greensboro was not invited.

"I will say pretty squarely that I feel safe in representing the general feel of people within the IRC experiencing homelessness as it related to this information," replies Kennedy, "as we've been talking about it non-stop since it happened."

The rest of her response is inaudible.

Marcus Hyde stands up and explains that he was the one who invited other members of the community. When he says this, Kennedy turns her back on him and walks out of the shot in apparent anger.

Much of what Hyde says is inaudible, but one of the clearer statements he makes is "No one is stopping you for having a meeting...uh...and you can go ahead and have your meeting, but I think it's pretty clear why people would question this, if these people on that list are invited, except for the Homeless Union, except for Graham Holt, and except for the family."

Much of Kennedy's response is muffled.

"The first phone call I got about this was at three o'clock in the morning, and I have been knee-deep in this ever since," says Kennedy. "You have stood in my office and asked me repeatedly for the phone number to this family when they were calling just to talk to us. Yes, you talked to her, that's fantastic. But the reality of the situation is that you have no idea what has happened in the last 24 hours, and to assume that you do, and then light into an attack about this is not helpful, EVER!"

At this point, Reverend Wesley Morris introduces himself as one of the people who were not invited and speaks about the information in the initial press releases.

"That hung out there in this community for too long, and never should have been out there in the first place. The next thing that happened was a press conference that called the attention of the city to the letter that was sent. There was no response. Formal, written, email or otherwise. That letter was asking for a community dialogue, in a room that would look like this, centered around the family who came up here on a couple of occasions. Those that signed on to the letter were asking for a kind of community dialogue that could have averted this kind of issue. I found out about this meeting today."

Mayor Vaughan then stands up and speaks.

"I do want to say that when we got the letter, I reached out to the medical examiner's office right away, because one of the concerns was how long it was going to take to get the toxicology report and the autopsy report finalized. I reached out to the medical examiner and the SBI to see if there was any way to expedite the final report. It was a little difficult. They don't play favorites to Greensboro or any other city, but I do think that working with them to get the final report may have helped a little bit. I have worked with them over the last month to get those reports finalized, to get them to the family. They certainly reported to the family and to their attorney before they came to the City."

Vaughan then describes how, once the medical report was released, "the first thing we did was go to Judge Bray and ask not only could we see the video, but could we release it to the community at large."

In their depositions, Police Chief Wayne Scott and City Manager David Parrish would state that they did not recall the mayor being part of that process.

Vaughan then addresses the issue of Marcus' killing being declared a homicide. "There were only five check-off boxes. He [Associate Chief Medical Examiner Craig Nelson] was very specific when he said that homicide doesn't mean murder."

Sharon Hightower stands up and addresses the room.

"I want to say that I've never known what was going on behind the scenes. I feel left out. That video, I saw it for the first time Friday, with the chief standing there with a prepared statement, and I don't know who ran that or set it up. I think maybe the intent was there to explain it, but it..."

At this point, her voice becomes inaudible, as the recording phone is again apparently dragged across a flat surface.

When Hightower becomes audible again, she appears to be addressing her remarks to Vaughan, although it's hard to tell.

"You can sit there and roll your eyes, but I'm a little tired of it. [Inaudible]. There are things, many times, that go on, that others are having conversations about, and I'm pulled in at the last minute. I asked a few weeks ago to see that video, but was loudly shouted down, as you know, by another Council member. We've got to have a dialogue about how to move forward, but also about accountability and how to address what we saw on that video."

Next, Goldie Wells speaks. Wells represents the district that includes the IRC and was, with Kennedy, one of two Council members who knew Marcus.

"We were under court order. We could not see it. On Friday, the Judge came out of the courtroom and gave us special permission. Has everybody in here seen it? Who has not seen the video? It's on the City website. A picture's worth a thousand words. A lot of times we have perceptions about it, and then when we see it, it's a different story."

"Politicians gon' politician."   167

She then makes comments for which she would be widely criticized in coming weeks and months.

"There could have been a lot of reasons for the death. It didn't look like a murder to me. The men were saying we're trying to help him, c'mon buddy, calm down, we're trying to help you, calm down. If they had kicked him around, or said nigger do this, or get in here, or something, I would have felt they were being cruel to him, but they were not, they did not."

The room fills with angry murmurs.

"Homicide does not mean murder," says Wells so emphatically it's almost a shout. "I feel that we have a lot to do in this city, to bring about calmly, but if we escalate and take something out of context and use that to divide our city, we have too far to go and too many good things to go, and to take one thing and blow it out of context, just blow it way out, and then we divide our city, and we do ourselves no good by doing that."

The next person to speak is Fahiym Hanna, a young Black community leader who in 2020 ran unsuccessfully for the Guilford County Board of Commissioners but was defeated in the Democratic primary by veteran Black community leader and politician Melvin "Skip" Alston.

Hanna takes exception to being told to move on. "We always beg you in these moments to stop the process and rebuild it in order to stop harming people, and you tell us we have to move on. Imagine if 30 percent of the population said their trash wasn't being picked up. That would get worked on right away. We're not lying about this. People don't just make up stuff about the police for no reason. Why don't we stop the process now? This Council is probably the most progressive it's ever going to get. So why not let us stop here and deal with this, rather than telling us we need to move on?"

Black Lives Matter organizer April Parker criticizes Michelle Kennedy for "the fancy racist misstep" of using the phrase "Black Lives Matter" while excluding Black organizers like herself.

Reverend Nelson Johnson then speaks, beginning by saying that he isn't sure whether or not he was invited to the meeting. (Marcus Hyde and Mitch Fryer would later allege that Johnson and the Beloved Community Center were deliberately excluded for being too radical.)

"However this meeting occurred, it is some reflection of how people see things, and the pain that people are [inaudible]. Every crisis carries with it the danger of that crisis, but it also carries with it the opportunity to do something different and creative, and I want to challenge you to do that tonight."

He also responds to the attempts by Vaughan and Wells to distinguish homicide from murder by saying "an ordinary person knows what that means, that but for the behavior of another human being, this wouldn't have happened, and how you spin it may be satisfying to you, but people who hear it don't believe you, so we've got to have a quality of conversation that we've not been able to have in this city. I know what our police are capable of doing and I know the lies that I've been told, and I've known the lives that are no longer here because of it. I know the lies that have been told, I know the things that have been done, and the things that have happened to other people that are even worse."

Johnson tells Kennedy, Vaughan, and Wells that "whatever y'all decide after this meeting, and whatever formation you're in, is not going to be adequate, because right now, your openness to hearing the criticism and critique is too narrow."

The next speaker is Julie Peeples, pastor at Congregational United Church of Christ, who is white. "Precisely because so many people have been at this for so long, I think we need more meetings. I hear the pain of being excluded and that was not the intention, and you have my apologies for my part in that. At the same time, I think if we are really going to have something different happen, we need meetings in the northwest of Greensboro, the southwest, the southeast. We need meetings of teachers, or business leaders. I think we've got to get a lot of folks on board with making substantive lasting systemic changes. I think the answer to this is not that nobody can meet unless it's a big public meeting."

Kennedy concludes the meeting by saying "I take responsibility for anything that became exclusionary, which was not my intention. It was really to find a small group of us to start building conversation about building to bigger ownership of that."

She then calls embedding social workers with the police "a critical first step" in preventing more tragedies like Marcus' death and said, "in the three years that I'll finish out my first term, we'll still have a boatload of things we're trying to figure out."

Kennedy will resign from City Council two years and 28 days later.

20 "OBVIOUSLY, A LIE."

On Monday, December 3, 2018, one day after the meeting at the IRC, a "Justice for Marcus Smith" meeting was held at Shiloh Baptist Church in Greensboro. It was the first visit to Greensboro by Mary and George Smith, Kim Smith, and Len Butler since they learned how Marcus died, and the first time they spoke publicly about it. It was also the first time video of Marcus' death was shown to a large group of people, which in this case happened before anyone from the Smith family spoke.

"These videos should have been five minutes," said Kim, her voice strong and determined. "It should have been of the police caring for him until the EMTs got there and took him to the hospital. I feel the paramedics are just as responsible. That's just like if I called 911 and the ambulance never showed. Each and every police officer and each and every paramedic that was there, your profession looks down on you. You need to find another job."

She said that every officer who interacted with Marcus should be held accountable. "There was no sense of urgency at all. This was somebody's life on the line. Nobody stopped this madness. Greensboro, you ought to be afraid, because if they're going to keep people like this on the street, you better leave."

Mary Smith spoke next; some of her statements appear in the second chapter of this book, "The Man Whose Life Mattered." After a few minutes, she concluded by expressing her gratitude.

"It's been rough. Only thing I can say is thank you everyone for coming out. You saw the videos. Only thing I can say about those officers is karma will be back."

George Smith got up to speak about his son, but he didn't get very far without choking up. Marcus' brother Len then took the microphone.

"I thank every individual under this roof today. Thank God for my mom putting a wonderful brother in my life. It's sad he couldn't get help. He was what we in the Masonic world call a brother in distress. That means somebody in need. Thank you all for being here. Keep the fight, no matter where it's at, no matter who else loses their life to police brutality."

Reverend Nelson Johnson invited Mayor Vaughan to take the microphone.

"I came here tonight at the request of Kim to listen to the conversation, to listen to the dialogue, and that is what I am here to do. This is a very painful video to listen to, to watch. I know that we all saw it and we were watching the last minutes of somebody's life. It has hit us all. It has brought us all to our knees to watch it. I don't know what to say tonight. We are all processing this."

"What are you going to do?" yelled someone from the audience.

"I am here tonight to listen to the family," said Vaughan. "I came here tonight to meet with the family, to listen to the community, and that is what I am here to do."

"Community says fire him," said someone in the audience, referring to Chief Scott. "What is your response?"

"First of all, the City Council does not hire the police chief. The mayor does not hire the police chief!"

There were angry murmurs from the audience. "Give her time to answer the question!" cautioned Reverend Johnson.

Vaughan composed herself. "I knew that coming here tonight was going to be very difficult. I know, believe me, I know. I know this is awful for you. I don't know that I could watch what . . ."

"Did you watch the videos?" asked an audience member.

"Yes, I did," said Vaughan. "I cannot tell you how awful I feel for you."

"Feel bad for these other people!" shouted an audience member.

"Brothers and sisters, let one person speak at a time," said Reverend Johnson. He then handed the microphone to a woman who said she had been at the IRC the day before.

"I understand what you're saying, but the thing of it is, you should have already been on the radar to be here, you shouldn't have had to be invited. And I just want to know why you sound so different than what you said last night. You sound different when you're talking in front of the family and when you're not."

As might be expected under the circumstances, Vaughan responded defensively. "As I said yesterday, we're still waiting on the SBI report, and we're still waiting for it to go back through the DA."

Several people yelled simultaneously from the audience, making it unclear what they were saying.

"You don't know what is in my heart!" said Vaughan with a flash of anger. "You can say whatever you want to say."

Reverend Johnson raised his hand for calm. "Let me ask you to do this. Can you answer the question as to whether you personally feel the police chief should be fired?"

"I want to tell you," replied Vaughan, "I feel lots of concerns over that first press release..."

"Answer the question!" shouted multiple people in the crowd.

"I am answering it!" said Vaughan.

"No, you're not!" shouted an audience member.

"And I don't appreciate..." said Vaughan.

Reverend Johnson waved for silence and admonished both Vaughan and her critics.

"We're not going to devolve into a shouting match. We're not going to do that! Be quiet right now, Sister Mayor, I'm talking. Be quiet. I want us to build the unity of this group. And if you would answer that question, and then just sit down. You don't have to have a running argument here."

"I am answering," said Vaughan. "I have great concerns on how this was handled. I have concerns about that first press release that was put out. I want answers on why it was said that he was suicidal and dropped to the ground. That obviously was a lie. And I think that has to be answered too. And we're going to ask those questions on who put that press release out and under what grounds, because obviously based on the video, which you were able to see, and we released that video and all the videos so you can see it, we're going to want answers. And based on those answers, you're going to see what our answer is. But that very first press release, obviously, is a lie."

When there were more shouts from the audience, Kim Smith came to Vaughan's defense.

"First of all, I'm going to say this, we're not going to attack Nancy. Because let me tell you somebody who I serve, and justice is going to prevail, because He said, vengeance is mine. We're not going to attack Nancy. Her conscience is going to tell her what to do. We're not going to fuss at her. Everybody is scared, Nancy, and I'm telling you, from heart to heart, your people of Greensboro, are scared, and they want something done, in a caring way. And they ask for you, and they put it in your hands. And they want you to hear them."

Kim then motioned toward where Michelle Kennedy is seated.

"And Michelle, you knew my brother, you knew what type of person he was. This is not what we do, this is not how we conduct ourselves as a family, and we're not going to let nobody tarnish his name."

Kim paused before continuing.

"He did what he did. Everybody has things that they do, they're just not out with it, and they do it in the comfort of their homes. And let me tell you all one more thing about Marcus. He was homeless by choice. Because you can tell by his family, we wanted him to come home. He didn't want to come home because of what he was doing, he didn't want to let us see it. It was just a phone call. But we're not going to do this. We're not going to attack her. When she makes her decision, whatever the decision is, that's when we'll get back on this board, and we'll figure out what we need to do going forward. But her conscience is going to talk to her, and we're going to pray that God talks to her. That's what we gonna do."

"Thank you, Sister Kim," said Reverend Johnson. He then called on Sharon Hightower to speak. The councilwoman took the microphone.

"A couple of weeks ago, I asked to see the video, and then I was told no. First of all, let me apologize to you for your brother and your son. I am sorry. I watched this video, and I hurt. I have struggled with this because he was a human being and should not have lost his life like that. That was wrong."

Hightower paused to compose herself.

"And then to know this, and the report came out, and that the statement that he was suicidal and collapsed was an outright lie. And under the police officer oath, you cannot lie and maintain your job. And that needs to be handled immediately, because my life is on the line, too. I am Black and I live in this community, amongst all of you, and I drive my car at night, and right now I am afraid. And I can't represent you if I'm afraid. That is wrong, for me to be in that position. You should live in the city and walk about as you choose, without fear of any kind of retaliation from a police officer. The police officer I grew up with as a child was your friend, to protect and serve, and that is no longer the case, ladies and gentlemen, and when I watched the video at the end, I thought of Eric Garner and 'I can't breathe.' I've lived with that since Friday. I want a full investigation and I am going to ask for that at the City Council meeting because I want to know what happened, and why, and why somebody wasn't looking at him when he was laying on that ground. And why that procedure was enacted on him, because it was not proper."

Hightower then nodded at Mayor Vaughan.

"I will also ask, and I told the mayor this, that procedure needs to be removed from the [GPD] directives, period. Not modified, as the chief has suggested, but removed. And other cities have done it. We need to find alternative measures to restrain people. So. I am 100 percent supportive of what you all were asking for, because it's not unreasonable, it is fair, and we must do what is just."

Although Chief Wayne Scott was not present, Hightower addressed him directly.

"Chief, I stood with you in a press conference this year. I did not want you. And I've been penalized ever since because of that. They don't patrol my neighborhood, they don't respond very well, but that's okay, because in the end, God is the ultimate judge and I know that."

"Obviously, a lie."   175

Mayor Vaughan again took the microphone:

"We haven't had a situation quite like this before, where a press release has gone out on something serious like this before where information has obviously been false and we will work on that tomorrow to find out how something like that went out and what the consequences of that will be, and we will work on that tomorrow. Sharon had asked for an investigation on how this unfolded and we will certainly do that. I am not prepared right now to say what those penalties will be, because a lot of that will be up to the city manager with our review. All I can let you know and can let people here know is that it is very important to us and we know that it is very important to you and that you need to hold us to that standard and that is something we will look into first thing tomorrow morning, how a press release like that could have gone out, and we will get to the bottom of that and how the rest of the information unfolded, so you have our commitment to make sure that we will make that right and I hope that's what I can tell you right now."

When deposing Mayor Vaughan, Flint Taylor asks her about calling the press release "obviously, a lie."

VAUGHAN   I was responding to a question that an audience member asked me, and they used the word "lie" in the question and the premise of the question.

TAYLOR   So, you could have said no, it wasn't a lie, it was misrepresentation; or you could have said it was not a lie, it was a misstatement; but you said, "it was obviously a lie."

VAUGHAN   That is what the quote is. I may have used—maybe I should have used other words at the time.

Taylor then quotes her statement that "I want answers on why it was said that he was suicidal and dropped to the ground."

VAUGHAN   You know, after speaking with the Smiths and seeing how hurtful the word "suicidal" was to them and their grandchildren, yes, I did go back and talk to the chief.

And you know, when you look at the press release, we can—you know, I think—the word "disoriented" was there. You know, it may have been my choice to have stopped at disoriented. But the fact is, he did at certain points say, "I want to kill myself" and "I want to die." So, it was not inaccurate.

TAYLOR   And you concluded that after speaking to Chief Scott?

VAUGHAN   Yes. I spoke to Chief Scott. There was—you know, also the portion where he fell to the ground, you know, after looking at the videos, he obviously, did stumble out of the car. You know, he—he did not get out of the car, you know, standing up wanting to get help. At that point, you know, he stumbled out of the car.

TAYLOR   You watched the video before you made this statement [the one at Shiloh Baptist] and you said at that point the drop to the ground was obviously a lie. What changed from the time you made this statement after you watched the videos until you came to the conclusion that, gee, he really did drop to the ground?

VAUGHAN   I watched the videos more than once, you know—you can watch videos and continue to see more facts.

TAYLOR   So, when you made this statement at the church on the 3rd of December, you watched the video and determined that the statement in the press release that he collapsed, or as you characterized it, dropped to the ground, was a lie, correct?

VAUGHAN   I would say, in reviewing the video, that he did stumble out of the car.

TAYLOR   Well, is that the same thing as collapsing, in your view?

VAUGHAN   He was not—yes, because he was not of his own—he didn't get out of the car. He didn't stand up. He did stumble out. He did collapse out.

TAYLOR   Did you know that the officers who were there and who put hands on Marcus Smith when he came out of the

	car characterize it as they grabbed him and escorted
	him to the ground. Are you aware of that?
VAUGHAN	I have not seen any of their depositions.
TAYLOR	So, your testimony is that you went back after you made
	the statement that dropping to the ground was a lie, and
	you watched it again and decided that, well, it wasn't
	quite a lie, he stumbled and went to the ground, correct?
VAUGHAN	I did go back and review the video after the meeting at
	the church.
TAYLOR	Okay. You saw him stumble and collapse; is that what
	you concluded after saying it was a lie to say that?
VAUGHAN	When I reviewed the videos, it appeared to me he stumbled.
TAYLOR	And you equated that with collapsing?
VAUGHAN	I didn't think it was completely wrong, no.
TAYLOR	So, it was inaccurate but not a lie; is that what you
	concluded after you rewatched the video?
VAUGHAN	As I said earlier, I might have used different word choices.
TAYLOR	Even if you agree that he collapsed when he came out of
	the squad car, even if one agrees to that, it leaves out that
	it was three minutes later, after he was handcuffed, RIPP
	Hobbled, and his handcuffs were attached to his ankles,
	that he died, and that death was at least partially caused
	by the prior restraint. Would you agree that essential
	fact being left out, left at the very least a misleading
	impression of how Marcus Smith died?

Defense attorney Alan Duncan interjects and there is much back and
forth about whether Taylor is badgering the witness and the meaning
of "combative."

TAYLOR	Let's go back to this statement for a moment. "The subject
	became combative and collapsed." Is that an incomplete
	and inaccurate statement about how he died?
VAUGHAN	It was incomplete.

TAYLOR   Did you talk to the chief about that aspect of the press release, that the maximum restraint part was left out?

VAUGHAN   I'm sure we talked about restraint. But you know, again, this is just a press release, it is not a police report. It has no weight of law or anything behind it. It was incomplete at the moment.

TAYLOR   And it remained as the only official statement from the City until almost three months later when the chief medical examiner came out with his report, correct?

VAUGHAN   I don't know that.

TAYLOR   Well, do you know any official statement by the City of Greensboro or its police department concerning the maximum restraining of Marcus Smith as an aspect of his death until November 30th of 2018?

VAUGHAN   Yeah, I don't think I could answer your question.

The review and public Council discussion of the inaccurate press release that Vaughan promised the audience at Shiloh Baptist Church never happened, and the only future public statement she would make about the press release was to walk back calling it a lie, just as she later did in her deposition.

On January 18, in a brief interview with WXII-TV reporter Bill O'Neil, she said: "It is one of those cases that are difficult. Somebody died and you want to hold somebody accountable but ultimately, those officers, I do not believe they had any ill intent. I am satisfied given all the factors that have taken place, that the concerns over the press release are overblown."

O'Neil also reported that "the mayor says those who oppose the decision to clear the officers involved, including the Smith family, can still seek appeal through the citizens review board."

A month before Vaughan told O'Neil that, she listened in silence as two members of the citizen's review board told Greensboro City Council that any investigation by that board would be worse than useless.

A Lawsuit and a Settlement

21 "A VICIOUS AND ABLEIST LIE."

Thirty-five members of the public spoke of the Marcus Smith case at the Tuesday, December 4, 2018, meeting of Greensboro City Council. All expressed outrage about what they had seen on the bodycam videos. Twenty-three called the press release a lie. Seventeen called for the firing of Chief Scott. Eleven called for a full investigation into what they termed a cover-up.

Before any spoke, Nancy Vaughan read the following aloud:

This is really my statement, and I haven't run it by the rest of Council. Last night, at the meeting at Shiloh Baptist Church, I had the opportunity to speak with the Marcus Smith family. I expressed to them our condolences on the loss of their loved one and I agreed to look into the initial press release. I believe releasing the body-worn camera videos was the right thing to do. The chief of police petitioned the court to release the videos so that anyone can view them. It should be noted that the officers involved did not object to the release of the videos and that all 17 officers anywhere in the vicinity that night agreed to the release. All unedited videos are on the City's website.

On Friday, the chief of police issued a special order that the maximum restraint method called the RIPP Hobble, commonly referred to as hog-tying, is no longer being used to tie the feet and hands together. This method had been in place for the last 15 years. The device will only be used to bind feet. The Greensboro Police Department will be exploring new methods for maximum restraint. At the suggestion of Michelle Kennedy and it had been talked about by other Council members in the past, but based on her experience at the IRC, in working with people experiencing mental and addiction crises, the city is going to embed mental health workers in our police department. These professionals will be new hires who are specially trained to assist police with their encounters with people suffering from mental health or drug addiction issues to help defuse and deescalate negative interactions. They will also provide follow-up and treatment options. The Guilford County Emergency Services director has seen the body-worn camera video. Questions regarding the level of service displayed by the Emergency Service providers should be directed to the County. We have been informed by the SBI that their report will be finalized by the end of this week.

I would like to apologize for not responding to Graham Holt's letter regarding the Marcus Smith case. I understand that had led to a great deal of frustration, which I regret. We are here to listen to your concerns, and we will hold our individual comments, if any, until the end. We ask that you do not engage in shouting, and that you address us from the podium, and we will respect your opinions.

Speakers included Black GCJAC members Cherizar Crippen and Irving Allen, who said that asking that board to investigate Marcus' death would be a useless diversion.

Comments of Cherizar Crippen

"I serve on the GCJAC, Greensboro Criminal Justice Advisory Commission, and apparently as a stand-in for the PCRB, which is the police accountability review board, in case quorum requirements need filling. I'm here to make sure this City does not try to pass off these committees as groups that can actually hold the police accountable."

According to Crippen, "the only power that these commissions have is the power of suggestion." She then described the nondisclosure agreement she and Allen had been asked to sign.

"If I violate it, then I'm facing 20 days in jail and a $500 fine. The nondisclosure agreement forces me to use the city attorney to advise me on what's considered confidential and what isn't. The city attorney works for the City. It would just create a conflict of interest."

She also said that the North Carolina house bill mandating that the City create a police accountability review board imposed no penalties on board members who revealed its findings, nor did it require the City of Greensboro to do so. "So, what are you all afraid of? What exactly would happen to you if you decided to say we're not going to do that here in Greensboro, we're going to allow the people on that Council to speak out?"

Crippen criticized what she characterized as "blind trust" that police are always truthful. "When they lie to cover their butts and it involves a death, they should lose their freedom and their jobs just like the rest of us. There aren't a few bad apples around here, this is a bad orchard, and it dates all the way back to policing's inception as slave catchers."

Crippen concluded by denouncing what she called "a vicious and ableist lie about Marcus Deon Smith, about him falling and collapsing like some type of cartoon, when we know that none of that happened."

Comments of Irving Allen

Allen began by stating that, as a member of GCJAC and the PCRB, he was "really glad" that the Marcus Smith videos had become public without the PCRB being involved in the process, "because we were woefully unprepared to deal with this situation."

"I'm also glad that the video was released ahead of time. I'm glad that the community was able to push for that to happen, I'm glad that the family was able to push for that to happen, and I want to say that we were tasked to work with the Council, and so far, we've failed to develop a process that will properly even intake these processes that we've been dealing with for several years."

After speaking about the nondisclosure agreement, which Allen said attorneys he and Crippen consulted had described as "one of the harshest they'd ever seen," he accused Council of "asking for volunteer citizens to stand up and put their freedom on the line and sign away their right to

"A vicious and ableist lie."   185

speak, when on the other side, we've seen false information that would have been presented to us in the same way that it was presented to you by the police department."

"It's a little disturbing for the volunteer citizens who have been following this process and have been asked put their time and reputations on the line, to face harsher consequences than the police chief who introduced the false information that you received to that same body. If we had watched this video, then I would've had to do 20 days in jail and pay $500 to let you know what you already knew, that something was wrong."

The hour and 48 minutes of public comments, which ended with Allen being asked by Mayor Vaughan to "wrap it up," had begun with Anna Fesmire of the League of Women Voters of the Piedmont Triad, who said, "Democracy cannot survive in the dark; you appear to have worked to keep the case of Marcus Deon Smith as dark as possible for as long as possible." Fesmire accused the mayor, Council, and chief of never responding to questions from the public and stated that Marcus' death "cries out loudly for an examination of the overall preparedness of our police department to deal with the mentally ill."

Homeless Union of Greensboro members Marcus Hyde, Eddie Brewer, Ryan Tardiff, Hester Petty, and Prasafany Outlaw all spoke, with Brewer giving his perspective as a homeless person and Outlaw giving hers as a formerly homeless mother who knew and had been helped by Marcus Smith. Petty alleged that, although the officers repeatedly stated their belief that Marcus was under the influence of drugs, "no one asked Marcus what he was on or when he had taken it."

Other speakers included North Carolina A&T student body president Delaney Vandergrift, who called her university "the Blackest school in the UNC system," and talked about Black student grievances against the GPD "every year without fail," citing previous cases of police misconduct.

Another was Signe Waller Foxworth, widow of Dr. Jim Waller, who was murdered in the Greensboro Massacre. She told Council, "We need a citizen board to review and oversee the police department actions, and that has subpoena power, and we need it right now."

Speakers from the Black clergy included Reverend Wesley Morris, Reverend Brandon Wrencher, and Reverend Nelson Johnson, who called the initial press release "the beginning of the cover-up" and asked Council "not to spin the medical report of homicide to avoid holding those responsible for this homicide accountable, including the highest level of police and yourselves."

When it came time for Council to respond to the public comments, the first to do so was Sharon Hightower, who said that City Attorney Tom Carruthers "told me I have to be careful about what I say today."

Hightower offered her condolences to the Smith family and apologized for not responding to the letter from them and Graham Holt. "I fell for what I was told initially, that he was suicidal and collapsed." She then noted she had asked to view the videos in mid-November.

"As you know, I got shouted down, disrespected, and dismissed out of the Council chamber. When I asked for something that was my right to ask for, I was told I had to wait for the process, and a process that apparently does not work. I've talked to Irving [Allen] so many times about this, and I said, Irving, are you sure this is the way we want to go, because this PCRB is not at all what it needs to be. I hope that we will fix it, I hope that it will change, because citizens need a voice, but they don't need a voice that's controlled, that's not the first amendment, that's not freedom of speech."

Hightower also said she had talked to Michelle Kennedy earlier that evening about "offering licensed clinical social workers as part of the team, but we need to make sure that we're covered seven days a week, 24 hours a day, not Monday through Friday." She then suggested funding it by taking away the GPD's Civil Emergency Unit and diverting those funds to the proposed crisis response team. She stated that the integral use of the RIPP Hobble should not just be modified, as Vaughan had reported, to only bind a subject's legs, but that the device should be abolished.

"Because, first of all, it's using a rope, and for African-Americans, we know what a rope is. It carries with it a horrible stigma of oppression and slavery. 'Strange Fruit,' you all remember the song. So, anything that has a rope attached to it should be totally done away with. I'm disturbed that we've used it for as long as we have."

"A vicious and ableist lie."   187

Hightower then became the first member of City Council to publicly call for an independent investigation of how Marcus had died and the department whose procedures had enabled his death.

"I think there's many questions that we don't know the answer to. Someone will say, Sharon, you're just playing to the audience. No, I'm playing to my conscience, because any time our citizens are upset, we should be upset, we should be disturbed. We have to make sure something happens here. What that is, I don't know, exactly, but I would say that we should look at it from beginning to end, and look at our County partners, because I'm concerned by some of the things that went on in the video. Maybe I can get some full disclosure. You deserve answers. We need to be the councilpeople that we promised and took an oath to be."

Unsurprisingly to anyone who knew her rhetorical history and uncritical support for the GPD, Marikay Abuzuaiter defended the actions of the officers who killed Marcus, and that's when the audience became angry.

"You may not like it," began Abuzuaiter, scowling as she often did at any allegations of police misconduct. "But I would like to be offered the same few moments to say what I'm going to say. I don't know if many of you know what mollies do to someone."

The room exploded in shouts, boos, and incredulous laughter. After both the mayor and Abuzuaiter shouted for the audience to let her finish speaking, Abuzuaiter continued.

"Not only do they cause so many things going on in your body, but they also create a form of superhuman strength."

According to the March 10, 2015, article "How Molly Works in the Brain,"[1] the amphetamine MDMA, a hallucinogenic rave drug commonly called molly (not "mollies") by its users, can have a wide variety of dangerous side effects. But it gained popularity not because, like so many such drugs, it merely causes euphoria, but due to its "prosocial" effects. "Molly makes users feel friendly, loving, and strongly connected to one another," which is why psychiatrists have become interested in its psychotherapeutic potential.

Abuzuaiter may have been confusing MDMA with the then-recent hysteria over "Flakka" or "bath salts." Regardless of the source of her misconception, the long history of ginned-up public hysteria over drug-induced "superhuman strength" has, as previously described, become a boilerplate defense for police using excessive force, but has little or no scientific basis.

"I asked some doctors," said Abuzuaiter, when the audience finally calmed somewhat. "I did some research, I'm not a medical expert, nor am I someone who can judge other people. What I was trying to say was when you have a situation like that, according to medical experts, not me, it has to run out of their system, I don't know if you all saw the whole video, I've seen the entire video, and Mr. Smith was running around for a long time, that is one way that it kind of gets out of the system."

There were more expressions of scorn and derision from the public in the packed Council chamber.

"I cannot judge Mr. Smith nor his actions nor what led up to his actions that evening," continued Abuzuaiter before making the remark that would offend Mary and Kim Smith. "I cannot judge Mr. Smith on why his family may not have been around. I cannot judge Mr. Smith on anything that happened to him that evening. Nor can I judge the officers."

There were more angry shouts, causing Mayor Vaughan to exhort the audience, "You may not agree with her, but let her speak!"

After giving her version of what transpired before Marcus was restrained, in which she noted the initial complaints from people in passing cars, but not that Corporal Strader said Marcus no longer seemed in danger of harming himself once the street was blocked off, she spoke of the device that killed him.

"Do I agree with the RIPP Hobble? No, but for maximum restraint, that is what is commonly used, I'm not saying I agree with it. It needs to be changed, and the chief has changed it to where it is only going to restrain their feet."

She also told the audience they needed to pay more attention to comments on the social media pages of local TV stations, as "they are running about 90 percent in support of the officers having patience, having compassion, giving the gentleman time, putting him unrestrained in back of the police car."

"A vicious and ableist lie."

Someone in the audience yells, "Can we talk about how you're a police informant? Can we talk about how you're in their pocket?"

There follow some moments of hushed inaudible conversation between Council members before District 3 representative Justin Outling voices concern about the call for embedding social workers with the police.

"The first time I heard we would be doing something in terms of engaging with social workers was yesterday after a Council member said it at a public meeting, and then tonight. I think in this situation it's really important for us to be deliberate and analytical in our response. We have to think through how we respond to the situation. I would like to understand what it is that I missed, as I wasn't even consulted as part of those five members of Council."

Michelle Kennedy replies, "The room I was in when I watched the tape consisted of Sharon Hightower, the mayor, Nancy Hoffman, and myself, and we quickly agreed that was something we can do immediately. It doesn't end systemic racism or other profound layers of this, but it is one thing we can do. I'm not sure how you found out about this yesterday, because I sent a link with all of this and some best practices from around the country to you on Saturday, but I never heard back."

Outling attempts to speak over her, as he had done weeks earlier with Hightower.

"Go ahead and tell me what I need to hear," says Kennedy, "but I can finish the time that I have to talk. I can keep talking too, but my name is on the mic right now."

"The audience is acting better than we are," says Vaughan.

There is more shouting from the audience, this time at Outling.

"I cannot tell you today where every dime of the money to support that will come from," says Kennedy. "I don't know. We've not had a conversation with the city manager to figure out the scaffolding behind it, but I'm damn glad it's happening, and that's what I know. Sometimes you do what's right because it's right and you figure out the details and you build the bike as you ride it, and when it's about somebody's life, something like providing mental health clinicians who are not police officers makes all the difference."

Shortly after that, the meeting ends.

A month after Cherizar Crippen and Irving Allen explained to the Council and the public why they considered Mayor Vaughan's repeated recommendations that Mary Smith take her complaint to the Police Community Review Board (PCRB) to be useless, District 2 representative Goldie Wells announced she was removing them from that board.

"I would like to take Irving Allen and Cherizar Crippen off the Greensboro Criminal Justice Advisory Commission and PCRB," said Wells on January 15, 2019, in the final minutes of that evening's nearly four-hour meeting, when there were no more members of the public in the audience.

On the video posted on the City's website, Sharon Hightower says something in response, but her microphone is not turned on and her comments are inaudible.

Grimacing, Wells replies, "We really... I'm not sure, but, uh, I think any Council member should be able to take somebody off of... off of it. And it's for reasons, so I'd like a second."

"So, do we have a second?" asks Mayor Vaughan. When no other Council member responds, she seconds the motion.

The motion passes 7 to 2, with Hightower and Mayor pro tem Yvonne Johnson opposing. The mayor, Wells, District 3's Justin Outling, District 4's Nancy Hoffman, District 5's Tammi Thurm and at-large members Michelle Kennedy and Marikay Abuzuaiter all vote to approve the removal of Crippen and Allen.

Sharon Hightower appears to make objections, but again, her microphone is not turned on. The only clear words are "we had a conversation."

"Uh, uh," says Wells, but does not complete whatever she is attempting to express.

"Well, they haven't, they haven't attended the trainings," says Vaughan. Hightower continues to speak without an operating microphone.

"It's for reasons," says Wells, "believe me, it's for reasons. Please accept my, uh, explanation, for reasons."

The meeting ended with no further discussion of the removal of the two PCRB members who repeatedly called that board muzzled and ineffective.

"A vicious and ableist lie."

22 "A QUESTION OF TRUST."

Having served 14 years as Guilford County District Attorney, Douglas Henderson announced early in 2018 that he would not be running for reelection that November and would retire at the end of the year. In a December 28, 2018, letter to Chief Wayne Scott, Henderson said the eight officers involved in the death of Marcus Smith were not criminally negligent in the death of the man they hog-tied. A press release about the decision stated, in total:

"The City of Greensboro and the Greensboro Police Department turned over the investigation to the North Carolina State Bureau of Investigation. The SBI concluded its investigations and turned the matter over to the Guilford County District Attorney's office and they have provided us with their response."

"I guess that means it's legal in Greensboro, North Carolina, for a group of white police officers to suffocate a Black man to death," said attorney Graham Holt to the press after the City released the news that Henderson stated the case was closed.

In his public letter to Chief Scott, Henderson made statements very similar to what Scott had told journalist Jordan Green in November, stating that, while departmental directives required a restrained subject to be placed in a seated position or on their side to avoid harm while being transported, "Mr. Smith became unresponsive immediately after he was necessarily placed in the additional restraints and before he could be transported to the hospital in the manner described. Mr. Smith was at no time transported while in the 'RIPP Hobble' device."

Holt called that letter a "boldfaced lie," as Marcus "was in the hog-tied position for at least a full minute before he became unresponsive. It's ridiculous to say that, so it's just more of the same of the City cooperatively working to cover up a man being killed by the police."

Speaking for the Homeless Union of Greensboro, Marcus Hyde told the *News & Record*'s Richard Barron[1] HUG was considering its options in response to Henderson's judgment, including the possibility of a civil lawsuit against the city.

"If the DA and the Police and Council all want to cover for each other, that's unfortunate for the people of Greensboro who are going to foot the bill for us to right these wrongs." Hyde also expressed hope that Henderson's successor Avery Crump would re-open the case, as Crump, the first Black woman to serve as district attorney in Guilford, was supported by a group of the same Black leaders who called for action in the Smith case.

Hyde told Barron this could be the "defining moment" for her new administration, but on January 4, Crump's Chief ADA Steve Cole announced the case had been thoroughly reviewed and at this point the matter should be considered closed.

At the City Council meeting on February 5, 2019, when Cherizar Crippen spoke about being removed from the PCRB, Hester Petty presented Council with important information about the RIPP Hobble which they seemed to disregard. Mayor Vaughan not only dismissed any notion of firing Wayne Scott but made her first public statement walking back her claim that the press release had been a lie.

"I'm here tonight to clear up a few things," said Crippen when she addressed Council during the public comments section of the meeting. She said the official reason given for her and Allen being removed from the PCRB was that they had missed three successive meetings. But, alleged Crippen, when she applied in the early fall of 2018, Council was aware that both she and Allen were working "60 hours a week" on voting rights campaigns and doing a lot of traveling and were "not aware of any meetings taking place until the fourth meeting."

Crippen said that when they attended that meeting on November 20, she apologized for missing the previous three and was told not to worry about it but was asked if she had signed her nondisclosure agreement.

"I said we have concerns about this, and would like to discuss it, and they said this is not the time now, but we will send you an email to set this up so that you can both go over your concerns and bring you up to speed. Then the December meeting was canceled for snow, and in January, we were unceremoniously dismissed."

Sharon Hightower publicly apologized to both Crippen and Allen for this treatment, but said that, as she had voted against removing them from the board, she was not allowed to make a motion to reinstate them. "The winning side has to make that motion," said Mayor pro tem Johnson, who had also voted against dismissal, and under those rules, she could not motion to reverse that dismissal.

Then Crippen said, "We are aware there is a silver lining here. We know that City Council can move very quickly when they want to. So, in the case of Marcus Smith, we hope you're going to apply some of that speed in getting justice for him."

She also asked Council to "be considerate and employ some level of tact when you are making off-the-cuff remarks." Crippen then referred to an unspecified previous incident in which, according to Crippen, Wells allegedly remarked of Marcus Smith "that maybe it was just his time to die." This, said Crippen, had been very hurtful to the Smith family. "It's disrespectful to them, and just gross." Wells did not respond to Crippen's claim that Wells had made such a statement, nor to later calls from activists for her to apologize to the Smith family.

After Hightower apologized effusively to Crippen, Wells offered a grudging apology for making the motion to dismiss the two board members without hearing them out. But, she stated, they deserved being dismissed for not signing the nondisclosure agreement when they were first told to do so. Seeming to disregard Crippen's claim that the absences were excused, she said that non-attendance was a deal breaker. Neither she nor anyone else who had voted to remove Crippen and Allen made a motion to restore them to the PCRB.

Wells, who was 76 at the time of this exchange, then made references to having been "accused of stifling young Black leaders" and "putting all the young Black people down." This, stated Wells, "is not my intention at all," but then launched into a tirade, admonishing Crippen that "you're gonna have to follow some rules."

When Crippen replied that she needed to be aware of rules to follow them, Wells shouted, "Just have manners!" After Crippen stopped trying to respond, Wells said "the younger ones have to learn also that elders deserve some respect."

"I have a great relationship with the elders in this community," replied Crippen, "and you have never tried to give me a piece of advice. All you did was remove me from a council. So, this narrative that you're trying to push is inherently false and more of the same, and we need to really do better."

Mayor Vaughan cut them both off by stating that Council needed to move on. Nobody addressed the apparent elephant in the room, which was that Crippen and Allen were dismissed after stating publicly that the complaint with the PCRB the mayor was urging the Smith family to pursue would have been both secret and ineffective.

Longtime activist Hester Petty then took the podium, and with the aid of an overhead projector, shared with Council the instructions that came with the RIPP Hobble she had recently ordered from the manufacturer to find out more about the device.

As Petty proceeded to demonstrate, the Hobble was packaged with a folded glossy cardboard sheet with bold large-print instructions to "NEVER Hog-Tie a Prisoner." The reverse side included illustrations depicting how to use it to prevent a prisoner placed in the back seat of a police car, as Marcus was, from kicking. The method shown does not involve attaching the ankles to the wrists or placing the person face down on their stomach.

In his introduction to the video compilation edited by the City, Scott called the restraint a "RIPP Hobble" five times. The only restraint sold under this name is the RIPP Hobble from RIPP Restraints International, Inc., a company created in 1987 to design and manufacture restraints marketed to law enforcement agencies.

Company President Joelle DeVane said in a statement: "RIPP has been training to NOT hog-tie an individual since at least 1994. That's the furthest I can find, for sure, and that was when my father, Bill DeVane, Sr. started training law enforcement on Sudden Custody Death Syndrome (SCDS), which covers positional asphyxia, positional restraint asphyxia, excited delirium and cocaine psychosis."

Two hours and 45 minutes into the meeting at which Crippen and Petty spoke, and at which Crippen received multiple responses and Petty received none, Mayor Vaughan spoke on Marcus Smith.

"There's been a lot of conversation about Chief Scott. You know, that decision is the city manager's, and I think we have a great city manager and personnel is in his purview, but I for one would not be in favor of taking a voting to fire the chief. I believe that is the city manager's job. I respect him, and I don't think the chief should be fired, period.

"But you said that he lied!" shouted someone from the audience.

"I was responding to a question," replied Vaughan. "I was responding to a question that used the word 'lie' in it. I have talked about the press release on a number of times... We sit here for two hours and we listen to people speak to us," admonished Vaughan, "and we try to be respectful and listen to everything people say, and then we speak, people decide to yell at us, stand up, and walk out. We can't get the same respect that we try to afford you."

She then returned to why she had called the press release a lie. "So, I was responding to a question. I have responded to it many times since then. You know, a press release is immediately after something that occurs, and often it is done without the entire information, often it is updated. When that initial press release went out, it didn't even go out with Marcus Smith's name."

What this argument does not acknowledge is that, while the omission of Marcus' name was corrected two days later, no press release for the next two months ever mentioned that Marcus had been hog-tied, and the City did not issue any information about the restraint that killed him until Graham Holt told the press what he and the Smith family had seen on the bodycam videos.

"A question of trust."   197

After more interjections from the audience, Vaughan shouted "Excuse me, this is my time to speak!"

"A press release is not a police report," said Vaughan, using language very similar to that of Chief Scott in his deposition. "It is notification to the media that something occurred! There are other reports that go into great detail!"

"Getting back to my original comment," said Vaughan, "I am not going to instruct the city manager to fire the police chief. One, I don't think that's our role. Two, I don't support firing him. So, I want to make those two points clear."

When Vaughan finished speaking, Sharon Hightower stated she had always been public in her opposition to hiring Wayne Scott and alleged that his department retaliated for this by not patrolling her district or responding to calls there. "My community knows that, and I apologize to them for that, because they don't get the same fair treatment as the rest of the city. But sometimes we've got to do what's right."

Hightower acknowledged that any disciplinary or punitive action against Chief Scott for his alleged lack of transparency was a personnel matter under the purview of City Manager David Parrish, for whom she expressed respect. "But I do believe there needs to be accountability in words and actions. We have to be very diligent about things that come out of these spaces, and sometimes, when the tail is not right, it's because the head is not right. And so, I'm very concerned."

So was Michelle Kennedy, who began her comments by saying that, for her, "the conversation rests on how do you take responsibility, whether for a lie or an error or whatever it is, there's something to be said for the way it is handled that makes a whole lot of difference, and for me, that's the piece that never quite leaves me."

She agreed with Vaughan that the personnel issues were the responsibility of the city manager, "but for me, the question about the press release is a question of leadership and a question of how you manage when things go wrong, intentional or otherwise." She concluded by calling it "a question of broader trust, and I can't get beyond that, and that's where I stand on that issue."

Two months later, her stance on that issue would lead Kennedy to call for an independent investigation into the death of Marcus Smith.

23 "WE WILL PROTEST AT YOUR HOUSES."

At the April 1, 2019, meeting of Greensboro City Council, a minister from Marcus Smith's hometown called Chief Wayne Scott a "lying racist."

Reverend David E. Kennedy, Pastor of New Beginning Missionary Baptist Church and President of the Laurens County NAACP, can be seen in a YouTube video[1] in which he leads a Council chamber full of Smith family supporters in singing "Wayne Scott got da hump! Humpty-dumpty-dump!"

This impromptu performance is met with looks of unease from several Council members. He also declaims, "We will protest at your houses, we will protest at your churches, we will protest and call for a boycott in the city of Greensboro."

Minutes after Reverend Kennedy spoke, Zalonda Woods, of the Homeless Union of Greensboro, presented Council with a box containing over 100,000 signatures collected by the national organization PushBlack, demanding the firing of Chief Scott. Before the next speaker could take the podium, a visibly emotional Michelle Kennedy (no relation to the pastor) made a statement met with cheers and applause, something unusual for anything said by Council members about the Marcus Smith case.

"I've had conversations this evening with Mayor pro tem Johnson and I think the two of us would like to ask the city manager to call for an independent investigation into the death of Marcus Smith."

"I would second that," said Johnson.

"The thing that I think is important," said Kennedy, "is a resolution, and we aren't any closer today to a resolution than we were when this happened." She then referred to the lame-duck district attorney who had closed the case.

"And we have a new district attorney who also hasn't taken up this case, but this conversation keeps coming to our feet. The only way we get to someplace on this is moving forwards to a resolution. To me, this means, whether you're giving examples from Charlottesville or other places in the country, if there's not trust at this level, then an independent investigation into this should bring that level of understanding."

She was referring to the independent investigation conducted by the City of Charlottesville, Virginia, after the white supremacist Unite the Right rally in 2017. In an earlier speech from the floor, Reverend Wesley Morris proposed an investigation modeled on the Charlottesville one, which exposed misconduct from the Charlottesville Police Department and resulted in the resignation of its chief. That city voted to commission an independent investigation even while defending itself from lawsuits resulting from that rally.

Kennedy said she had not talked to any Council members other than Johnson, "but I can't sit here any longer and not move forward."

"Several months ago, I called for that independent investigation, and it was ignored," said Sharon Hightower. "I hope it's not ignored this time around."

Hightower acknowledged such an investigation might not resolve all concerns, "but we must find some answers and some solutions to the issues that are occurring. We have a city right now that is fractured by race and economics. We've got to fix those items and raise people's quality of life. We have a community who doesn't trust the police. I think we've got to start addressing these issues that really are prevalent in this community. There is an imbalance of treatment that is going on, and I think that, if we are a Council concerned about human rights, then we must address this and start to fix it. I would third your motion for an independent investigation, separate and apart."

Mayor Vaughan spoke of the challenge of finding an investigative body acceptable to everyone and acknowledged Charlottesville as a possible model. She also said that "there's not a day that's gone by that I've not thought of Marcus Smith."

"I know how this has fractured our community," said Vaughan. "This causes me many, many sleepless nights."

Several audience members expressed skepticism and disapproval when the mayor talked about her own anguish over Marcus Smith's death. "[Vaughan] needs to just listen and let the family do the grieving," muttered someone in the crowd. Others expressed the same sentiment more loudly.

"I am speaking!" shouted Vaughan angrily. Then, in a calmer voice, "This is something I think about every day. I would love to find a way to resolve this."

"Fire Chief Scott," said a young Black woman in the audience.

"I don't interrupt you, don't interrupt me!" shouted Vaughan. She then pointed out that, in a town-hall style meeting like this one, Council voting is not allowed. "If it's something we need to do between now and the next meeting, to talk about what an independent body looks like, and who it would be made up of or what organization would do it, then that's something we'll do between now and our next meeting and put it on the agenda. But that's not something that we as a body can do at this meeting."

From where she was standing in the back of the room, Mary Smith asked why, if the death of Marcus troubled Vaughan so much, the mayor had told the press there was "no reason to re-open the investigation."

"Did you hear what I just said?" snapped Vaughan.

"Did you hear what I said?" replied Mary.

District 2 representative Goldie Wells, who with Marikay Abuzuaiter was possibly the last person in the chamber that Mary Smith wanted to hear from, lectured the mother in the tone Wells frequently used on her young activist critics.

"It's your son, but we have protocol for meetings. The mayor is the leader of this meeting. Now, she's asked to speak, and we should give her respect."

A young Black woman in the front row, angered by the way in which Wells was speaking to the mother of a man killed by the Greensboro police, began shouting.

"We will protest at your houses."

201

"We have listened to you speak since September! You have silenced people in this city since September! This man is dead!"

"EXCUSE ME, SIT DOWN!" shouted Wells.

"Sit down or we'll have you removed!" shouted Vaughan.

"Have her removed, have her removed!" shouted Wells.

At that point, District 3's Justin Outling, who'd been silent the entire time, rose and left without comment or explanation, and did not return. Meanwhile, Reverend Wesley Morris walked to the agitated young woman threatened with ejection and hugged her, speaking quietly. She then left the room.

"It is about respect!" said Wells. "African—young people have to learn to respect!"

"Did y'all respect my brother?" shouted Len Butler. The mayor shouted back at him to "be quiet or be removed!" Wells shouted, "Protocol, protocol!"

After calling for calm, Mayor pro tem Johnson said, "One of the things I hear coming from the people is that we want an independent investigation. That's what we want to do. How do we do that? That's what we need to work out."

"And we'll have it on the next agenda," said Vaughan.

"On the next agenda to vote for," said Johnson.

Taking the podium, Kim Smith addressed her comments to Vaughan. "Ms. Mayor, you say you think about this, you think about this, but imagine us! I watched the video, my dad watched the video, my other two brothers, only my mom hasn't watched it. Imagine seeing your sibling die. Just give me a little bit of pity for that right now."

She turned to Michelle Kennedy. "Michelle, you knew him for years, you knew what type of person he was, you knew he did not pose a threat to these officers, he did not deserve to die this way. We will be out of you guys' hair if you can just give us justice. We hate coming up here."

While Kim did not address Marikay Abuzuaiter by name, she said her mother wanted her to mention the at-large representative's statement at the December 4 Council meeting, in which Abuzuaiter said that it might have been necessary to hog-tie Marcus Smith because the designer drug "Molly" may have given him "superhuman strength."

"There were too many professionals on scene for my brother to die," said Kim. "Nobody says, 'Stop guys, his breathing is changing, hold on, he's not sounding right.' Nobody said anything. Nobody stopped this lynching, all these officers on top of this one man. And they literally folded him like a piece of paper to toss in the trash."

She then asked, "How many RIPP Hobble restraints was done successfully before my brother? Has it ever been done?"

"The RIPP Hobble device had been used for ten years," replied Nancy Vaughan. "It had been used many times a month, it has been used hundreds of times."

Someone in the audience shouted a question asking if it had previously been used to attach the subject's ankles to their wrists while they were placed face down on their belly.

"Excuse me," snapped Mayor Vaughan. "Do not speak, or I will have you removed. But the RIPP Hobble device had been used hundreds of times a year, for ten years."

"We just want to know what kind of justice is going to be done on my brother," said Kim. "That's what we want to know."

Mayor Vaughan said, "I can't answer your questions this evening." Goldie Wells said something inaudible at the same time.

"I'm sorry, Miss Wells?" said Kim.

"I said maybe the independent investigation will bring some of these things out," replied Wells. "I think we're so divided that even when we say we're trying to do what you'd like us to do, you're still not satisfied."

"The division was already here," said Mary Smith from the audience.

"I'm not saying you brought the division; I'm saying the city was already divided," replied Wells. "We're sitting here, and we listen, and we've been called everything but a child of God. I've never been called a demon before in all my life." She was referring to a speech from the podium by Billy Belcher of the Working-class and Houseless Organizing Alliance, who said "the demons torturing Marcus Smith's family are the City Council of Greensboro."

"We will protest at your houses."

Wells suggested there were no immediately forthcoming answers. "If we knew the magic, we could wave a magic wand, and it could all be settled, so that it satisfied you and we could pull the City together. But we don't have it, and that's what we're trying to tell you."

"And that's supposed to be comforting to me?" asked Kim.

"I can't say if it's comforting to you," said Wells. "I'm just giving my answer, and whether you accept that answer or not, that's you and perception is reality."

Kim turned back to Kennedy. "Michelle, you know the love we had for Marcus, and I kind of feel you had a little love for Marcus as well, because you grew to know him, So I just want you to stand up for Marcus, if it's in any way possible."

Kennedy did not respond.

At the end of the public comments, Yvonne Johnson suggested that an independent investigation might not be conducted by the City Council. "Because there are people who, whatever we did, would not trust it." Instead, she suggested it should be done by "an entity considered trustworthy by the majority of the people."

Sharon Hightower suggested that "the Charlottesville investigation" could be a model for how to proceed. "Who did they use and how did they go about it? I think we need to look at that particular model and go about it. With haste. We're already six months into this."

The City of Greensboro would react very differently when the Marcus Smith lawsuit was filed a week after Hightower suggested using Charlottesville as a model.

24 "I DON'T GET INVITED TO THAT PARTY."

At an April 10, 2019, press conference at Bethel African Methodist Episcopal Church in Greensboro, attorneys for the family of Marcus Smith announced the filing of the federal civil rights lawsuit *Smith et al v. City of Greensboro et al.* One of those attorneys was Graham Holt, who had represented the family since he petitioned the GPD to allow them to see the videos depicting Marcus' death. The other was Flint Taylor of the People's Law Office of Chicago.

The Smith family had acquired a very big legal gun.

Taylor, who made the announcement at Bethel AME with Holt, was on the 2011 legal team that obtained the first judicial decision naming former Chicago mayor Richard M. Daley as a defendant in a civil police torture case, after taking part in the decades-long campaign to bring criminal charges against Chicago Police Commander Jon Burge, convicted in 2010 for lying about torturing suspects. This led, in 2015, to a historic $5.5 million reparations package to those tortured while in police custody during Burge's command, as well as an apology from famously unapologetic Mayor Rahm Emanuel.

The veteran Chicago attorney was co-lead trial counsel in the 1985 federal district court case that found two Klansmen, three Nazis, two Greensboro police officers, and a police informant liable for the wrongful death of one person and the injuring of two others during the 1979 Greensboro Massacre. This was the first time in US legal history that

KKK members, Nazis, and police officers were found jointly liable for a wrongful death.

In 1982, Taylor, and the People's Law Office which he co-founded, obtained a historic $1.85 million civil rights settlement against the Chicago Police Department for the death of Black Panther Party chairman Fred Hampton, shot in the head during a 1969 police raid while he lay sleeping under the influence of a drugged drink given him by an FBI informant.

Taylor announced the City of Greensboro and Guilford County were named as defendants, along with officers Justin Payne, Robert Duncan, Michael Montalvo, Alfred Lewis, Christopher Bradshaw, Lee Andrews, Douglas Strader, and Jordan Bailey, and Guilford EMS paramedic Ashley Abbott and EMT Dylan Alling. While the charges against the County would later be dismissed, those against its two employees were not, and the County would pay for their defense and contribute to the eventual settlement.

The complaint's preliminary statement included allegations that "Greensboro Police Officers caused Marcus' death by brutally restraining him prone on the ground and hog-tying him like an animal until he stopped breathing" and that Guilford County EMS "failed to intervene to protect Marcus from the use of unreasonable force and failed to promptly attend to his serious medical needs." It also stated that Marcus Smith was not engaged in any criminal conduct, was unarmed, made no threats to the police or others, presented no immediate danger to the officers, himself, or others, and was not actively resisting arrest.

It alleged that "written and *de facto* policies, practices and customs of Defendant City of Greensboro and its Police Department contributed to and were a moving force behind Marcus' death, as the Defendant officers were acting pursuant to these policies, practices and customs, that included the use of restraint devices to hog-tie people who are in a prone position, and the treatment of people who experience mental health crises."

The complaint alleged that, while and after restraining Smith, the officers and paramedics allowed him "to remain prone on his stomach, with his knees bent well beyond 90 degrees" while "they failed to continuously monitor" his condition, and that the paramedics were aware he was "unconscious, unresponsive and not breathing, yet waited longer than two minutes to begin any resuscitative efforts."

The complaint also described "a concerted effort to cover up" Marcus Smith's death, beginning with the police statement that he "had collapsed while he was in police custody (he did not), that he was combative (he was not), that officers rendered aid (they did not), that he died at the hospital (he died face down on the street), and blatantly omitting that Marcus was taken to the ground by the police and forcibly restrained and hogtied."

Six days after the Smith attorneys filed their complaint, Greensboro City Council announced there would be no independent investigation.

The first item on the April 16, 2019, agenda was "Council Discussion for an Independent Review of the Marcus Smith Incident," but there was no discussion.

After declaring the meeting in open session, Mayor Vaughan said that public comment is allowed on all agenda items and instructed those wishing to speak on agenda items to sign in at the City staff table in the back of the room. She also makes the standard request for courtesy and decorum and warns that those who cause disruption will be removed if they don't comply with a request to stop.

She then announces the first item on the agenda.

"Item Number One. We do have a motion, Council Discussion for an Independent Review of the Marcus Smith incident. Do we have a motion?"

There is a pause before Sharon Hightower answers. "Yeah, unfortunately, due to pending litigation, while I certainly support an independent review of the case, I make a motion that we table this item until after litigation has been resolved. But I want people to know that I absolutely do support an independent review, but because of the timing of everything right now, we are unable to move that forward. So, I would like to make that motion to table the item."

The motion is seconded by Michelle Kennedy, who in 2021 would apologize for doing so and attempt to reintroduce the motion. However, in April of 2019, she gives no evidence of those second thoughts. "I just want to follow up and echo what Sharon is saying. This is something we have very strong feelings about and I don't want to say this is not going to happen, but is delayed due to current litigation."

There is no further discussion and the Council votes 8–0 to table the investigation.

There are angry shouts from the audience. "I'm going to ask you to please be quiet or we're going to have to have you removed," says Mayor Vaughan.

"Marcus died, the chief lied, fire the chief of police!" chant multiple people in the audience. Vaughan asks for them to be removed. When Abuzuaiter starts to respond to the chants, Vaughan pats her hand and says, "We have a procedure now," apparently indicating for Abuzuaiter not to respond.

"Why can't we do a public comment about this?" shouts activist Rachel Wieselquist, whom Vaughan calls to be removed. Wieselquist leaves with other protestors when security arrives. Council whisper among themselves for a moment before moving to the next agenda item.

After the meeting was adjourned, Vaughan stated: "The motion was to table the item and the motion to table is non-debatable, which means you vote on it right away, so there's really no comment from Council and there are no speakers from the floor."

She confirmed the review was tabled due to the announcement of the Smith family's lawsuit and called it a "strategic blunder" on their part.

"I think it's common sense that, once the lawsuit is filed, you turn it over to the lawyers. I think that would probably be the same advice that the plaintiff's lawyers would have given their clients. I do think that, as a Council, we would have been willing to do a professional legal review of the way that the investigation was handled."

When asked what she meant by "strategic blunder," she replied:

"I do think it was a strategic error. They could have waited until an investigation was complete. I think the majority of Council was considering a professional review similar to Charlottesville, which could have been done reasonably quickly—most of the documents are already assembled, and unlike Charlottesville, there weren't a whole lot of different players. But in the end, the timing just didn't work."

As stated by many, including Michelle Kennedy when she made a seemingly anguished 2021 call for reopening the investigation that appeared to shock her fellow Council members, the Charlottesville investigation Vaughan cited as a model was conducted while the City was under litigation from both anti-racist protesters and neo-Confederates. Other than stating that the city attorney advised against it, no Council member or City official would ever give an explanation for why an investigation couldn't proceed while the family was suing the City.

"The same outrage from the community was manifesting at City Council meetings three years ago," said Lewis Pitts, who had helped bring his old friend and former co-counsel Flint Taylor to Greensboro and was present with the Smith family and their legal team when the lawsuit was announced. "As is the same lack of transparency and abrogation of duty by the Council."

Pitts was referring to an October 18, 2016, closed meeting in which the Council debated examining information regarding former GPD officer Travis Cole's use of excessive force against Dejuan Yourse, whom Cole punched multiple times after aggressively demanding to know why Yourse was sitting on the stoop of a house that belonged to Yourse's mother. As the *News & Record* reported, at the public meeting immediately following the private one, Sharon Hightower accused fellow Council members of "trying to shut me down," and implied that a vote had taken place at the closed session.

Mayor Vaughan asked Tom Carruthers, then city attorney, if that vote could be made public. "I don't consider what was taken a vote," replies Carruthers. "I consider it consensus of Council. We don't take votes in closed session." In the minutes and audio recording from that closed session, which the *News & Record* hired a lawyer to obtain, the Council can be heard taking two formal votes on the subject, each with a seconded motion, and each Council member voting.

In the 2016 audio recording released by the *News & Record*, Hightower asks to be allowed to view information on the Cole case.[1] At-large representative Marikay Abuzuaiter expresses concerns about the public image of the police department. At-large representative Mike Barber (who would lose his seat to Michelle Kennedy in 2017) cites "potential pending litigation in this matter" and advises "that we make no further public statement." Abuzuaiter then states, "There's possible litigation on this one which could really put us in a tight spot."

Reflecting on the Dejuan Yourse controversy in 2019, Lewis Pitts condemned what he characterized as repeated covering-up of police misconduct, both in the 2016 assault on Yourse and the 2018 death of Marcus Smith. "When this City Council gets credible evidence that the police are engaging in wrongdoing," said Lewis Pitts in 2019, "they bury their heads in the sand. Their sworn moral and legal obligation is to the best interests of the community, not to protect themselves from civil liability."

He also suggested the tabling of the independent review was a punitive action against the Smith family.

"They're saying, well, if they're going to file a lawsuit, we just won't hold the investigation. That's spanking the family on the hand because they had the audacity to sue."

Pitts believed the lawsuit would bring to light the Greensboro Police Department's past history with the Black community. Mayor Vaughan said she did not believe the currently tabled review would have addressed those claims. "I think there are people who thought there would be a wider-ranging investigation, looking at GPD over the years, but I don't think that was ever under consideration."

At least not until Michelle Kennedy proposed it again two years later, only to see that proposal quashed in another closed session.

In August of 2022, Sharon Hightower expressed regret for voting in 2019 to table the investigation. "I respect lawyers, I really do, but some of the things they told us we couldn't talk about, I think we've got to look back and say, maybe that wasn't a legal opinion. And that's what so many folks say about Greensboro, that we just cover up stuff.

"Well, of course, cover-up indicates conspiracy. I really believe in my heart there was a cover-up initially. After all details hit the street, it was kind of hard to continue that. I just think we could have gotten to a quicker resolution if all cards had been on the table, and we had been straight-up and honest. That press release was very deceptive. Because, when I read it, I thought, okay, this was a person in custody, he was in some kind of distress, they tried to help, and when he did, he just collapsed. And then when I saw the letter from Graham and the word 'hog-tie' really came across to me. I thought, excuse my language, *Oh, Hell no, I need to see the video*, I need to understand how he died. And that's when I asked to see it and was told no. When I finally did, I remember being pissed off when I walked out of the room where they'd shown it to us.

"I was going to that Council meeting [in 2019], prepared to remind everybody we'd said we were going to have investigation, prepared to vote for one. When I got there, I was told they had filed a lawsuit. I asked if that meant I couldn't bring it up, and they said no, you can't. Now I think we should have gone ahead and conducted one. The public trusts very little what government does about police interactions gone wrong, and I think that one way we could try to help restore people's trust in the system—not necessarily their faith—is if we at least had done that. I think it could and should have been done, and that an investigation could have been simultaneous with the lawsuit.

"Wayne Scott never policed [the majority-Black] East Greensboro. How do you put someone in charge of a department that serves the whole city when you yourself haven't truly served the whole city before? When their only relationships with that East Greensboro community are negative dealings? I've even had people who said, 'Wayne Scott, where did he come from, did you all hire him from somewhere else?' I said no, he's a police officer here in the city, but nobody in East Greensboro knew him. Even some leaders didn't know, really, who he was. That was troubling for me, that someone who'd never had any type of relationship over in our community, was given that job.

"I don't think it was just [Scott]. I think there are things that continue to go on in this city, and that they want things to remain the same, and I think there was some people saying, listen, we don't need this, this is bad publicity, we're trying to grow economic development and bring more jobs here. I think a lot of that conversation went on, but I'm never privy to that, because I don't get invited to that party. Which is okay, because

I don't want to be there, as it ain't gonna be my kind of party, and if I'm there, I'm gonna be on the menu."

In the deposition of City Manager David Parrish, Flint Taylor asked, "Did you take a position as to whether or not there should be an independent investigation?"

"In my capacity as city manager," replied Parrish, "I felt like we had enough investigations completed on this. It's the City Council's decision, and I work at the will and pleasure of the City Council, but my decision would have been we've already had enough investigations related to this matter."

"THE ONLY PLACE THEY WILL
25   EVER AGAIN SEE MARCUS..."

At the end of the long and contentious meeting on December 4, 2018, at which 35 speakers accused the City of a cover-up and called for the firing of Wayne Scott, Mayor Vaughan and the Council's two most conservative Democrats, Nancy Hoffman and Marikay Abuzuaiter, had a discussion about how the town hall format might "need tweaking."

"I would like to get some feedback," said Vaughan, "because I think, right now, this town hall style meeting is a little bit stalled."

"I think it's been hijacked, depending on the subject matter," said Hoffman. "We hear the same thing, month after month, from basically the same people."

Actually, between December of 2018 and May of 2019, over 40 different community members took the podium to call for an independent investigation and/or the firing of Wayne Scott, with several at each meeting introducing themselves as first-time speakers.

In June, after months of being denounced by public speakers at town hall meetings, Vaughan made the following announcement:

""Starting with our first town hall meeting in July, we're going to change the structure a little bit. We've all been talking about what we can do to get out into the community to make these meetings more accessible, and we had thought that we would do district meetings, so we're going to start with District 1, and it will be at the Ruth Wicker

Memorial to Women, which is a beautiful building over by Barber Park." She explained that the first meeting of each of the next five months would be held in a different district.

She also said that "those meetings will not be televised, because they are going to be in libraries or City buildings that don't have the ability to televise."

This also meant that those meetings would not be recorded on video, livestreamed by the City, or posted to its website.

One person repeatedly alleging that meetings were being "stalled" by "the same half-dozen" speakers on the Marcus Smith case was John Hammer. He had little respect for Vaughan, Hightower, or Kennedy, but even less for the "far left" speakers accusing the City of a cover-up.

After Vaughan's announcement, both Hammer and the activists he regularly dismissed in his coverage agreed on one thing; this move by Vaughan was an attempt at depriving the Smith family's supporters of a media platform.

"The City Council won't say it publicly," wrote Hammer,[1] "but not having the town hall meetings televised seems to be the main reason the meetings are being moved out of the Council Chamber. The off the record stated belief of members of the City Council is that if the meetings are not televised that the same people who have now been coming to meetings for over a year speaking about the same topics and being disruptive won't bother to come if they aren't going to be on television."

In her initial announcement, which as Hammer noted, was made without public discussion or a Council vote, Vaughan stated the audio would be recorded and the minutes of the meetings would be posted, but that the meetings would not be livecast or televised. Typically, it takes several months before the minutes of a Greensboro City Council meeting are available on the City website, and Vaughan said nothing about speeding the process.

At the June 18 work session, Sharon Hightower asked if the offsite town hall meetings could be recorded on video and posted to the City's website, even if the City didn't have the capability of streaming the meetings live as it customarily did with those in the Council chamber. City

Manager David Parrish replied this could be done, but due to technical issues involving processing offsite video, they would not immediately go online. The result of this was that the July, August, September, October and November town hall meetings could not be viewed live by anyone not physically present at the meeting, and videos of each meeting were not posted on the City's website until days later.

Activists and community members demanding the City fire Chief Scott and settle with the Smith family did attend each offsite meeting, but their numbers were smaller than at previous town halls. While it was never true that only "the same half-dozen people" were calling for justice for Marcus Smith at every Council meeting, the number of those doing so declined throughout 2019. Late that year, several activists stated that, in the future, they were going to focus on voting every City Council member out of office rather than persuading them to change their minds. One reason that ultimately didn't work may be that not enough voters cared, but it's not the only one.

In April of 2021, one City official alleged that Council was "in a quiet panic" over an upcoming NBC interview with Mary Smith and were worried that "this may kill us if we don't settle before the November election." But due to redistricting issues arising from the 2020 census, Greensboro would have no municipal elections that year. A tentative settlement of the Smith case was announced in February of 2022, three months before the postponed municipal primary, and the name "Marcus Smith" was not a major campaign issue of the general election held that July.

In 2019, however, election season seemed very far away.

In April of that year, the civil case of *Smith v. Greensboro et al* was assigned to Judge Loretta C. Biggs, an Obama District Court nominee, who in 2015, became the first Black woman appointed to the federal bench in North Carolina.

On June 13, a defense motion to dismiss the charges against the eight officers alleged the restraint used on Marcus Smith was not excessive and stated such a device has never been declared unconstitutional. One filed by County attorneys alleged EMS responded appropriately under intense pressure.

On March 25 of 2020, Judge Biggs dismissed all counts against Guilford County, but allowed many of the ones against the City and its officers, as well as the individual claims against the two County employees. Biggs also let stand claims that Marcus Smith's 14th Amendment right to equal protection under the law and due process had been violated, but dismissed claims that the officers violated his 4th Amendment right against illegal search and seizure. She also ruled that attorneys for the officers had not demonstrated entitlement to immunity on excessive force and wrongful death counts, and the EMTs were not immune to the plaintiffs' due process claims. This meant excessive force and state law wrongful death claims against the officers and City could move forward, and that plaintiffs had plausibly argued Marcus Smith's death was in part due to the City's alleged failure to properly train its officers. "Plausibly," in this context, simply meant those claims would be argued in court rather than summarily dismissed. Biggs also dismissed claims that Marcus Smith's rights under the Americans with Disabilities Act had been violated.

Flint Taylor called the ruling "a long-awaited victory for the Smith family."

"It recognizes that the use of brutal hog-tying on defenseless persons is a clear violation of their constitutional rights and that the GPD had woefully inadequate training procedures and practices concerning the use of restraints which were a direct cause of Marcus' death," wrote Taylor in an email statement. "Will the City and County leaders stop paying their silk-stocking private lawyers (at least $250,000 to date) to defend this case and instead admit official wrongdoing by their sworn officers and apologize and make right by the family and the entire Greensboro community?"

Taylor said the Smith legal team's next step was pretrial discovery, which would entail "taking the sworn testimony of the officers, supervisors, and other involved witnesses, such as former GPD Chief Wayne Scott and Mayor Nancy Vaughan."

Mary Smith also made a public statement.

"The family of Marcus Deon Smith thanks Judge Biggs for the decision to move forward. Marcus' father said in tears that he will

I AIN'T RESISTING

forever be haunted by seeing his son take his last breath on the Church Street pavement. Marcus' sister Kim and brothers Len and Jay also wept when they said that the only place they will ever again see Marcus is in their memories."

In the months between the June 2019 defense motion and the judge's March 2020 ruling, several controversial actions taken by representatives of the City of Greensboro were denounced by supporters of the Smith family as attacks on free speech.

In a September 5 press conference at the International Civil Rights Museum, Dr. T. Anthony Spearman, president of the North Carolina NAACP, called Graham Holt "a courageous attorney...being brought under attack by the City Council and the legal entities here in the City of Greensboro for something that he has done and is doing on behalf of the African-American community."

What Spearman described as an attack was not, on the surface, a response to Holt's work as a plaintiff attorney in *Smith v. Greensboro*, which was still in pretrial discovery, but something Holt had done on behalf of his former client Zared Jones, who in 2016 alleged that he and his friends were racially targeted, brutalized, and falsely arrested by two Greensboro Police officers following a 2016 incident outside a downtown bar.

In 2017, Holt filed a complaint on Jones' behalf, alleging that Jones and his friend Aaron Garrett were standing on the sidewalk outside and complaining to GPD Corporal Corey Johnson that the two young Black men had been assaulted by a bouncer inside the bar. While Jones and Corporal Johnson were talking, Sergeant Steven Kory Flowers and officer Samuel Alvarez approached. According to Holt's complaint, the new arrivals escalated the situation into a struggle between Officer Alvarez and Jones' friend Aaron Garrett that ended with Garrett being slammed against a car and tased. A 2017 *NC Policy Watch* article by Joe Killian reported that this was the second time Alvarez was accused of racial profiling and brutality.[2]

In May of that year, all charges against Zared Jones were dropped.

In January 2018, Guilford County Superior Court Judge Susan Bray ruled that Graham Holt and Zared Jones could view GPD body-worn camera videos of the incident, but only if they signed a pledge of confidentiality, in which they agreed not to "disclose or discuss the body-worn camera recordings except with each other or in association with any official hearing where they are present together with the Police Community Review Board [PCRB]." Soon afterward, additional petitions were granted to members of the Greensboro City Council, including the mayor, the city manager, legal counsel, the Police Community Review Board, and the chief of police, allowing them to view and discuss the footage amongst themselves. The mayor and Council also received gag orders that prohibited them from discussing the footage with outside parties.

The City appealed the gag order, and no City Council members viewed the video they were allowed to see but not discuss. The State Court of Appeals upheld Bray's 2018 gag order in August of 2019.

On August 9, Holt sent an email with the subject line "CONFIDENTIAL Zared Jones" to the mayor and City Council via the "E-mail City Council" portal on the City of Greensboro website. In it, he wrote, "While I no longer represent Zared Jones, Clifton Ruffin, Aaron Garrett and Alfonso Thomas, I urge you to watch the body-worn camera footage of their unlawful arrests." His email acknowledged that the gag order "prevents disclosure or discussion with third parties about the body-worn camera footage," but alleged that discussing that footage with City Council was not a violation of the gag order, as they had also been granted permission to view it and were not third parties.

The email stated that Holt had been allowed not only to view videos of the incident outside the bar, but also footage from the body-worn cameras of Alvarez and Flowers as they approached the scene, recognized the young Black men from an earlier encounter that evening, and engaged in conversation that indicated they were conspiring to arrest them without probable cause. Holt urged the members of the City Council to view this footage and stated that doing so would reveal racial profiling on the part of the two officers, as well as a stated intent to provoke an incident for which the Black men could be arrested.

On August 27, Bray initiated disciplinary proceedings against Holt for allegedly violating her gag order by sending that letter to

Greensboro City Council. In her motion, she wrote that Holt, "may have acted with impropriety calculated to bring contempt upon the administration of justice."

Holt was traveling when the press conference was held at the Civil Rights Museum. Retired civil rights attorney Lewis Pitts Jr. described his friend Holt as "being illegally and wrongly singled out" for his efforts to expose alleged GPD malfeasance. Another speaker in defense of Holt was Reverend Cardes H. Brown, president of the Greensboro NAACP and religious chairperson of the state NAACP, who called the censure "an egregious act to try discredit him."

"If we allow the City to just continue to roll on, crush up and spit out people like Graham, we might as well not call ourselves a city," said Reverend Wesley Morris.

Reverend Nelson Johnson, organizer of the press conference, stated the case was not really about Holt violating a court order, but "the cover-up of police abuse of power." He called the proceedings against Holt a calculated attempt "at stopping the investigation of that process in its tracks."

Both Johnson and Pitts decried the "hypocrisy" of Holt, and not the Greensboro City Council, being held accountable for information that "the City of Greensboro chose to release." Both alleged that City Attorney Chuck Watts had informed Judge Bray of Holt's email to Council, in an attempt to get the Smith family's Greensboro attorney discredited, censured, and possibly even disbarred. Dr. Daran Mitchell, pastor of Trinity African Methodist Episcopal Zion and president of the Pulpit Forum of Greensboro, alleged that the proceedings against Holt were part of an ongoing pattern and practice of "coverups smearing over these issues, especially when it comes to police misconduct."

After the press conference, Pitts pointed out that Holt had described the alleged actions of the two officers, in almost identical words, in a previous letter to City Council in 2018.

"He was also under the gag order then, but nothing happened to him for writing that letter. I think it's only happening now because he's part of a major civil rights lawsuit against the City over the death of Marcus

Smith. And City Attorney Chuck Watts personally delivered Graham's email to the judge, with the clear intention of having Graham hauled before her for allegedly violating her order."

Chuck Watts acknowledged he had a copy of Holt's email printed out and hand-delivered to Judge Susan Bray's office. "She chose not to look at it, and instead asked the parties, meaning my office, police lawyer Amiel Rossabi, and Graham to show up for a meeting, which we did. And she did ask us to see if there was some way we could resolve the matter. Which was curious to me, but my main concern was, what should I do with the document."

Watts acknowledged both City Council and Graham Holt had the right to see the videos, but that neither could disclose what they saw to the public. The problem, alleged Watts, was that Council was trying to get the gag order lifted via the appeals process, but that Holt had allegedly directly violated the order by writing to Council about what he had seen.

"So, we're together with Graham in the sense that we don't think that she should be gagging people. But Graham's mistake is that he's apparently disrespected the Judge's authority to issue such an order. That's gonna be his problem. I'm not the prosecutor of his case; I don't have a dog in that hunt. We'll be curious, of course. It may inform us, by how she treats a similar order, about how she may treat any of the Council people if they were to behave in a similar fashion."

On September 30, 2019, Holt appeared before a disciplinary panel appointed by Bray to determine whether he had violated her gag order. One member of that panel was attorney Don Carter, who asked the court, "How do we punish somebody for something that's not valid?"

At that preliminary proceeding, Holt's attorney Robert O'Hale asked for a stay until the North Carolina Supreme Court ruled on the City's appeal to overturn Judge Bray's gag order. O'Hale stated that, should the gag order be overturned, the entire matter could be moot, as his client should not be censured for violating an order found unlawful by the State Supreme Court.

Special Prosecuting Attorney Walter "Kirk" Burton disputed this claim by stating that Holt was not part of the City's appeal of the gag order but acknowledged that a reversal of that gag order could impact any sanctions brought against Holt. Both the defense and prosecution stated they were unaware of any existing case law that specifically addresses these issues, which presiding Judge Allen Baddour called "uncharted territory," although Baddour stated that some rough analogies may exist, such as rulings that "a person who resists an unlawful arrest is not guilty of resisting arrest."

The proceeding began with all parties expressing confusion as to the role of the panel appointed by Judge Bray, with Judge Baddour calling the panel "a new beast to me." Ultimately, all agreed that they "should not proceed in a substantive hearing" until after the State Supreme Court ruled on the City's appeal.

On December 16, 2022, that court overturned Judge Bray's gag order. On June 8, 2023, Mayor Vaughan said that she and several other council members had watched body-worn camera video from the incident, and that "I can't speak for the others, but I disagree with Graham Holt's description of what can be seen or heard on that footage."

October of 2019 brought a new dispute involving the City of Greensboro, transparency, and free speech, although this was tested at that month's City Council meeting and never got the point of judicial action. Mayor Vaughan began the October 2 town hall meeting by announcing a new code of conduct for members of the public speaking to the Council.

Vaughan said anyone violating these rules might be declared out of order and asked to leave. She then read aloud from the document she and the city attorney had prepared without any consultation with other Council members.

"Comments primarily focused on the performance of particular City employees will not be entertained in this forum and be ruled out of order. That does not mean that we can't talk about departments and performance of departments, but we do not want to talk about specific employees."

This meant any criticism by public speakers of Chief Scott, or any of his officers, would not be allowed.

"The only place they will ever again see Marcus..."

"Comments primarily focused on matters that are in litigation will not be entertained in this forum. Litigation occurs in the courts, and I will rule out of order comments by individuals that appear to be intended to impact the litigation process through public comment during our meetings. This is not an alternative public forum for promoting any particular citizen's view of matters that are being addressed in the court."

This rule would prohibit speakers from calling on the City to settle *Smith v. Greensboro*, or even mention the incident that resulted in the litigation.

District 1 representative Sharon Hightower stated later that evening that she was not comfortable with the new rules.

"I think it gets into matters of freedom of speech, and I'm a little taken aback by tonight's regulation. First, we've not had any discussion around what was being presented, and I was a little shocked as I listened. Are we targeting certain people who've been consistent about talking about certain individuals, or are we just saying we don't want to open ourselves up to personnel issues? But I think there's nothing wrong with allowing people to talk about certain issues. This was a forum started to allow people to come get it off their chest, no matter what it is they're frustrated about. And I feel like now we are putting too many constraints on freedom. So, I'm very concerned and would like to have more discussion about what the thought processes are. Sometimes you've got to say what you think in the presence of people who elected you to serve."

At the next town hall meeting on November 4, multiple speakers challenged the new rule and the mayor appeared to back down. Vaughan repeatedly told several speakers they were violating those rules but did not cut them off or have them removed.

When Lewis Pitts took the podium, he announced his intention of defying the new rules, and did so by talking about the Smith lawsuit. Pitts' microphone was not cut off, and he was neither removed from the room nor arrested.

"Had my bail money and everything," he joked afterward. More seriously, he stated his belief that arbitrary enforcement of the rules "is even more insidious" than enforcing them against everyone. "Having the rules in place, but only using them to silence those who the mayor or other Council members decide, at any particular moment, is safe to silence, is extremely dangerous."

In his time at the podium, Pitts called Mayor Vaughan's rules "preposterous" and quoted Dr. Frayda Bluestein of the University of North Carolina School of Government as saying they were unconstitutional. Pitts then said, "I'm going to violate them right now," to applause from the spectators. Pitts accused the city of "having spent, of taxpayer's money, $181,286 for attorney fees for pin-striped patronage, paying lawyers $300 an hour to fight the lawsuit brought by Marcus Deon Smith's grieving parents."

Pitts was one of six speakers to defy and denounce the Council rules. Another was frequent Council critic Hester Petty, who said, "Mayor Vaughan, your attempt to regulate the content of my public comments is unconstitutional and self-serving" and "your new rules are meant to limit public discussion of subjects you and some Council members simply don't want to hear about."

Petty then named GPD officers Lee Andrews, Michael Montalvo and Justin Payne as the ones who applied the restraint that killed Smith and said they should be fired, along with Corporal Douglas Strader and Sergeant Christopher Bradshaw, the two ranking officers on the scene. She also said Chief Wayne Scott should not be allowed to resign but should be fired for perpetuating the cover-up.

"It is a legal issue and is being decided in a court of law," said Vaughan.

"And I have a constitutional right to talk about it here," said Petty, to applause from the audience.

Assistant professor Dr. Justin Harmon of UNC Greensboro's Department of Community and Therapeutic Recreation said that some City Council members appear to "prefer the citizens of Greensboro...sit on their hands and bite their tongues, and become good little supplicants, embracing the image of voice and fellowship in a city where both the past and present often indicate otherwise."

The rules announced by Vaughan were never mentioned during a Council meeting again. District 3 representative Justin Outling, an attorney who would later unsuccessfully challenge Vaughan in the 2022 mayoral election, told the press that the rules Vaughan had attempted to impose were unconstitutional. Vaughan later acknowledged that the announced code she had drafted with the city attorney was "quietly dropped" due to lack of support from other Council members.

Vaughan's critics accused her of trying to impose the new rules not just to silence discussion of the Smith lawsuit but calls for the firing of Wayne Scott. Those calls became moot in August of 2019, when Scott announced he would be retiring at the end of the year.

On June 7, 2020, more people heard and said the name Marcus Deon Smith than at any previous public gathering, when a rally titled #BlackoutNC: An Anti-Police Brutality Demonstration, brought thousands to Greensboro's LeBauer Park.

The gathering was organized by Greensboro Rising, a group founded in the late spring of 2020 to demand racial accountability, social change, and nonviolent policing from City leaders.

"We traveled this road many times, only to be almost laughed at by City Council," said Kim Smith from the park's stage. "We won't ever stop fighting for Marcus. Greensboro, you had a George Floyd in your city. Marcus Smith was the George Floyd of Greensboro!"

"You would not want to be standing where I am today," said Mary Smith, who said her son "died just the same way George Floyd died" and that "their autopsies were exactly the same."

"Greensboro City Council and [now former] Police Chief Wayne Scott have played us," said Mary. "And Nancy Vaughan said she found no wrongdoing. She could have avoided all this if she'd acted like the mayor of Minneapolis after George Floyd's death."

"We fully support the protestors naming of Marcus Smith, together with many other Black victims of police suffocation and asphyxiation," said Smith family attorney Flint Taylor, "including George Floyd in Minneapolis, Eric Garner in New York City, and Derek Williams in Milwaukee, as victims of racist and illegal police violence, and we call on Mayor Vaughan, the Greensboro police chief and the *Greensboro News & Record* to emphatically and definitively follow suit."

Five days after Taylor called on the City of Greensboro to "follow suit," private attorneys hired by the City filed a motion to halt discovery in the lawsuit Taylor was litigating.

26 "THEY'RE BEING PIMPED."

On June 12, 2020, Alan Duncan and Gray Russell, the private attorneys defending the City of Greensboro and the eight GPD officers in the federal civil rights lawsuit over Marcus' death, filed a motion to temporarily stay the start of discovery. Discovery is a pretrial procedure in which each party to a lawsuit can obtain evidence from the other party by methods including depositions. In their motion, Duncan and Russell cited another ongoing court case in which Mary Smith acknowledged that her late son may have one or more minor children. They asked that the discovery process be delayed until the paternity of those children could be determined.

The same morning, at a press conference hosted by the Beloved Community Center, every speaker called for the Greensboro City Council to "stop delaying" and come to terms with the Smith family.

The press conference was organized and hosted by Reverend Nelson Johnson and Reverend Wesley Morris. Other speakers included Byron Gladden, chair of minority affairs at NC 6th District Democrats; Adrienne Spinner, second vice chair of the Guilford County Democratic Party (GCDP); Greensboro Rising organizers Irving Allen, Kiera Hereford, and Casey Thomas; and retired civil rights attorney Lewis Pitts.

At the press conference, Gladden stated that the GCDP had recently passed a resolution calling for the City of Greensboro "to publicly atone for the homicide of Marcus Deon Smith, adequately compensate his family, and hold the presiding officers and their supervisors accountable." Spinner was there on behalf of the GCDP "to stand with the Smith Family, Greensboro Rising, and the Beloved Community Center in solidarity, as we demand an end to the continuous stalling taking place regarding justice for Marcus Smith's death."

Near the end of that night's Council meeting, Mayor Vaughan asked City Attorney Watts for an update on the litigation, including "a stay that may have been filed by your office or by our attorneys."

That stay was not actually filed by the City Attorney's office, which had no official role in the lawsuit. However, this was the first public occasion on which Watts, who had been hired as chief city attorney in May of 2019, would become a very vocal part of the ongoing public controversy. It was also the first occasion in which he would make a statement that some activists and advocates for the Smith family would denounce as a lie.

In response to the mayor's query, Watts stated that "there is no stay being requested, no stay whatsoever."

Watts described the motion entered by the defense as a request to delay only the start of the discovery process, whereas "a stay would stop all litigation processes." After describing the probate issue, Watts concluded by stating "we are not asking for a stay" and "we don't expect the delay that we've asked for to delay the date of trial."

Watts' critics would later call this statement not only deceptive but disingenuous. Any stay that did not delay the start of the trial would inevitably curtail the discovery process. Flint Taylor had stated several times in press conferences and interviews his intention to depose former Greensboro Police Chief Wayne Scott, Mayor Nancy Vaughan, City Attorney David Parrish, and others to determine not only the facts of Marcus Smith's death, but whether GPD training procedures (or lack thereof) were a factor in that death, and if City or police officials attempted a cover-up. If discovery was delayed but a trial was not postponed, Taylor would have less time to do that.

Despite Watts' claim that "no stay" had been requested, the June 12 request by the defense was titled "DEFENDANTS' JOINT MOTION TO TEMPORARILY STAY THE START OF DISCOVERY" [capitalization in original]. And according to Cornell Law School, a stay is a "ruling by a court to stop or suspend a proceeding or trial temporarily or indefinitely." By this definition, the June 12 motion is indeed a stay, even though it is requesting a delay in an individual proceeding (the discovery process), rather than the entire trial.

In a statement the next morning, Watts wrote: "Typically, a 'stay' and the way that this term was generally being used by Mr. Pitts and his crew was that the litigation generally would be stopped such that no civil litigation activity would be going on. As I said last night, all we were asking for was a delay of the start of the discovery period."

The reference to "Mr. Pitts and his crew" was the first indication of Watts' seeming obsession with Lewis Pitts, who had been regularly criticizing the City and its legal team at Council meetings.

Watts, who is Black, had recently moved to Greensboro from Raleigh, where he had been a general counsel and deputy secretary for the North Carolina Department of Transportation. Statements made by Watts in correspondence and conversations during the spring and summer of 2020 demonstrated he had little familiarity with Greensboro's Black community leaders Nelson Johnson and Wesley Morris, or the Beloved Community Center, of which they were members. Instead of acknowledging the efforts of Johnson and Morris to focus media attention on the controversy over Marcus Smith's death, Watts claimed that the protests were the work of their fellow activist Lewis Pitts.

He also denied any claims "that our goal was to delay the completion of litigation and any ultimate payment to the plaintiffs as much as a year," which he described as "the fundamental point of the protesters" and "the fundamental untruth." His statement continued:

"We have agreed to a one-year discovery period, but we could reduce that by the time it takes the plaintiff's team to figure out who are the real parties in interest. While we did not know that there were children, the parents did and continued to pursue the case as though they [the parents] were the next of kin. Now they have acknowledged that there may be as many as three children."

"They're being pimped."

Watts sent an email to Guilford County Democratic Party Chair Betsy Fox which indicated not only an obsession with Lewis Pitts, but a belief the man who had resigned from the state bar was somehow one of the plaintiff attorneys in the civil rights lawsuit his employers were fighting. "Is the Democratic Party part of Mr. Pitts' litigation team?" was the subject line of his email.

He wrote, "I was shocked to see the party participating in a 'press conference' put on yesterday by Lewis Pitts where lies were spread in connection with a matter in the litigation process. Was that participation approved in the regular way?"

Watts stated that "Mr. Pitts' efforts to make this civil litigation matter into a public cause and to fan legitimate flames of discontent in the wake of Mr. George Floyd's murder is deplorable. And it would be different if it was all about finding a just outcome, but it's not. He has but one goal in mind and it's not justice. I would hope that the Democratic Party would not participate in his efforts to take advantage of the terrible murder of Mr. George Floyd and the legitimate protests that have ensued. The unfortunate death of Mr. Marcus Smith was totally different from what happened to Mr. Floyd and both cases deserve to each be addressed on their own merits."

In a telephone interview, Watts responded to questions about his statement concerning Pitts.

"Well, he's been at the forefront of everything. He's before Council all the time, talking about this issue, this litigation. In one of the articles that's been written about this, he was named as the lead attorney here in Greensboro, and he's not an attorney."

No article published by *YES! Weekly, Triad City Beat*, or the *News & Record* had described Lewis Pitts as an attorney in the Marcus Smith litigation.

Asked if he was aware that the press conference held that week, like many others at which Pitts has spoken, was organized and hosted by Black ministers and activists, and if he was familiar with the Reverend Nelson Johnson's decades-long history of activism against police brutality, Watts responded:

"I don't know all the players involved, but it's clear to me that [Pitts] is the leading force behind the stuff." Watts expressed his concern over what he described as "the ethical" issue of Pitts' involvement in the protests. "He's also playing the role of a lawyer, and he's not a barred attorney. So, it creates a lot of angst on my part that he's in the middle of it, and I'd just like his role to be clarified."

When told his remarks could be interpreted as stating prominent Black clergy were holding these press conferences at the behest of a retired white attorney, Watts replied with agitation, "I think they're being pimped! That's my view of it."

He also stated that "all the deceit and duplicity" is on "the whole other side."

"All I'm trying to do is make sure the City's money is not paid to the wrong party if it's to be paid at all. With respect to the discovery process, if we start discovery today, and we don't know who the real party of interest is, it's a whole different game plan. Two or three months later, we find out it's some kid, the process gets restarted. Why should we do that so that they have three months of basically run time on the year clock that we agreed upon, that they can do all the discovery that they want to do. They know who we are, and everything they're looking at is public. Their job is nowhere near as challenging as ours. They shouldn't get a three-month head start on it. That's all we were arguing for. There was no intent to delay the ultimate conclusion of this litigation."

Despite Watts' repeated use of "we," the city attorney was not litigating anything in the Smith case, as neither Watts nor his staff were part of the defense team. Instead, he was doing what he accused Lewis Pitts of doing, attempting to "argue" the case in the court of public opinion.

In response to Watts' tirade, Flint Taylor called it "beyond disgraceful that a high-ranking City official is falsely and maliciously calling Mary Smith and her lawyers liars" and asked if Watts was speaking for Mayor Vaughan and City Council when he made those statements. He alleged Watts' "rambling" description of the probate proceedings involving Marcus Smith's children demonstrated "a profound ignorance of how the issue of heirship and the distribution of money will be managed" and stated that the probate issue "would in no way will be affected by the hog-tying case going forward now."

The June 12 defense motion argued that discovery should be delayed until the completion of a separate State Probate Court proceeding related to a petition filed by Mary Smith as administrator of her son's estate. Mary's petition asked the state to determine whether Marcus Smith's adult son Marquis Zyquarius Smith and two minor children were heirs to the Smith estate. As Marcus' children were not named as heirs in the wrongful death litigation, defense argued that discovery should be delayed until heirship was determined, as that determination may be that the true heirs are Marcus Smith's children rather than his parents.

In their response, plaintiffs contended discovery should begin immediately, arguing most of discovery will be on liability rather than damages, as the latter would be where heirship might become an issue. Magistrate Judge Joe Webster agreed. His order filed July 2 in the United States District Court for the Middle District of North Carolina ruled "the Court will deny Defendants' motion to stay discovery and enter an order to commence discovery immediately," as "any hardship to Defendants as a result of moving forward with discovery is minimal."

Flint Taylor gave the following statement to *YES! Weekly*:

"We are pleased that Judge Webster unequivocally denied the City and County defendants' motion for an indefinite stay of all proceedings and cleared the way for us to expeditiously obtain all of the documents relevant to the homicide of Marcus Smith and the cover-up that followed and to question under oath all of the officers and EMTs involved, those who trained them, former Chief Scott, and the mayor."

Taylor also condemned "City Attorney Charles Watts' irresponsible and false statements to the City Council, the Mayor, and the media, about our lawsuit, the City's motion to stay, the Smith family, Greensboro's Black clergy, our legal team, and Lewis Pitts."

Taylor was not the only one outraged by Watts' statements. On July 1, the Beloved Community Center issued a three-page statement titled "Truth and Integrity: A Requirement for Genuine Democracy," which

I AIN'T RESISTING

accused Chuck Watts of lacking the second quality and disregarding the first in his allegations about Lewis Pitts.

The statement began with an introduction by Executive Director Reverend Nelson Johnson describing Pitts as "a white retired Civil Rights Attorney and a dear friend of mine, who was viciously slandered by Greensboro City Attorney Chuck Watts," and stated, "being demonized myself in this city for many years, I know the process."

The body of the statement began with a quotation from the North Carolina State Bar Rules of Professional Conduct, in which Rule 4.1 states "in the course of representing a client, a lawyer shall not knowingly make a false statement of material fact or law to a third party."

After describing a June 16 press conference at which speakers called on the Greensboro City Council to stop "delaying and come to terms with Smith family," the statement then accused Watts of a "two-day tantrum, insulting and slandering Lewis Pitts and other Greensboro residents, clergy and advocates." It also noted Watts' email to Guilford County Democratic Party chair Betsy Fox.

The response stated that the press conference had been conducted by their organization, not Pitts, that the death of Marcus Smith was "already a public cause," as Marcus was killed by City employees, the City and those employees are named as defendants in the lawsuit, the City has paid "hundreds of thousands of tax payer dollars" to its defense team, and dozens of Greensboro residents had spoken about the lawsuit and related matters at City Council meetings.

The statement responded to Watts' "I hope the Democratic Party would not participate in these efforts" with the following passage:

"What efforts are these? The efforts in which Lewis is joined by a large, diverse group of clergy, civil rights leaders, advocates for the homeless, policing reform advocates, and other Greensboro residents?"

It also took issue with Watts' statement to GCDP Chair Fox that the "unfortunate death of Mr. Marcus Smith was totally different from what happened to Mr. Floyd," by stating that both cases involved Black men who said they couldn't breathe while they were killed by police.

Of Watts' statement to *YES! Weekly* that Pitts has "been at the forefront of everything" and is "before Council all the time, talking about this issue," the statement declared:

"Finally, Watts got something right. For well over a decade, Pitts has been among the advocates at the forefront of the fight for racial and economic justice. Instead of bemoaning Pitts' admirable efforts, Watts should do his job—for which he's paid handsomely—and take a page out of Pitts' book when it comes to truth-telling and social justice advocacy."

It responded to Watts' allegation that Pitts "is playing the role of a lawyer, and he's not a barred attorney" and that this "creates a lot of angst on my part that he's in the middle of it, and I'd just like his role to be clarified" by offering the following "clarification" for Watts:

"In January 2016, Lewis became the first person ever to resign from the North Carolina State Bar, after convincing the Board to establish a new procedure for resignation. He decried lawyers who 'approach law practice as a business,' 'hunt for profit,' and serve corporate interests. Watts should consider whether his vendetta against Lewis is fueled, at least in part, by the fact that Lewis' critiques apply to most of Watts' career. Since resigning from the bar, Lewis has neither claimed nor implied that he's a licensed practicing attorney, and he has not practiced law. Watts' personal angst and mission to attack Pitts' good name can't justify his baseless accusations."

On July 2, Johnson said that Watts offered him an apology.

"He reached out to me by phone and said that he wanted to apologize, and I asked him if he could be more specific about what he was apologizing for. He said that he misspoke. And that's the extent of it. My thinking is, I wasn't mentioned in all of what he said to the Democratic Party and what he said about Lewis. My further thinking is that he needs to apologize to these young people and to Lewis, but I didn't feel called to engage him in a back and forth. I received it and that was it."

In his June 2021 deposition of Michelle Kennedy, Flint Taylor repeatedly asked whether she found Watts to be "trustworthy." Defense attorney Alan Duncan objected that the question was "interference with an attorney-client relationship" and thus "an inappropriate question." He then instructed Kennedy not to answer.

After some verbal sparring with Duncan, Taylor asked Kennedy if she was familiar with Watts' claim that Lewis Pitts "was pimping the Black community." Kennedy said that she was.

Taylor then asked Kennedy if she considered the statement by Watts to be part of her "attorney-client relationship" with him.

"No, I do not," replied Kennedy.

"And do you find that statement to be trustworthy?" asked Taylor.

"I find that statement offensive," replied Kennedy.

The next year, she would condemn another public statement by Watts, which she would call both offensive and untrue. Before that happened, she would challenge the veracity of statements made by multiple GPD chiefs to City Council and the press, when she angrily said "we've flat-out been lied to again" at the November 2, 2020, meeting of City Council.

She was referring to the question of whether the Greensboro Police Department had actually banned hog-tying.

That summer, the police department of neighboring Winston-Salem issued an order that "placing a subject with their hands secured behind their back, legs secured together, and their legs and hands connected together behind the subject's back with the subject's legs flexed at the knees" was "STRICTLY PROHIBITED" [all-caps in original directive].

At the November 2 Council meeting, Kennedy, Sharon Hightower and Mayor pro tem Yvonne Johnson all stated they had been led to believe by former Chief Wayne Scott that his department had formally banned this restraint technique over a year before Winston-Salem did. After sustained grilling by the three Council members, Assistant City Manager for Public Safety Trey Davis, who had been a GPD deputy chief when Marcus was killed, acknowledged that this was not the case. He and City Manager David Parrish told Council that language would be added to the GPD directives manual explicitly prohibiting the technique.

The subject came up in the public comments section of the meeting, which began with speaker Catherine Holcombe asking, "Has hog-tying been deleted from the police training manual?"

No City official responded to Holcombe's question. The next speaker, Lewis Pitts, addressed the wrongful death litigation by alleging that the

City had already spent over $414,000 on "lawyers asking to have the lawsuit thrown out," a cost which Pitts predicted would soon climb to over a million dollars. He then referred to Hester Petty, the next speaker announced by Mayor Vaughan. "I think Ms. Petty's going to bring up the fact that there's been no banning of hog-tying by you."

"I'm told we had an order against hog-tying," said Mayor pro tem Johnson.

"I don't want to address it in context of the terminology of hog-tying," interjected Assistant City Manager Davis. "I think the question is mainly surrounding if we maximally restrain, which was the practice when the RIPP Hobble was used. The previous administration removed the RIPP Hobble from the equipment officers use." In its place, said Davis, the GPD now used "a device that is two Velcro straps, one that goes around the ankles, and the other that goes around the area just above the knees. With those devices, officers are not able to bind a person's hands to their feet."

Hester Petty then began her remarks by stating. "Let me just say that, with flexicuffs and the limb restraint, you certainly can still hog-tie somebody."

Although several Council members, particularly District 2's Goldie Wells, expressed confusion on this point, Petty's statement was correct, as Mayor Vaughan later acknowledged. The 2018 edition of the GPD Directives Manual stated that flexicuffs can be used in such a matter, with the following statement: "If further immobility is needed, the secured wrists and ankles of the arrestee may be linked together using flexicuffs or the Hobble device."

Linking a person's wrists and ankles behind their back in the position that killed Marcus Smith is the essential definition of "hog-tying" as it pertains to human beings (when pigs and other livestock are restrained in this manner prior to slaughter, their four feet are not tied behind them).

"There has been an outcry over the death of George Floyd," stated Petty. "Brian James, Greensboro's police chief, has condemned the officers involved in George Floyd's death in custody. But you don't have to go eleven hundred miles away to Minneapolis to find a Black man killed in police custody, when we have our own tragedy right here in Greensboro, with the homicide of Marcus Smith by Greensboro police officers."

After stating that "the newly released GPD directives do not contain a prohibition of this deadly and unnecessary restraint technique," Petty reminded Council that Winston-Salem banned it. She then asked, "Why is this simple statement absent from the new GPD directives?" She stated, "When a police department refuses to take measures to protect citizens from the use of deadly force in situations where it's unwarranted, as was the case with Marcus Smith, it becomes your duty to protect the public from police abuse."

Unlike it had in its non-response to Lewis Pitts, Council took up the question. "Have we done it or not?" asked Yvonne Johnson of Trey Davis. "Because the last chief told us that it was going to be banned!" Michelle Kennedy agreed, stating that former GPD Chief Wayne Scott had told her the same thing. "I've been telling people it was banned," said District 1's Hightower. "And that's because we were told that. We do need to get it right."

Kennedy asked Davis to answer Hightower and Johnson's question.

"Again, the police department's direction was to change their practice for the restraints," said Davis, apparently using "restraint" to mean a device and not a position. "And the restraints they currently have don't allow officers to perform the actual function."

"Can I just ask a really direct question?" said Kennedy, with a note of irritation. "The definition of hog-tying is binding the feet of something. That is actually what you do when you hog-tie something. Are we or are we not, just yes or no, are we still hog-tying people?"

"Let me answer Councilwoman Kennedy," said Davis. "The practice is relevant to binding hands to feet. GPD's current practice is not to either instruct or have officers bind people's hands to their feet that are in custody, as well as a further step of insuring that, if they do have a person in a prone position to restrain them temporarily, then they are to immediately assess the condition of that person and place them in a position that is much more safe, or safe for that person."

"I understand that's what you practice," said Kennedy, "but what I'm asking is, what is the written policy regarding this?

"We did not explicitly state that police may not hog-tie," said City Manager David Parrish, "because that language is not in the directive and

"They're being pimped."

never was. We also don't explicitly state that you can bind hands to feet. We are looking at language to be a little more clear. Because it doesn't state that you can do, but to Hester's point, it doesn't state that you can't."

That's when Kennedy stated with exasperation, "Then we've flat out been lied to, again."

Council then argued over terminology for several minutes, with Davis, at-large representative Marikay Abuzuaiter, and District 2's Goldie Wells insisting the language was a moot point, as restraining a person in such a manner was "impossible" with the new flexicuffs, despite the old directives manual's reference to them being used in precisely that manner.

For once, the GPD's staunchest defender was not Marikay Abuzuaiter, but Goldie Wells, who stated, "If you can't put the hands and the feet together, then you can't hog-tie, whether you say it or not, in terms of the new device, you can't use it to do that." Wells also expressed dismay that Chief Brian James "isn't here to defend himself."

"We could ban hog-tying all day long, but there is no tool that an officer has that would allow hog-tying at all," said Abuzuaiter.

Sharon Hightower referred to Hester Petty's statement that this wasn't true, and then said that, without a ban in writing, "a whole 'nother administration could come in and bring back the RIPP Hobble."

Both Abuzuaiter and Wells protested the statements by Kennedy, Hightower, and Johnson that the previous GPD administration had "lied" (a word only used by Kennedy), but the trio remained firm in their recollection of being told that the procedure had been explicitly banned.

"We will get it changed," said Parrish. "It's not a stretch to make that simple statement that hands and feet will..."

"And that executive memo was not put into the directives," interjected the mayor, referring to a memo that, unlike the directives manual, was not made public. "The executive memo is separate from the directives. People can't find that in the directives."

"We will make the change," said Parrish.

On Wednesday, November 4, Assistant City Manager Davis sent an email to the mayor and City Council. It contained the following paragraph.

"To provide further clarification surrounding the "Handling Persons in Custody, Restraint, and Transport of Individuals" policy, Chief James and his staff have implemented a policy change to this Directive, and have begun the process of implementing that policy change. While the restraint device currently issued to officers (the 'limb restraint' device) does not allow officers to bind an individual's hands to their feet, GPD staff has instituted language in the policy that will provide further guidance to officers. Effective immediately, all Greensboro Police Officers are strictly prohibited from connecting a detainee's hands to their feet, regardless of the restraint device used."

Section 11.1.4, page 263 of the directives manual was revised to include the following sentence: "Connecting a detainee's hands to their feet, regardless of the restraint device used, is strictly prohibited."

For Michelle Kennedy, that was not good enough. After the revised directives manual was posted, she made the following statement:

"While GPD asserts that limb restraints cannot be used to bind hands to feet, the fact that further guidance was necessary to indicate the prohibition against hog-tying is troubling to me. The fact that the prohibition was issued on November 3rd and not per Council's initial directives is unacceptable."

Three weeks later, City Attorney Watts made another statement that Kennedy would also denounce, although he did so in an email to activist Hester Petty that Petty did not make public until speaking to Council in January of 2021.

27 SIX FIGURES AND A HISTORY OF HOG-TYING

At the January 5, 2021, town hall meeting of City Council, the first speaker, Hester Petty, criticized City Attorney Chuck Watts for describing Marcus Smith's life as being worth no more than six figures.

Watts had sent her an email three weeks before, in which he responded to questions originally asked by Petty and Lewis Pitts during the previous month's meeting. Pitts had said the City had spent nearly half a million dollars defending the case so far, and was likely to spend five times that amount before it was done. Pitts also cited previous lawsuits over misconduct by Greensboro police officers in which settlements were between $6 million and $13 million.

"Lawsuits are not guarantees of victory," wrote Watts to Petty. "If this case goes to trial, given the video evidence of the incident and the officers' defenses under the law, it is my view there will be a verdict for the Defendant, thus giving the Plaintiffs nothing. Should the Plaintiffs clear both of those hurdles, the court is likely to award the Plaintiffs the actuarial assessment of Marcus' earning potential over his expected life span. Given his illnesses, lifestyle, and employment history, that is not likely to be a large number, probably less than six figures. It would be unprecedented for Plaintiffs in North Carolina to receive anything in the range of the comparables listed by Mr. Pitts. That is not to say that it won't happen, but it is highly unlikely. So, if the Plaintiffs are looking for that high a sum in a settlement, then you might understand why the

City will likely continue to pay outside counsel to defend itself and its tax payers by pursuing this litigation to conclusion."

In a response to this email, Flint Taylor accused Watts of being "profoundly contemptuous of the value of Black and Brown lives in general and Marcus' in particular, and of the humanity of a fairly selected North Carolina jury," and condemned the city attorney for "misunderstanding how the value of a life is calculated in a civil rights case lawsuit versus some sort of insurance actuarial table."

"The City has already paid $550,000 to defend this case and will pay at least another $1.5 to $2 million more before trial. So, is Mr. Watts contending that Marcus Smith's life that was taken by a brutal hog-tying is worth 1/25th of the City's lawyers' pretrial fees? Less than 1/65th of Eric Garner's life that was taken by a police choke hold in New York? Less than 1/120th of Breonna Taylor's life that was taken in a police raid in Louisville? Less than 1/???? of George Floyd's life that was taken by a police knee on his neck in Minneapolis?"

Lewis Pitts also responded to the city attorney.

"The email renews my concern about the city attorney's stability and therefore his advice. Among his striking history of bad advice is the colossal error of advising the mayor she could legally ban speakers during public comment period from mentioning specific litigation against the City or even criticizing City employees by name. The policy developed pursuant to his advice was immediately and roundly criticized by legal experts as violating the constitutional rights of free speech and quietly revoked."

"It's painful to hear people talk about a six-figure offer," said Michelle Kennedy. "And I completely understand when the community is saying, well, you spend $600,000 in legal fees. Well, we have. But we made an offer that was five times that amount of money in October, that we never got a response to. So, it's not completely fair to say that we're not in serious negotiations. Going to the table with a $3 million offer is much different from going to the table with a $100,000. That causes distrust and further breeds devaluation of this man's life. I'll use Hester Petty because she talks about it a lot, and fairly so. If I'm coming to Council and saying, you spent more than half a million dollars defending this lawsuit, and I think that all you're willing to offer for this man's life is a $100,000, I'm livid. And the fact is, we've offered more than five times what we've spent in legal fees, and didn't get a response to that offer, so we've had no choice but to continue down the legal process at that point."

When asked about Kennedy's claim that the City of Greensboro offered $3 million to settle the case, Flint Taylor called the statement a "goddam lie!" He made it clear he believed the alleged liar to be Watts rather than Kennedy.

"We categorically deny that the City has offered us $3 million dollars or anything that is in anyway even remotely close to that number. If they had offered $3 million, the mediation would not have been suspended by the mediator last October, and negotiations would have continued, which they unquestionably have not. It is important to determine how and by whom the City Council members and the mayor were fed this false information because it appears to be yet another attempt to falsely attack Mary Smith and her lawyers and to make us unjustifiably appear unreasonable to our supporters and to the public at large."

When asked about the supposed $3 million offer, the mayor, city manager, and all eight members of the City Council, chose not to respond. The only one to respond was Chuck Watts, who expressed outrage at Pitts' allegation of "bad information."

"Mr. Pitts has on numerous occasions asked questions or made statements during the public comment period of Council meetings that seemed to be intended to essentially invade and disturb my relationship with my client. The attorney-client relationship is a privileged relationship of trust and confidence. His assertions that Council is getting 'bad information' and even 'terrible advice' are attempts to undermine their trust and confidence in their lawyer. He does that tactically but without any basis for knowing what I may have said to my client and, therefore, no idea whether Council received good or bad information or advice. I do not believe that any of my clients have taken any of those statements seriously. I would suggest that you ignore them as well."

Responding to a question about whether he told Council members the Smith family had been offered $3 million, he wrote:

"I am quite confident that you are aware that these conversations and communications occurred in a confidential setting. I try to comply with these requirements and will neither confirm nor deny anything that happened in the context of our confidential mediation. The reason that these communications are confidential is to allow negotiations to occur between the parties without having a concern that the discussions will in the short-term become public, particularly in piecemeal fashion where they can be taken out of context. The fact of that confidentiality is believed to enhance the potential for a successful negotiation. All that I can say about that mediated negotiation is that the parties were not able to reach agreement regarding a settlement of the case though all sides gathered for a day to try to see if an agreement could be reached."

He also accused Flint Taylor of violating rules of confidentiality regarding mediation.

"You may believe that you have some sort of right to this information, but that is not true. In fact, the opposite is true. The people in that room that day have a right to expect that those conversations will remain confidential. What is also true is that I have an obligation to respect that right and not to share confidential discussions of a mediated settlement conference with you."

He then argued that those same confidentiality rules prevented him from answering the question.

"Similarly, for me to disclose to you or anyone what I have said privately to my client not only breaches the confidentiality of that relationship but could also render those conversations discoverable, in other words not protected by the privilege that they deserve. Such a disclosure by me could result in significant litigation delay and expense to the City. So, for all those reasons, I cannot disclose any part of those discussions. Further, I don't think that you should speculate about what I may have said to my client based upon things that others may say. Part of the reason for the confidentiality that parties agree to when they engage in mediations is that putting the proper context around partial disclosures is nearly impossible. And, of course, piecemeal disclosures tend to be strategically designed to represent something other than what would fairly represent the discussion during a mediation. So, I won't engage in such disclosures."

Taylor's deposition of Michelle Kennedy, conducted in June of 2021, suggests the city attorney did indeed tell City Council that the Smith family had been offered a $3 million settlement, and that this claim was false. This is supported both by what Kennedy said under oath and what was redacted.

Taylor asked Kennedy if it was true Watts wrote that Marcus' life was "not worth six figures." Kennedy replied, "Unfortunately, yes" and called Watts' statement "an extremely poor choice of wording." Taylor asked Kennedy, "Do you find Chuck Watts to be trustworthy in his statements to you and the Council?"

Defense attorney Alan Duncan objected that Taylor is "intermeddling" in the "attorney-client relationship," and instructed Kennedy not to answer.

"And, in fact, you told Ian McDowell, back when he was interviewing you in either April or May, that the City had made a $3 million offer and we had turned that down, right?"

"Correct," said Kennedy, who then said this statement was "based on what was explained to me by Mr. Watts."

"And you also know that we protested like stuck pigs when we heard that Watts was saying, and you were saying publicly, that we had been offered $3 million, correct?"

"Yes," said Kennedy.

"So that's another example of how Watts is completely untrustworthy, correct?"

Duncan objected.

"It is an example of something being communicated in a way that was not actually the way it took place," said Kennedy.

"So, in other words," asked Taylor, "the communication that Watts made to you and to others on Council, according to another article that Ian wrote, was not accurate, in terms of what had been offered to us, if anything?"

The next 18 lines of the publicly released deposition are blank, other than "REDACTED AS 'HIGHLY CONFIDETIAL' [sic] BY CITY OF GREENSBORO."

Six Figures and a History of Hog-tying   245

A month before that interview was conducted, the City's defense attorneys attempted to censure Flint Taylor for releasing previous depositions to journalists, even though those documents were already redacted of anything deemed confidential. Had this motion succeeded, the discovery process might have ended prematurely, and the litigation stalled. This would have also prevented further public disclosure of even redacted transcriptions of depositions taken after that date.

On May 12, 2021, three documents were filed in Federal District Court by Alan Duncan, one of the attorneys defending the City of Greensboro and its eight officers in *Smith v. Greensboro*. These were a defense's "Joint Motion to Show Cause or for Other Relief with Respect to Potential Violations of Protective Order and Local Rules," a brief in support of that joint motion, and a declaration from Mayor Nancy Vaughan filed in support of the brief.

In her declaration, Vaughan stated she received an email from activist Hester Petty and several press releases from the Beloved Community. The motion and supporting brief argued these were evidence that Taylor violated the court's protective order of July 16, 2020.

The motion alleged the "accelerating campaign of public communications made directly by counsel, or with their apparent coordination, raises significant concerns about fairness, about compliance with the Court's Orders, and about compliance with the Court's Code of Professional Responsibility." While not directly seeking to penalize any journalist or activist for passing on information from depositions allegedly received from plaintiff attorneys, which the Court would not have had the power to do, the defense attorneys were attempting to prevent future releases of information acquired via discovery, as well as punish the attorneys who had released it.

In an interview with Sayaka Matsuoka,[1] Flint Taylor pointed out the depositions he released had already been heavily redacted of anything the City deemed confidential. "It wasn't us that made the redactions. They can't have their cake and eat it too. They made their redactions so that no information that they thought was confidential would be publicly released and none of that has been but now, they are trying to throw a blanket over all of it."

I AIN'T RESISTING

As to the claims of both City Attorney Chuck Watts and defense attorney Alan Duncan that plaintiffs were attempting to "litigate the case in the court of public opinion," Taylor pointed out the City and police department had been doing that months before the lawsuit was filed, through press releases, the defense of Marcus' killers by City Council members Marikay Abuzuaiter and Goldie Wells, the controversial statements about the value of Marcus' life and the attacks on activists and the local chapter of the Democratic Party by the city attorney, and the skepticism that Mayor Vaughan and other Council members had expressed about plaintiff assurances that Marcus' children would receive their fair share of any settlement, which Taylor characterized as implying that Marcus' mother intended to cheat her own grandchildren.

On August 2, 2021, Magistrate Judge Joe Webster ruled on the motion. The reason the ruling was made by Webster rather than Superior Court Judge Loretta Biggs is that it's standard practice for a magistrate judge to rule on discovery matters, while the higher-ranking judge handles the major motions, such as calls for dismissal or summary judgment, as well as the actual trial.

Webster sided with the plaintiffs and opined that plaintiff attorneys had sufficiently demonstrated that any information they shared with the public and press was "available from sources other than the discovery designated as confidential by Defendants." He rejected the defense claim that the released depositions were under the protective order for the first 30 days after they were filed, as the filed transcripts already had any confidential information redacted.

"The PO [Protective Order] does not expressly prohibit a party from speaking to the press or disseminating public information not designated as confidential." Defense, opined Webster before denying the motion, had not presented sufficient evidence that plaintiffs violated North Carolina's Rules of Professional Conduct.

The next major battle in pretrial discovery had been brewing since January, when plaintiff attorney Graham Holt filed "Motion to Compel Defendant City of Greensboro to Produce Body Worn Camera Footage of Prior RIPP Hobble Incidents."

Six Figures and a History of Hog-tying   247

The motion stated that plaintiffs had requested all documents related to previous instances in which GPD officers hog-tied people and that, in response, the City produced police reports of over 150 instances from 2014 to 2018. However, "none of them describe the manner in which the RIPP Hobble was applied." The motion then stated that evidence of the manner the restraint was used "does exist in the form of the body worn camera (BWC) footage from the officers who were involved in those incidents."

The motion concluded by requesting that the Court compel the City of Greensboro produce BWC footage corresponding to those police reports of RIPP Hobble incidents two years prior to Marcus' death, from September 8, 2016, to September 8, 2018, as well as "all RIPP Hobble incidents in which any of the Officer Defendants were involved, either as a participant, witness or supervisor, without limitation as to time."

On February 18, 2021, this motion was referred to Magistrate Judge Joe Webster. On April 28, Webster granted that motion to the extent of ordering defendants to produce footage from the 50 incidents "in which the RIPP Hobble device was used that most closely precede the death of Mr. Smith on September 8, 2018."

The City's attorneys fought this order vigorously, filing a motion to stay and multiple objections over the next few months, while simultaneously attempting to censure Taylor for releasing the redacted transcripts and reports that Webster would eventually rule were not confidential. On May 21, Webster ordered that "Defendant need only produce the BWC footage that depicts the actual deployment of the RIPP Hobble device, in other words, the video footage running from the time at which the device is applied to the individual in custody through the time the device is removed."

On May 28, the City filed another objection, another motion to stay, and a declaration by GPD Chief Brian James in support of these motions. On June 3, due to these objections, the case was referred to US District Judge Loretta Biggs.

On June 25, Judge Biggs heard arguments about whether Webster's ruling should be upheld. "Our task here is not to relitigate the motion to compel," said Biggs. "We are here to make a determination on whether Judge Webster made a determination erroneously."

After three hours of testimony, Biggs upheld Webster's April order compelling the City of Greensboro to produce body-worn camera footage from 50 incidents in which individuals in custody were hog-tied, prior to the killing of Marcus Smith. This ruling did not make that footage public but did order the Greensboro Police Department to provide it for private viewing by plaintiff attorneys.

Biggs dismissed arguments by defense attorneys Duncan and Russell that the production of the footage was irrelevant because it did not depict Marcus Smith and that "most" of the incidents recorded on it did not involve the eight defendant officers.

Prior to this court proceeding, *Triad City Beat* reporter Sayaka Matsuoka submitted a public information request to the City of Greensboro for incident reports in which officers hog-tied people from September 2014 to September 2018, but the City denied that request, alleging that the documents are not public records because they were part of legal proceedings.

Although Biggs expressed irritation with Duncan and Russell for protesting the magistrate judge's order, the next time that the City's defense team objected to a plaintiff motion, Biggs and Webster ruled against the plaintiffs.

THE END OF DISCOVERY AND OF MICHELLE KENNEDY'S TENURE
28 ON CITY COUNCIL

On April 20, 2021, the Greensboro Council member who'd privately called for the firing of Wayne Scott, and disciplinary actions against Chuck Watts, publicly apologized for voting to table an independent investigation into the death of Marcus Smith. She then moved not only to re-open that investigation, but to expand it into the "climate and culture" of the Greensboro Police Department. Although Nancy Vaughan, like many other Council members, appeared shocked, the mayor stated the Council would soon publicly debate and vote on Kennedy's recommendation.

In a May 26 interview with the *News & Record*'s Richard Barron,[1] Kennedy condemned the "fear and mistrust" created by the actions of the Greensboro Police Department, not only in the death of Marcus Smith and its aftermath, but other interactions between the City's police and the Black community.

On June 1, 42 days after Mayor Vaughan and City Manager Parrish said Kennedy's motion would be publicly debated and voted on, Council went into a closed session. Two hours later, Vaughan announced there would be no investigation, and a visibly angry Kennedy, appearing via Zoom, made a statement to that effect prepared for her by City Attorney Watts.

On August 17, Kennedy announced her resignation from Greensboro City Council.

In the final minutes of the April 20 meeting, Kennedy spoke of watching the jury verdict in the trial of Derek Chauvin for the murder of George Floyd, saying, "All I could think about was Marcus Smith." She said she had two regrets.

"The first thing is that I regret voting to table an independent investigation into his death, particularly as we were discussing Charlottesville as our role model for how we wanted to move forward with this situation. If you recall, Charlottesville launched an independent investigation even as they were under litigation in the events that occurred there."

The other thing weighing on her was what she called a matter of transparency. "This Council has fought really hard against a gag order in relation to the Zared Jones case, and it would be hypocritical for us to simultaneously fight the release of videos that allegedly depict other hog-tying incidents that took place before the death of Marcus Smith. Sitting here and taking a stance of silence, while what we know is an incredibly broken and racist system continues to exist, makes me complicit, not just in the death of Marcus Smith, but in the death of every Black man at the hands of that system."

In a voice suggesting anguish, Kennedy said "the only thing that I can do at this point to try to move back in the direction that my conscience was telling me that I should have stayed in the whole time, is to ask for us to go back to following that model that we discussed, of Charlottesville, which is calling for an independent investigation even though we are in the midst of litigation." She concluded by calling for "closure" and "understanding of the reality of the events that occurred on that day," ending with "for me, that's real transparency."

After a pause in which multiple councilmembers appeared either troubled or angry, Mayor pro tem Yvonne Johnson said she would "not be opposed to such an investigation." Kennedy then made a motion to authorize an investigation, which Johnson seconded. "I'm not prepared to vote this evening," interjected Mayor Vaughan before any votes could be cast. "I think we need to have a discussion on what the complete ramifications are. I'm not adverse to talking about this. "

I AIN'T RESISTING

Kennedy suggested Council should, at their next scheduled meeting, discuss what "framework may be possible for that independent review body." Vaughan asked the city manager and city attorney how quickly a work session could be scheduled. City Manager David Parrish said there were already four items on the next week's agenda, and that there might not be room for this new item until late in May.

That wasn't soon enough for Yvonne Johnson, who suggested that Parrish determine what other agenda items could be pushed back. "If we could come to some resolution, it would be good for our city and good for our residents."

The mayor suggested Kennedy change her motion. Kennedy agreed: "I make a motion that we have a special work session regarding an independent investigation into the death of Marcus Smith."

"We don't need a new motion," said Vaughan. "A direction would…"

City Manager Parrish interrupted, and said "Considering the topic, I think it would be helpful to at least have a consensus."

Kennedy restated her motion. It was seconded by Johnson and passed unanimously.

Speaking to reporter Richard Barron on May 26, Kennedy not only expressed her grave concerns about the Greensboro Police Department, she criticized former District Attorney Douglas Henderson's clearing the officers who killed Marcus, while indicating she expected no redress from current District Attorney Avery Crump. She told Barron that an inherent conflict of interest exists between a district attorney and any police department, and that if officers are under suspicion of breaking the law, DAs are rarely effective or neutral.

"In an instance where there's a question of police misconduct that may need prosecuting, it's irresponsible to leave it in the hands of a DA. We want an independent look at how our police department has behaved." She also said there needed to be "a broader conversation" about the GPD's culture and conduct, and that the City should "identify a truly neutral third party" to conduct the investigation.

She acknowledged this could not happen without the support of at least five members of City Council.

Also interviewed by Barron, Councilwoman Marikay Abuzuaiter, always a staunch advocate for the police department, said there was already a mechanism to conduct independent investigations into police conduct in the form of the Greensboro Criminal Justice Advisory Commission, the body two Black members were dismissed from after stating that commission was neither independent nor effective. Abuzuaiter told Barron the killing of Marcus Smith by eight members of the department she strongly supports had "been investigated thoroughly," and that she saw no need for further inquiry.

While the June 1, 2021, Council work session was broadcast live on the City's website, it is no longer archived there. The meeting was called to order at 2 p.m. and went into closed session at 4:14. At 5:19, Council reconvened in open session. The minutes posted to the City's website tersely describe what happened next: "Councilmember Kennedy made a statement regarding an independent investigation; and stated under advisement City Council would take no further action." These minutes, which are the only public record of what happened in that closed session, don't even state the subject of the quashed investigation.

Minutes after Council entered back into open session, Mayor Vaughan said that Kennedy, who was absent due to a family illness, would be making a statement about the investigation via Zoom. After a pause, Kennedy appeared on Zoom with an expression that appeared both angry and resigned. She stated the city attorney was preparing a statement for her to read. When she received it a few seconds later, she read it from her phone.

"So let me say first, that, yes, I am the person who asked us to have an independent investigation, both as it relates to the events connected to Marcus Smith, and a larger investigation around institutional culture and essentially an agency-wide conduct review of the Greensboro Police Department. And so, on the advice of the city attorney, Council met in closed session and received advice from an attorney who practices exclusively in the area of independent investigation. Council has decided not to pursue any such investigation at this time."

Kennedy later said the only part of the statement that was her own words, rather than scripted for her by Watts, was the reference to "a larger investigation around institutional culture and essentially an agency-wide conduct review of the Greensboro Police Department."

According to Kennedy, she "was told" that "I had to make that statement myself because I was the one who called for re-opening the investigation."

The City of Greensboro has refused all requests for records of the closed session in which it was determined there would be no investigation and that Kennedy would make that announcement. When asked if a vote had occurred in closed session and without public debate, actions against Council's own by-laws, Watts invoked attorney-client privilege.

In the redacted transcript of Kennedy's June 29, 2021, deposition by Flint Taylor, a document that would never have been made public if the City's defense team had succeeded in their attempts to place even redacted depositions under seal, Kennedy tells Taylor she requested and believed the work session to be public. She then stated that, when Council went into that closed session, she did not expect the question of whether to conduct an investigation to be decided until after they were back in open session.

"I assumed we would get some information around possibilities for an independent investigation, but no, I did not anticipate that we would finalize a discussion on the Smith case."

When Taylor asks Kennedy if Council voted in that closed session, defense attorney Duncan interjects, "I would advise the witness not to answer this question," but adds "I will allow Ms. Kennedy to respond to what was the precursor for reading that statement."

Taylor then reads aloud Kennedy's statement that "consensus was reached that there would be no pursuit of an investigation" and "that I should be the one to read the statement prepared by Chuck Watts." When he asks if she was included in that consensus, she replies "I did not support the conclusion made."

Taylor responds, "And so then it wasn't a consensus, was it?"

"No," says Kennedy.

When Taylor asks if anyone else didn't support the "consensus quote-unquote," Duncan shuts down that inquiry by invoking legislative privilege for a closed session. Taylor then asks Kennedy if she felt "she was under some kind of compulsion from the rest of the Council" when she read her statement aloud, Kennedy answers, "Yes."

"I agreed to do it, but I did not agree with the statement we were making or anything it said."

Just as the time allotted for Taylor to question Kennedy ends, he requests "that we continue to have a dialogue about this, as you are potential witness in this case," and asks, "Would you be willing to talk to me?"

"In terms of any statement I have ever made or my personal views on this," replies Kennedy, "Absolutely."

On August 17, 11 weeks after Council quashed Kennedy's proposed investigation, and 18 days after she made statements under oath so critical of the City's former police chief and current attorney, Kennedy resigned from her elected office in order to accept a paid position with the City.

Two days later, the Interactive Resource Center (IRC), for which Kennedy had served as Executive Director since 2014, released a letter from Kennedy announcing she was also resigning from that organization.

"I am not leaving this work; I am simply transitioning to a new role," wrote Kennedy. "I will be joining the City of Greensboro as the Director of Neighborhood Development, continuing the work of ending homelessness and advancing safe, decent, affordable housing. As many of you know, the IRC has worked in tandem with the City on critical issues to address homelessness for years. I look forward to continuing that partnership." Her salary at the nonprofit was $80,500. With the City, it would be $130,111. In a conversation the next day, Kennedy called the transition "the right fit for me in terms of where I'm best positioned to support the community" and said her priorities would include improving housing, particularly for people with low incomes or who are experiencing financial difficulties.

"One of the things that the City has worked hard on is code enforcement, and I'm excited to make sure we are moving forward in that area and in ensuring that our housing is safe and decent and meets housing code regulations. I want to move the needle on eliminating substandard housing. Neighborhood Development oversees homeless services, housing services, and code enforcement, so it's still the same kind of framework that I've always worked in."

Mayor Vaughan said she looked forward to working with Kennedy, particularly on issues of code infractions. "Michelle has a lot of experience with minimum housing and a lot of good suggestions. I've enjoyed working with her on this issue and look forward to seeing real improvement."

In her on-the-record statements, Kennedy emphasized that her ongoing disagreements with Council and the city attorney had nothing to do with her decision to resign.

"This, for me, is really about my career and professional work that I've been doing for more than 15 years. It has nothing to do with any decisions that were made as a Council member, any conversations, discussions, or anything else."

"ALL OF US WERE COMPLETELY
29   SHOCKED BY WHAT WE SAW."

On August 2, 2021, four days after deposing Kennedy, and 15 before she announced her resignations, plaintiffs filed a new motion. The motion requested that the Court "permit Plaintiff to re-depose Defendants Payne, Duncan, Andrews, Bradshaw, Lewis, Strader and Bailey, to re-depose a limited number of the City's police trainers, City policymakers, and GPD command and supervisory personnel, and to depose a limited number of other material witnesses recently revealed in the BWC footage."

Filed with the motion, but under seal, were detailed summaries of what the produced videos purportedly revealed, along with the relevant footage. Exhibits not under seal included excerpts from Michelle Kennedy's deposition and a statement by Flint Taylor summarizing what he purportedly witnessed in the videos.

Taylor stated that BWC footage of those incidents, filed with the court under seal, "revealed, *inter alia*, the following facts:"

- A Black woman hogtied by a Defendant with her legs at less than 90 degrees from her body, left prone on the ground for more than five minutes, with her breasts exposed, yelling and screaming in pain, outrage and humiliation;
- Other persons expressing pain with one also saying he cannot breathe;
- Indifference and verbal abuse by the Defendant hog-tiers to the pain and suffering of the victims;

- Numerous examples of persons with their legs bent at an angle of less than 90 degrees from their back, including during an incident only hours before Marcus Smith was hogtied;
- The tightening of the RIPP Hobble beyond the 90-degree angle despite being told by a fellow officer not to do so;
- A Defendant complaining that they "don't make the Ripp Hobbles like they used to", and that "the new ones hurt more;"
- A Defendant responding to an older Black woman peacefully asking for her lawyer by hog-tying her while she screams out in pain;
- A Defendant, while hog-tying a black victim without apparent cause, saying that he ends up Ripp-Hobbling people all the time for some reason;
- Of the 12 incidents within the produced range, 9 of the victims are Black, one is a Pakistani-American, 2 are white, and two are females.

According to Taylor, his team had also reviewed footage of hog-tyings by 38 non-defendant officers, which revealed:

- Comments about training, including one officer doing on-the-job training, with commentary, on a victim;
- During that "training," the officer saying just about every time he's had to use a RIPP Hobble, he's had to go back and get a new one because it's covered in blood;
- On one occasion, an officer has knee on the neck of a pregnant Black female victim, similar to how George Floyd was fatally restrained, for more than 2 minutes while she is being hog-tied; she is prone, hog-tied, and crying out that she can't breathe;
- An elderly woman suffering from dementia is RIPP Hobbled while she repeatedly complains that it is hurting her arms. She is crying, on the ground, facedown, with her dress up throughout the RIPP Hobbling;
- In between 10 and 12 incidents, officers pushed the legs to less than 90 degrees from the victim's back while or after hog-tying;
- Officers put pressure put [sic] on the head, back, buttocks on numerous occasions while hog-tying;
- An Officer pushed a victim's face into the ground;
- In seven incidents, the victim cried out that they could not breathe;
- Victims were left in a prone position after hogtying on numerous occasions;
- Several hog-tied victims were placed face down in squad car;

- 29 of the 38 victims were Black, 15 of whom were female and 4 were juveniles;
- 21 of the 38 victims were women, including 3 juveniles.

Taylor stated that his team's review of the BWC footage revealed that "38 of the victims (76 percent) are Black, and 39 (78 percent) are of color," and that, in "the vast majority of the 148 hog-tiers in the 50 incidents, 124 (84 percent) are white, 24 of the victims (48 percent) are women, and that all of the women were hogtied either exclusively by male officers (14) or by a crew of majority male officers (10)."

These statistics were cited in a September 2, 2021, letter to Department of Justice special litigation chief Steven Rosenbaum, which was sent by the Beloved Community Center and signed by 25 Black ministers, community leaders, and organizers, as well as former local and state politicians. In a September 29 press conference in front of the building that contains both Mayor Vaughan's office and the City Council chamber, many of those who signed the letter made speeches accusing the City of a cover-up.

Reverend Bradley Hunt, president of the Greensboro NAACP, condemned "the devaluation of Black bodies, whether it's by the hands of the police department or those in our community," and stated, "those in leadership continue to neglect the fact that poverty persists in our community and allows violence to take place, over and over again." Describing the death of her son, Mary Smith asked how "professionals that get paid by our tax dollars allow a man that had no weapons and no charges to die like that?" Reverend Nelson Johnson condemned the Greensboro Police Department for "a history of questionable leadership for years."

For these allegations, the letter sent to the Department of Justice on September 2 relied substantially on Taylor's descriptions of August 2. Unlike the presumably much more detailed sealed summaries, as well as the sealed BWC footage those summaries purported to describe, Taylor's declaration was a public document that anyone could download from the online docket, read, quote from, and share.

At the October 5 meeting of Greensboro City Council, both Mayor Vaughan and City Attorney Watts expressed irritation with activists for doing just that. This happened during the public comments section of

"All of us were completely shocked by what we saw." 261

the meeting, when multiple speakers sought Council's response to claims made in the appeal to the DOJ.

When activist Paulette Montgomery took the podium, she denounced Council for spending "$1 million to defend this case when all evidence shows overwhelming culpability by the Greensboro Police Department," and quoted multiple descriptions as well as statistics cited in the letter.

"What about the pregnant Black female who was hog-tied for more than two minutes while the officer has his knee on her neck, just like George Floyd? This woman was pregnant, placed on her stomach, with one officer's knee placed on her neck, having air supply cut off to her unborn child while she is being RIPP Hobbled? What if that was your daughter, sister, or mother? Would the child have any issues at birth from this hog-tying? Maybe, maybe not, we'll never know. And that's just completely shameful."

Montgomery also stated that "former GPD Commander Nathaniel 'Trey' Davis recently admitted that there was racial disproportionality as to who was hog-tied, while former chief Wayne Scott admitted to supervising 135 to 200 hog-tyings. Our current Chief Brian James, who was the command supervisor over the officers who hog-tied Marcus Smith, approved the report that exonerated those officers. The cover-up is so blatant it's hard to believe Council is still toeing the line. And honestly, is this the Greensboro you really want? It appears that we have tons for business development, but not for our community members that need housing, food, and mental health support. Not sure how you sleep at night, knowing this is how you run your city."

Before calling on the next speaker, Vaughan responded to Montgomery's comment as well as previous ones.

"It was said earlier that we could have watched the videos when we wanted to. In fact, we only got the ability to watch the videos, I believe, last week. Some of us have watched some of the videos. And I would caution the speakers not to just reiterate things that the plaintiff attorneys have said. None of you have seen the videos, and all you are doing is reading the plaintiffs' words, and that's all I'm gonna comment at this point."

Montgomery replied that, at the last Council meeting, neither Vaughan nor any of the other members acknowledged having seen the videos.

"No," said Vaughan, "because we have the ability from the judge to watch them, and I would caution people who just parrot the words of the plaintiff attorneys."

Two weeks later, Judge Webster denied the plaintiff motion that included Taylor's brief public descriptions of what he claimed to have seen on the videos, along with the sealed footage and longer summaries. His ruling stated that reopening discovery would "cause significant prejudice to Defendant City of Greensboro."

Webster called the plaintiff summaries of the BWC footage "subjective, one-sided accounts," but this does not necessarily mean he either watched the footage or considered Taylor's descriptions factually inaccurate, although both Greensboro's mayor and city attorney described him as saying as much. His statements can also be interpreted to mean that any descriptions of the videos coming solely from either plaintiff or defense attorneys is inherently "one-sided and biased."

In October of 2022, during the final proceedings in *Smith v. Greensboro*, Flint Taylor responded to Mayor Vaughan's statements of the year before, in which she alleged that the descriptions in his much-quoted declaration about what he'd allegedly seen on the BWC footage depicting previous hog-tying incidents were distorted and inaccurate.

"All I can say is that when we got these videos," Flint Taylor said, "myself, Graham Holt, and Ben Elson, the three lawyers in the case, and then a remarkable legal intern we had, watched, analyzed, and summarized these videos. And all of us, but particularly our intern, were completely shocked, traumatized, and outraged by what we saw. She wrote a lot of the summaries; we wrote some of the summaries. We're lawyers. We write the evidence in the light that we see it. Of course, the defendants, who are agents of the City, are going to minimize this, in the same way they would have minimized it at trial, or in summary judgment motions."

Taylor said he absolutely stood by the accuracy of his team's descriptions.

"Of course, we picked out some of the strongest ones. I defy Nancy Vaughan and Chuck Watts to stand in front of the public, show these videos to the public, and try to justify women having their breasts exposed, for example, and being hog-tied clearly in violation of the City's own regulations, again and again. And the statistics that almost all of those doing the hog-tying were white males and a huge predominance of the victims were Black and almost 50 percent were women, all being subjected to a cruel device that had been strongly denounced by the United States Justice Department 25 years ago."

He then turned to the word that Vaughan spoke with apparent sincerity and anger in early December of 2018: "The mayor had a chance to take a brave and honest stance, and for a short time, she seemed to be doing that, when she said that initial press release was obviously a lie. But then, she got a phone call and had meetings that I strongly believe resulted in her saying something mandated by Wayne Scott. Even going back to her apparent promises to the concerned public at Shiloh Baptist Church, when she not just once but repeatedly called the press release a lie, you can read what she said next, 'We need answers,' in two ways. One is that she's sincerely demanding answers, and then someone in power gives her an explanation, or the powers that be tell her to change her ways, that she's jeopardizing the police department and giving it a bad name."

Taylor emphasized that, while he agrees that the press releases were lies, those weren't the only ones. "One sub-thread in the case was our attempt to expose their defensive lies about hog-tying. We were able to get these documents that referred to hog-tying and defined it in a manner consistent with what they did to Marcus Smith, but they simply wouldn't admit that they hog-tied him, after having started out in their press release by not even admitting that they touched him, by stating that he simply died in police custody."

Taylor alleged that the falsehoods went beyond what happened to Marcus, or even past instances of misconduct, but that the GPD refused to be honest about its own terminology, training, and directives.

"There was another level of denial, about whether they had hog-tied him or what it meant to hog-tie. We found in their training materials references to hog-tying that were almost completely, as lawyers say, "on all fours with" what they did to Marcus. "All fours" in lawyer speak means completely the same. When we confronted their trainers and their supervisors, they tried to maneuver around the documents that defined hog-tying in a way that applied to Marcus Smith, and in various ways tried to talk about how their training never used that term even though they had PowerPoint slideshows and training manuals that used the term and told them not to do it."

Taylor accurately pointed out that, in the early days of the controversy after the videos were released, Vaughan responded to activists by saying that Chief James told her his officers had RIPP Hobbled hundreds of people.

"Think about it, she says, in defense of the City and herself, that Greensboro cops had been hog-tying people all the time and it wasn't a big deal because, she says Wayne Scott told her, nobody had been hurt. Yet it apparently never occurred to her that the City should investigate that, and look at some of those videos. So, it doesn't surprise that, when she allegedly does look at those videos two years later, she doesn't see anything wrong in them."

That, said Taylor, is what led plaintiffs to try to determine just how much hog-tying was the pattern and practice of the Greensboro Police Department.

"At the very end of discovery, we were finally able to get the magistrate judge to order that they give us those 50 videos or previous hog-tyings, because it never was something they considered serious enough to actually make detailed reports about, much less investigate the use of. So that became a question how Greensboro, which likes to hold itself up as a bubble of blue in a reddish-purple state, had covered up police complicity in the Greensboro massacre and, 41 years later, was still routinely doing this."

He then spoke of how Magistrate Judge Joe Webster had shut down further discovery regarding that pattern and practice.

"That's a case of the City benefitting from their own misconduct. They ran out the clock filing objections and resisting production of these videos, so we had to build a case based on police reports that made these references to maximum restraint without any details about the nature of that restraint, whether in terms of if the hands were connected to the feet, how long people were in the position, and what caused them to do that. Over many months, we are able to put together a case sufficient to demand the videos. But the court had set a deadline that discovery would end in late summer of 2021, and because of the City's obstructions, we

"All of us were completely shocked by what we saw."   265

did not get the judge's order compelling production of those videos until the spring, and then defense moved to reconsider the order, and since the order was from a magistrate, they were allowed to appeal to the federal judge, and that took time. She upheld the magistrate's ordering of the production of the 50 videos, but we did not get those videos until discovery was over."

Taylor said that, without the time constraints, he believes his team would have been allowed to make a broader pattern and practice claim against the City.

He wanted to make it very clear that the videos of the 50 previous hog-tying incidents, and his team's detailed descriptions of what could be seen on them, were not excluded as evidence. If the case had come to trial, plaintiffs would have been able to show those videos to the jury.

"They weren't thrown out. Judge Webster found that this video evidence could be used to show a pattern and practice that would help to support our existing claims that the City had failed to properly train its officers. What he denied was our motion to amend our complaint to make a new claim based on this new evidence. That was a disappointment but did not change the fact that the Court ordered the defendants to give us those videos, which they did after a long fight, and that we retained the right to use them in evidence, even though the judge stopped us from expanding the case beyond the evidence we received at the very end of discovery."

Was there any connection between the City finally producing those videos at the end of discovery and then agreeing to settle shortly before the case would have gone to trial?

"Yes," he replies, "it was a Sword of Damocles hanging over their heads. We called it a game change in our briefs, and I believe it speaks volumes that none of the city officials who claimed our descriptions were inaccurate made any effort to prove us wrong."

"MY BROKEN HEART WOULD RATHER HAVE MARCUS BACK THAN ANY SETTLEMENT."

In 2022, Greensboro lost its fourth Black police chief. Brian James, the GPD insider hired in January of 2020 to replace the controversial Wayne Scott, announced his retirement in March and left office in May, making his tenure as chief the shortest in memory.

Unsurprisingly, his sudden departure released a flood of rumors that set the gossip mill wheels turning.

Within hours of his announcement, conservative social media was rife with unsubstantiated rumors that James had either been pushed out by Mayor Vaughan or quit in frustration over what several commenters on *Rhino Times* articles called Vaughan's "micro-management" of the GPD.[1] Progressives had criticized Vaughan for walking back her denunciation of the GPD press releases and actual socialists continued to denounce her as a police stooge. Now, those who called her a socialist for not being as reactionary as themselves accused her of seeking to defund the police.

Amiel Rossabi, the Greensboro Police Association attorney known for belligerent public statements defending any GPD officer accused of brutality, frequently characterized Vaughan as hostile to the police. Yet in the July 2022 election, Vaughan was endorsed by the association Rossabi represents as an attorney, and she has defended the actions of not only the officers who killed Marcus Smith, but the professionalism and integrity of controversial officer Samuel Alvarez.

Alvarez allegedly dumped 15-year-old Jose Charles onto his head during an altercation at a 2016 Fourth of July celebration and was accused by attorney Graham Holt of profiling Holt's client Zared Jones and three of Jones' friends in a 2017 incident in downtown Greensboro, during which Alvarez was caught on a bystander's camera grabbing one of the young Black men from behind and slamming him into a car. When explaining her reasons for trying to prevent speakers at Council meetings from criticizing City employees by name, Vaughan cited Alvarez as someone who was being "attacked without the opportunity to defend himself."

Brian James never publicly cited any friction with, or lack of support from, Greensboro's mayor, city manager, or Council as a reason for his retirement. "I'm 52 years old, certainly old enough to retire," he told WFMY News 2, "but still young enough to hopefully start another career at some point."

"I'm very disappointed," said Mayor Vaughan to the *News & Record.* "He has left a great legacy. We talked about the importance of family and the toll that it takes."

On May 13, 2022, Kevin M. Guskiewicz, Chancellor of UNC Chapel Hill, released a public statement that "I am pleased to announce that Brian James, a highly respected leader in law enforcement, has been named Chief of UNC Police, effective July 1."

"I am confident," stated Chancellor Guskiewicz, "that Chief James will have the same positive impact on our community that he did for more than two decades in Greensboro." At the time of this book's completion, Brian James' first full year as UNC's second Black police chief ended without controversy.

With James' resignation, Teresa Biffle became interim chief after having served as the deputy chief of the management bureau since being promoted by James in 2021. During her previous tenure as commander of Professional Standards under Wayne Scott, then-captain Biffle wrote the press release stating that Marcus "collapsed in custody" without mentioning that he was hog-tied, and weeks later, recommended that

Scott return four of the eight officers whose actions killed him to active duty (which the other four had never been removed from), even though the internal investigation was not yet complete.

In December of 2022, former Assistant Chief John Thompson was announced as Greensboro's new police chief after what a City press release described as a "competitive, national search and extensive interview process." Thompson, who is white, first joined the GPD in 2003, and served in various roles over the years.

On October 24, 2022, one month and three weeks before Thompson was sworn in, US District Judge Loretta Biggs issued her final motion in *Smith v. City of Greensboro*, placing under permanent seal a number of exhibits in the case, which Biggs ruled "filed pursuant to the parties' settlement to provide additional arguments about the basis for sealing in light of the resolution of the parties' dispute."

"The City of Greensboro and the family of Marcus Deon Smith have reached an agreement to settle the lawsuit brought by the estate of Marcus Deon Smith," stated City Attorney Chuck Watts at the February 1, 2022, meeting of the Greensboro City Council, three years and 145 days after the police homicide of Marcus Smith. The prepared joint statement, which Watts was invited to read aloud by Mayor Nancy Vaughan, continued:

"Importantly to these parties, the total settlement of $2,575,000, the majority of which will be paid by the City of Greensboro and the remainder by Guilford County, will financially benefit both the parents of Marcus Deon Smith and his children, and will formally acknowledge, with a commemorative plaque, that Marcus Deon Smith's life mattered. These parties will soon request judicial approval of the settlement and dismissal of the lawsuit without any findings of wrongdoing and liability. After the settlement is concluded, these parties intend to move forward in the spirit of respect and reconciliation."

Later that evening, plaintiff attorneys Flint Taylor and Ben Elson of the People's Law Office of Chicago and Graham Holt of Greensboro issued the same statement, but with this preface:

"As a result of much blood, sweat and tears by the Marcus Smith family, community activists, and the Smith legal team, the Greensboro

City Council voted last evening to settle the Marcus Deon Smith case by releasing the following joint statement."

Plaintiffs' announcement of the joint statement also added the following coda:

"While the details of the agreement are still confidential, we on the legal team and on behalf of the Smith family want to thank the activists of Greensboro and all those of goodwill in the Greensboro community for standing shoulder to shoulder with us in this long struggle for transparency and justice in the Marcus Deon Smith case. We are gratified that this agreement will honor Marcus's deep love for his children and that the City of Greensboro will formally recognize that Marcus Deon Smith's life matters."

After reading the joint statement aloud at the Council meeting, City Attorney Watts stated, "It is my expectation that this process of drafting a longform settlement and getting the necessary approvals will take some time." He told the mayor and Council that "further comment regarding the facts and circumstances or the settlement would be inappropriate."

The next day, Mary Smith said: "My broken heart would rather have Marcus back than any settlement."

Cherizar Crippen praised the settlement, but said, "it should not be mistaken for justice."

"Every single person who aided in the miscarriage of justice for Marcus Smith," she continued, "has been allowed to avoid accountability for their actions leading up to and following his murder at the hands of the Greensboro police. GPD and City officials worked diligently to cover up this murder. All of them were allowed to retire, resign, stay with GPD, or go to another police department. They even get to run for elected office again. So, what's preventing this from happening to someone else? This isn't a fluke, it's a pattern."

Those running in the then-upcoming July election included not only Mayor Vaughan, but District 2's Goldie Wells, the one Council member other than Michelle Kennedy, who by then was no longer on Council, to have known Marcus.

Vying with Wells for the District 2 seat was Cecile "CC" Crawford, who was one of the few challengers to make the Marcus Smith case a campaign issue. "This money won't bring Marcus Smith back," said Crawford, "but his family deserved to have recognition that his life had value. I hope this brings Mary Smith and her family at least some small amount of peace. Council may not be able to speak on the case, but we all need to speak about the need for transparency from our elected leaders."

The young Black community organizer from District 2 did not succeed in unseating the veteran Black incumbent, but she came closer than any other challenger that year, with 48.3 percent of the vote to Wells' 51.5 percent. Her friend and fellow organizer Franca Jalloh did not do as well in the at-large race, where the three seats were retained by incumbents Yvonne Johnson, Marikay Abuzuaiter, and Hugh Holston (in his first election after being appointed to replace Michelle Kennedy).

On April 15, a document titled "Settlement Agreement and Release of All Claims" was filed in the Middle District of North Carolina. It was signed by all parties of the settlement and awaited only a ruling by US District Judge Loretta Biggs.

The agreement stated that the City of Greensboro will pay $2,220,000 of the settlement and Guilford County will pay $350,000, with the funds disbursed within 60 days of the settlement's final approval. $1.21 million will go to the parents and estate of Marcus Smith. $1.35 million will be apportioned between his three children. $10,000 will go to Greensboro's Interactive Resource Center (IRC), for the installation of a plaque stating: "This courtyard is named and dedicated in loving memory of Marcus Deon Smith with funds for this dedication provided as an expression of respect and reconciliation by the City of Greensboro."

The two minor children and Marcus' adult son Marquis would each receive $450,000. Within 60 days of the effective date, the payments to the daughter designated as "A.D." and to Marquis Smith would be made to accounts administered by Toussaint Law, PLLC. The agreement stated that none of the parties have been able to locate the child designated as "K.S.," nor the child's mother, but that all parties must cooperate "with reasonable efforts by the Guardian ad Litem to identify and locate K.S." and that "the Guardian ad Litem shall report to the other Parties" every six months until K.S. has been located, or until the child is no longer a minor.

"My broken heart would rather have Marcus back..." 271

It then stated that:

"The undersigned attorneys of record for Mary Smith will counsel her not to call for the termination of employment of the Officers, Paramedics, or any other past or current employee of the City or County. Moreover, Mary Smith and her counsel specifically acknowledge that the settlement of this litigation should not negatively impact the employment status of the Officers, Paramedics, or any other past or current employee of the City or County."

"Nothing came easy in this case," said Flint Taylor, speaking hours after Judge Biggs issued that order. "Certainly, the settlement did not."

Taylor said it might not have happened at all without the efforts of John Harkavy of the North Carolina Association of Superior Court Mediators.

"He had to come up with a proposal that took into account a situation without any precedent, because there was an outstanding contest about who the heirs were. There was that shameful North Carolina law that refuses to recognize unlegitimated children as heirs."

Taylor was referring to North Carolina General Statutes Chapter 29, of which § 29-19 states that, for a child born out of wedlock to become an heir, that parentage must have been must have been acknowledged by the father in writing before a certified officer and that acknowledgement filed with the Clerk of Superior Court in the county in which the child resides. It further states that, for purposes of heirship, the father can only be established by DNA testing if he died within a year before or after the child's birth. Therefore, there was no way of legally determining that Marcus Smith's adult son Marquis and his minor children A.D. and K.S. were his heirs.

"The City had always—we thought somewhat pretextually—made a big issue that the children should get the lion's share of the money, not the parents. The parents and, we thought, the children should be compensated whether they were the legal heirs. But that all had to be worked out in terms of the shares that everybody got. It seemed that, for such a long time, the mediation was going nowhere because both sides were so far apart not only on the financial question, but the question of proportionality to the potential recipients. And that's when the mediator came up with a double-blind proposal. That means that both sides got to vote yes or no without knowing what the other side voted. We had decided to say yes almost nine months ago, and they also decided to say yes, and for the last nine months, we were working out language and parameters in terms of money and all of that."

The devil, said Taylor, was in the details.

"We did so much negotiation on the language. They wanted statements in there that protected police officers from our calling for them to be fired or disciplined. We had to compromise on that. A lot of what happened was that we had to soften language they put in, and they consistently opposed any kind of apology. The statement about the importance of Marcus as a human being was our compromise on that. We made it stronger, but it was still a compromise on the idea that they should concede he was wrongly killed. But we did strengthen that language in terms of what would be on the plaque."

Taylor pointed out an aspect of the settlement which he said "put the lie" to any concerns expressed or implied by either the City or its attorneys that Mary Smith was out to deprive her grandchildren of their fair share.

"All of the work we did comes out of the parents' share of the money. The mediator made that a part of the proposal, that the children would not have to pay those fees. You could call us shortchanged in that deal, but we were glad to do it. If it was about the money, we would never have taken the case, considering the logistics of my coming down here all the time and the amount of work we did."

Taylor said that, as an experienced Chicago attorney, there was one aspect of the case he least anticipated. "The whole question of transparency in regard to the litigation. That was an extremely significant part of the whole story, going the gamut from the very restrictive anti-transparency laws of North Carolina applied to police documents compared to Chicago and Illinois. Not just the protective orders, but how the City and County lawyers attempted to silence us around stuff that wasn't under protective order and keep us from part of our role, which is, within the confines of the law and the court's rulings, to maximize public transparency in terms of such an important piece of litigation."

"The outrageous thing," said Taylor, "is that it wasn't just a cover-up, but a justification, with the two-facedness of, on the one hand, finally doing away with this racially and sexually discriminatory 25-year practice, and on the other hand, defending it in Marcus' case and all these other 50 cases. God knows what the other 250 videos might have shown. We only had a fraction of the videos depicting what the defendants in Marcus' case had done in other cases."

His harshest criticisms were for Nancy Vaughan.

"It's shocking as well that the mayor would continue, after having a pang of conscience when facing a roomful of angry citizens, to consistently, publicly and in depositions, and even after reporting to have watched the 50 videos, rather than to say, oh my God, this wasn't necessary, whether it was the case of the woman who hogtied while in a jail cell, or that of the person hogtied hours before Marcus was and by the same officers, who said to Hell with what we were trained, hog-tie them. The weight of all of it is just insurmountable. It's appalling that the City and its leadership, with the possible exceptions of Michelle Kennedy, who was moved out of City Council, and of Sharon Hightower, who was silenced and ignored, never condemned the practice or admitted any substantial wrongdoing."

When asked whom he considered complicit in the alleged cover-up, Taylor replied:

"City Manager David Parrish, who said under oath that he didn't think there should be an independent investigation. Chief Wayne Scott, who ordered and approved the press release that Kennedy, Hightower and even for a few days Vaughan called a lie. Teresa Biffle, then commander of the Professional Standards Division and currently the interim chief, who wrote the press release, and who recommended that the four officers be returned to the streets before the investigation was over. And Sergeant Stein, who conducted the investigation. They were all its architects."

Epilogue

31   FIVE YEARS LATER

Nelson Johnson and Cherizar Crippen

"If you have to build pressure to get a modicum of justice every time there is an injustice, the system is not working. People shouldn't have to hold press conferences and do monkey flips in order to get justice from law enforcement officials. It's all of this stuff up underneath the police department, and it's still there, just like it was in 1979. It wasn't all cleared out then and the Marcus Smith case is its legacy."

Nelson Johnson found small solace in how public outcry may have led the City to settle *Smith v. Greensboro*, and possibly played a role in Chief Wayne Scott's departure. He disagreed with Michelle Kennedy's statement—both when deposed by Flint Taylor and in interviews—that the "buck stopped" with Wayne Scott.

"I think there absolutely was a cover-up at the City level. In the context of a group meeting, for the mayor to say—and it was clear she meant it—that the chief lied, and then to change that statement, actually implicates her. I think that's partly the way the City operates, that what they call the interests of the City are oftentimes against the interests of the people who populate that city. It's almost impossible to shake off the culture that you are such a part of. To some degree, I think that's what Mayor Vaughan was dealing with, the City's culture that she's been part of for so long."

He was not optimistic that the organization Vaughan initially urged Mary Smith to appeal to, the Greensboro Criminal Justice Advisory Commission, would ever be able to investigate or correct the abuses created by that culture.

"We need an oversight mechanism for the police department that is not filtered through the City and is completely independent of it, particularly when complaints are made."

Nelson Johnson's North Carolina activism did not begin with the 1969 protests that led to the Siege of A&T by the National Guard. In 1965, the 22-year-old Johnson enrolled at that university following his discharge from the United States Air Force. In 1967, he joined the Foundation for Community Development (FCD), a statewide organization promoting community activism in low-income neighborhoods. That summer, he also joined the Grassroots Association of Students (GAS), which organized Black student activists on North Carolina campuses. And in 1968, he co-founded the Greensboro Association of Poor People (GAPP), a coalition of A&T and Bennett College students and community members opposing city policies that marginalized Black citizens.

Cherizar Crippen's local work as a Black organizer began 50 years later. In 2017, Crippen, then in her early thirties, moved from New Jersey to North Carolina, where she enrolled in Guilford Technical Community College and co-founded Black Lives Matter Greensboro. In 2020, she organized both first aid and legal aid for protesters tear-gassed and arrested during the protests that erupted downtown after the murder of George Floyd.

Crippen, who was removed from GCJAC after stating to Council that neither that body nor its subcommittee, the Police Community Review Board, could effectively investigate the death of Marcus Smith, agreed with Johnson that any such review board is useless unless independent of the city and its police.

"[Councilwoman] Goldie Wells tried to convince Irving Allen and me that it was in our best interest not to serve on the PCRB. She posited that being kicked out would give us the freedom to do the real work without threat of imprisonment and fines. Irv raised this point: 'You take your car to a mechanic to fix it. You should take your policing issues to organizers to fix them." We've both spent years examining policing, alternatives, and societal issues. But in truth, GCJAC wasn't created to address any of that. Its purpose seems to be regaining the public trust that the police have squandered. What has it done for victims in the community since it was formed?"

Crippen was referencing the 2021 killing of Joseph Lopez Jr. and the 2022 killing of Nasanto "Duke" Crenshaw, neither of which were investigated by either GCJAC or its PCRB subcommittee, and both of which resulted in wrongful death lawsuits against a police officer and the City of Greensboro by the parent of a person of color. *Lopez v. Hamilton et al* was filed by Graham Holt and Flint Taylor in June of 2022 while they were still negotiating the settlement of *Smith v. Greensboro*. *Doriety v. Sletten et al* was filed on March 9, 2023, by attorneys for Wakita Doriety, Nasanto Crenshaw's mother.

The unarmed Joseph Lopez was shot and killed by GPD officer Matthew Hamilton on November 19, 2021, after more than 20 officers responded to a 911 call from the house where Lopez was living with his girlfriend. When they arrived, Lopez was discovered hiding in a storage shed. Hamilton, the K-9 officer on the scene, ordered Lopez to come out. Seconds after Lopez announced his intention of doing so,[1] Hamilton released his dog into the dark shed, then followed it inside and fatally shot Lopez in the face as Lopez grappled with the animal.

For the first six months after Lopez's death, Greensboro police and the Guilford County district attorney announced no action beyond Hamilton having been placed on administrative duty while the case was under investigation. On June 7, 2022, attorneys Holt and Taylor held a press conference announcing the lawsuit by the victim's father, Joe Lopez. Hours after they spoke to the media, interim GPD Chief Teresa Biffle fired Hamilton and District Attorney Avery Crump indicted him for manslaughter, the first time a Greensboro officer ever received a criminal charge for killing someone police were attempting to take into custody.

As of the end of May 2023, a criminal trial had not yet been calendared and the civil suit was still in discovery.

On August 22, 2022, GPD Corporal Matthew Sletten noticed a white Nissan driving with its high beams on near FantaCity International Shopping Center on West Market Street. Sletten followed the vehicle into the complex and pulled up behind it after it temporarily stopped. Running the license plate showed the Nissan had been reported as stolen. As Sletten stepped out of his patrol car, the Nissan pulled away at a low speed.

Sletten followed it through the shopping center and attempted to block it in a cul-de-sac. Multiple juveniles emerged from the Nissan and fled on foot. The driver, 17-year-old Nasanto "Duke" Crenshaw, attempted a three-point turn, causing the Nissan to scrape bumpers with the patrol car. He then backed away from Sletten's vehicle. Sletten emerged, ordering Crenshaw to get out and lie face down.

Instead, the teenager accelerated. Sletten later claimed the driver was "trying to run me over," but on his bodycam video, it appears Crenshaw was attempting to drive around him, as Sletten neither moved out of the vehicle's path nor was struck by it.[2] According to GPD Departmental Directives, officers should only shoot at a moving vehicle when an occupant of the vehicle is using or threatening to use lethal force by means other than the vehicle itself and there are no reasonable means of avoiding its path.

Sletten fired two shots into the Nissan as it passed him and a third from behind it. Crenshaw was declared dead at the scene. A remaining passenger, whom the GPD has described as fifteen-years-old but whom Crenshaw family has claimed was 14, was also in the front seat when Sletten fired, but was unharmed. On March 30, 2023, Guilford County District Attorney Crump declined to indict Sletten on criminal charges, but the GPD investigation, which is still ongoing at the time of this writing, will determine if he contravened policy.

When asked what consequences she would like to have seen for the killers of Marcus Smith, Joseph Lopez, and Nasanto Crenshaw, Cherizar Crippen quoted an anti-racist chant: "Indict, convict, send those killer cops to jail. The whole damn system is guilty as hell!"

"A system enslaved us," she continued, "A system disenfranchised us politically and economically, a system maintains the status quo. Currently the status quo includes the murder of Black people without consequence. In the murder of Marcus Smith, the system of oppression targeting Black people was upheld by the mayor, city manager, almost all the city council members, city lawyer, police chief, EMTs and GPD."

Crippen considered Mayor Vaughan's talk of the Police Community Review Board to be cynical obfuscation.

"She misrepresented the power of the PCRB so much that she either had no idea what it was capable of doing, or she purposely attempted to mislead. Given her history, I'm thinking the latter is true."

Crippen did not share Nelson Johnson's opinion that things have gotten even slightly better.

"During the first few days of the 2020 global uprising, there were a lot of megaphones in the streets calling for justice in Minneapolis. I asked them to call for justice at home for Marcus Smith. One night I changed the 'request to join' question on our local Black Lives Matter Facebook page to say, 'Do you know about Marcus Smith?' Over the next weeks, 5,000 people joined that page and the vast majority answered 'no.'"

Crippen condemned Vaughan's reaction to the protests that erupted in the wake of George Floyd's murder.

"Two years after Marcus Smith's death, Nancy responded to calls for justice with tear gas. She turned Greensboro into a sundown town by enacting an unlawful curfew. They brought sound cannons to protests. White supremacists were allowed to post up around the city with guns. The county commissioners gave the police a tank. They increased their tech surveillance budget."

Crippen was referring to the $295,000 armored "critical incident vehicle" Guilford County Commissioners approved in June of 2020, just weeks after protests erupted in downtown Greensboro. While it was purchased for the sheriff's department, that agency's headquarters is two blocks from those of the Greensboro police, and Sheriff Danny Rogers announced the vehicle would be available to the GPD on "a 'call-out' basis."[3]

"A couple years later, the blood money for the murder of Marcus Smith was paid by taxpayers, just like it always is. No further consequences were visited on any of the players who sought to cover up his murder, like usual. Nancy was reelected. People still join the BLM page and answer that they do not know about Marcus Smith. GPD killed more people. The rich and powerful in Greensboro are dead set on making it a tourist destination, and tourist destinations will use anything to keep up a facade of peace, even violence. So, no, I don't think it's changed. Not for the better anyways. But that isn't unique to Greensboro."

The aftermath for the officers

Although the eight officers involved in the fatal hog-tying of Marcus Smith were cleared of both criminal and procedural wrongdoing and returned to active duty, since the killing one has been fired, three have resigned, and one has retired, leaving only three still employed by the City of Greensboro as of May 2023.

Christopher Bradshaw resigned from the GPD in June of 2022. As described in Chapter 11, Bradshaw repeatedly imitated Marcus' distress with a theatrically high-pitched voice, stood to the side while Marcus stopped breathing, and did not call a superior until another officer suggested he do so.

At the time, Bradshaw had the rank of police sergeant, making him the senior officer on the scene, although he testified under oath that he never gave any orders. He was the second-highest paid, at $67,118 a year. Three months after Marcus' death, that was raised to $68,717. Bradshaw continued to receive raises and merit increases, and in December of 2021, his salary was $78,193.

On February 1, 2022, the same day a settlement in the lawsuit was announced, former Sergeant Bradshaw was demoted to Police Officer I and his salary reduced to $66,464. He resigned in June of 2022. Under North Carolina law, the reasons for an officer's demotion, dismissal, or suspension are part of a public record, but as of June 6, 2023, the City of Greensboro had not responded to a request for that information.

Corporal Douglas Strader, the second-highest ranked officer at the scene of Marcus' killing, was fired in September of 2020 for an unrelated incident involving deadly force.

When Strader took part in the hog-tying, his salary was $58,348, which was raised to $59,738 three months later. In December of 2019, he was making $61,126. Two months before that merit raise took effect, Strader shot at a vehicle fleeing a crime scene at the intersection of South Elm Street and Washington Street in downtown Greensboro. The incident occurred 700 yards from where he had encountered Marcus 379 days earlier. Due to the appeals process, Strader did not receive his official letter of dismissal until October of 2020. In it, City Manager David Parrish wrote Strader: "I believe that, given the circumstances of the night in question, your use of deadly force against the driver and occupants of a fleeing vehicle was unnecessary and in violation of GPD Directive 1.5.13(A)."

At the time of his 2021 deposition by plaintiff attorney Flint Taylor, Strader stated he had been hired the week before by the City of Graham at the rank of Police Officer I, and was still on probationary status. An officer who leaves or loses their position after being investigated for alleged malfeasance or liability is often quickly hired by another department, as happened in the case of Timothy Loehmann, the white Cleveland police officer who shot 11-year-old Tamir Rice.[4]

Graham, the town whose police department hired Strader, is 26 miles from Greensboro and the seat of neighboring Alamance County, where law enforcement has often appeared supportive of the neo-Confederate counter-protestors who claim to "guard" that town's Confederate monument from anti-racist activists. The same month Strader was fired in Greensboro, on October 31, 2020, Graham police officers and sheriff's deputies attacked a peaceful voting rights march with pepper spray, an incident that received international attention. Despite condemnation of the attack by Governor Roy Cooper, neither Graham Police Chief Kristi Cole nor Alamance County Sheriff Terry Johnson were investigated or reprimanded for what happened that day, which resulted in an ongoing voter intimidation lawsuit from the American Civil Liberties Association.

In April of 2022, Graham activists circulated video and photos of Strader punching, choking, and pepper spraying a teenager while serving papers at an apartment complex. A "Change.Org" petition demanding his firing gathered 1,116 signatures.[4] Graham Police Chief Cole told press the incident was investigated, but according to state law, results were not public because the officer was not suspended, demoted, or terminated. She also stated that Strader had met all the requirements for being hired by her department.[5]

In April of 2021, Jordan Bailey, the last officer to arrive at the scene of Marcus Smith's death, and second-youngest present that night, resigned from the GPD.

Bailey had the rank of Police Officer II and a salary of $42,240 when he joined six other officers hog-tying Marcus while then-Sergeant Bradshaw watched. His salary was raised to $48,225 three months later, to $49,201 in December of 2019, and to $51,150 a year later. In February of 2021, he was demoted to Police Officer I. He resigned two months later. As of June 5, 2023, the City of Greensboro had not responded to a request for information on why he was demoted.

Lee Andrews resigned from the GPD in December of 2019. At the time he took part in the hog-tying, his rank was Police Officer III and his salary was $50,147. He still held that rank when he resigned a year and three months later, but his salary was $54,384. When Flint Taylor asked why he left the force, Andrews responded that Pond Lake Management, the LLC he had owned since 2012, "was doing extremely well, and, financially, it made better sense for me to go that route." He also stated that he would receive a partial pension beginning in 2024.

Michael Montalvo, the highest-paid and oldest of the eight officers, retired in April of 2020, after 25 years on the force. He told Flint Taylor that "the way our retirement is set up is, essentially, at 55, you start losing your city supplement if you don't retire," and this financial consideration was his only reason for leaving the force. At the time of Marcus' death, Montalvo was a Police Officer III with a salary of $69,970, and his rank and salary were the same when he retired seven months later.

The Behavioral Health Response Team

At a City Council meeting on December 4, 2018, Mayor Nancy Vaughan said she and the then-director of the Interactive Resource Center had been discussing the need for a crisis intervention team.

"At the suggestion of Michelle Kennedy, the city is going to embed mental health workers in our police department. These professionals will be new hires who are specially trained to assist police with their encounters with people suffering from mental health or drug addiction issues to help defuse and de-escalate negative interactions. They will also provide follow-up and treatment options."

The next time this proposal was publicly discussed at a Council meeting was December 17, 2019, one year and two weeks later. At that meeting, Council voted 8–1 to approve agenda item number 51, "Resolution Authorizing Award of Contract to The S.E.L. Group for Behavioral Health Response Program in the Amount of $500,000."

The Social and Emotional Learning (SEL) Group was a Greensboro-based organization founded by husband and wife Minister Keith Funderburk and Dr. Nannette Funderburk. The purpose of the approved contract was to create "a Behavioral Health Response Program (BHRP)" providing city employees with a "real-time response from a mental health professional during crisis interactions with customers/residents." As part of its contract, SEL Group was required to "equip city staff with the knowledge of how to handle crisis situations with clients in the absence of a mental health professional." The contract stated that SEL staff would be on call to "de-escalate crisis situations, minimize crisis situations that lead to arrests, and more effectively connect citizens who experience crises to the appropriate services in a timely manner" and that SEL clinicians would provide real-time response 24 hours a day, 365 days a year through December 31, 2020, with the option of two one-year renewals.

The program did not begin until March of 2020. Nine months later, the City declined to renew its contract with SEL Group, which would be replaced by a new team of counselors who would work directly with a select group of police officers who had been given additional training. The clinicians would not only train the officers who were also part of the new team, but would be dispatched to the scene with them.

This decision was not publicly discussed prior to Council's virtual work session on November 17, 2020. At that session, Assistant City Manager Dr. Kim Sowell told Council that a licensed professional had been hired to run the new team and the City was in the process of hiring six counselors.

This new city-run crisis intervention program, known as the Behavioral Health Response Team (BHRT), began with little fanfare in January 2021, and has been the subject of no Council discussion in open sessions since. The only significant press coverage has originated from *Triad City Beat,* in the form of an article from December 2021 and a second article from March 2023.

In the first,[6] Sayaka Matsuoka quoted Trey Davis, assistant city manager for public safety, as stating the BHRT answered 3,274 calls for service in the first year of its existence. She also reported the city would receive $330,000 from the recently passed state budget to expand the program.

Davis described the program as a "co-response model," in which "behavioral health specialists, also called clinicians, respond in partnership with law enforcement on mental health-related calls that would otherwise be handled solely by law enforcement."

Kay Brown, who at the time served on GCJAC, told Matsuoka that she considered partnering clinicians with police a good first step.

"I originally felt that a model without police would be best, but I think that there is still some work that needs to be done with mental health professionals to get more consensus around the implementation of those models. The number of calls that the team has been able to take and resolve has far surpassed expectations and there has been good feedback from the community with the model's implementation. My hope is that one day we, as a community, can do more preventative work that allows for the removal of police from models like this and make mental healthcare more widely available. But with that being said, the model is a great start and it will take more from local officials prioritizing economic development, proper wages for all residents, and funding education to make true long-term impact."

Matsuoka asked to speak to some of the officers and counselors involved, but the GPD denied her multiple requests. "We are not going to make anyone available for an interview at this time," said GPD Public Information Officer Ronald Glenn. Neither Glenn nor Davis gave any reason for this response. Matsuoka's article did not report on how the BHRT team would be dispatched to the scene.

In March of 2023, BHRT released what was billed as its first annual report.

In reality, the *Behavioral Health Response Team 2022 Annual Report*[7] posted to the City's website more resembles a promotional brochure, as much of the information on its four pages consists of "client testimonials" such as the statement by "Kim R" that "the Behavioral Health Response Team has saved my mother from harm and definitely from living on streets."

The "report" states that, when the BHRT team is called to the scene of a mental health crisis, either by other officers or by 911 dispatch, the officers secure the scene and "provide guidance around legal statutes and processes," while the clinicians, whom the report implies (but nowhere directly states) arriving with the BHRT officers, utilize "de-escalation techniques" and assess "suicidal or homicidal risk, and treatment options."

Additionally, the report states the BHRT team "often needs to meet with a person more than one time to ensure they receive appropriate help" and that "BHRT's community outreach coordinator assists with following up on GPD referrals," but does not describe this process. It gives the team's operational hours as Monday through Friday, 8 a.m. to 10 p.m. and states that the clinicians are "also available to GPD officers by phone after hours," but does not explain whether "available" means they merely advise the officers over the phone, or can be called to the scene after their regular hours.

According to the report, BHRT staff consists of eight police officers, including a corporal and sergeant, seven clinicians, a team leader, an outreach coordinator, and a paramedic. It describes the clinicians as including three "fully-licensed Clinical Mental Health Counselors" and two "provisionally licensed Clinical Social Work Associates," and states that one counselor "is also a dually licensed Clinical Addiction Specialist Associate."

An infographic on page 3 of the report describes BHRT as having responded to 2,357 "mental health calls" in 2022, in which the team "contacted or attempted to contact" 1,220 people.

On May 15, 2023, Latisha McNeil replied to an email query about how BHRT might respond to someone having a mental health crisis after midnight on a Saturday, as Marcus Smith was in 2018, with the following statement:

"Currently the BHRT Clinicians work an on-call schedule after 10 p.m. and on weekends. Officers can reach the clinicians via phone and clinicians will respond to the scene as needed. Officers also have the ability to submit referrals electronically to BHRT. Those referrals are assigned to a BHRT clinician for follow-up the next business day."

According to McNeil, when calls are received during the hours of 8 a.m. to 10 p.m. on Monday through Friday, "the unit would respond under their normal operational protocol," which is "a co-responder model where the BHRT clinician, and BHRT officer respond together to the scene."

So, if BHRT had been in place in 2018 and Marcus' mental health crisis had resulted in a 911 call before 10 p.m. that Friday night, BHRT officers and clinicians would have theoretically been dispatched together to the scene. After midnight on Saturday, when the incident actually occurred, the responding officers would not have been members of BHRT and would have needed to call whatever clinicians were available to the scene.

While the press has been denied interviews with BHRT clinicians or officers, a city 55 miles east of Greensboro has been more transparent about its recently formed mental health crisis response team. For "Durham's New Model for Public Safety," a May 9, 2023, article in *The Assembly*, Jeffrey Billman was allowed to accompany three unarmed first responders to a 911 call from a man suffering paranoid delusions brought on by his drug use. Billman was also given access to staff meetings and to Durham Police Chief Patrice Andrews, who stated that many of her officers originally expected regular calls to rescue clinicians from risky situations, but instead they were impressed by the pilot program's success in safely diverting 911 calls away from law enforcement.[8]

When asked in May 2023 for her opinion of BHRT, Cherizar Crippen did not express the guarded optimism that Kay Brown had in 2021.

"I'm all for experimenting with alternatives akin to BHRT, but it's going to take radical imagination and some trials and errors to disentangle policing and mental health services. And it needs to be disentangled. The Diagnostic and Statistical Manual of Mental Disorders [the standard classification of mental disorders used by mental health professionals in the United States] is inherently biased towards the experiences of white cisgender men, and so is policing. Police and mental health personnel have walked people hand-in-hand to their incarcerations and deaths."

Crippen then put it even more bluntly.

"No, I wouldn't let a cop near someone in a mental health crisis. They don't even have enough training to know the laws they are sent out to violently enforce, let alone how to help someone having a psychotic break or feeling suicidal. They've been heavily infiltrated by white supremacist groups. They don't seek help for their own mental health issues."

"...that Marcus Deon Smith's life mattered."

At the February 1, 2022, meeting of Greensboro City Council, city attorney Chuck Watts announced that a tentative settlement had been reached in *Smith v. Greensboro*. On October 11, 2022, the *Amended Settlement and Release of All Claims* was filed in the Middle District of North Carolina. Section 2c, "Payment for IRC Plaque", stated:

> The sum of Ten Thousand and 00/100 Dollars ($10,000.00) shall be paid to the IRC (or in such other manner as the IRC and City may agree) for installation of a plaque in the front courtyard of the IRC reciting that "This courtyard is named and dedicated in loving memory of Marcus Deon Smith with funds for this dedication provided as an expression of respect and reconciliation by the City of Greensboro."

Whether "an expression of respect and reconciliation" constitutes what Watts described as a formal acknowledgement that Marcus' life mattered is subject to interpretation. "We fought very hard about that wording," said Flint Taylor, "but it was clear from the start that anything actually resembling a formal apology, much less admitting responsibility for his death, was always going to be off the table."

According to Kristina Singleton, who succeeded Michelle Kennedy as executive director of the Interactive Resource Center, that plaque had not been installed as of May 2023. "I received a response from the City today that the plaque is currently in fabrication and is estimated to take three to four months to be completed and shipped. After that, the vendor will schedule installation."

If the plaque is delivered according to schedule, it will be available for installation soon after the fifth anniversary of Marcus Smith's death.

"My broken heart would rather have Marcus back than any settlement," said Mary Smith in 2022. "We all would. But the Smith family can hardly find the words to express how much we appreciate the love and the people in Greensboro."

She also thanked "our attorneys, organizers and advocates like Hester Petty, Reverend Nelson Johnson, and the Beloved Community Center, the Working-Class & Houseless Organizing Alliance, Greensboro Justice Coalition, and so many good folks I can't mention them all. But I can't leave out the homeless community that loved Marcus so much and appreciated what he did for them, from haircuts to giving them socks, and the folks who worked with him and them at the Interactive Resource Center. I love you all, and so does my husband George and our children."

Cherizar Crippen, who pushed back more publicly and strongly against the narrative from the police department than any other person with any official connection to the City of Greensboro, praised the settlement, but said, "it should not be mistaken for justice."

"City officials made the Smith family, our community organizers, and lawyers, fight for three long years, and I hope that everyone gets to rest and heal now. Sending all my love to the Smith family. I'm glad there were consequences for what they did to your kin. But I'm worried that it won't last long in a city where justice is more of a hashtag than a reality."

NOTES

Chapter 2

1   Richard Barron, "Family of man who died in Greensboro police custody mourns his loss, treasures his memory," *News & Record*, July 6, 2019, <https://greensboro.com/news/local_news/family-of-man-who-died-in-greensboro-police-custody-mourns-his-loss-treasures-his-memory/article_a9ab5334-51bf-5f20-885c-54ca0665f40e.html>

2   Jordan Green, "Few details in death of man after police encounter," *Triad City Beat*, September 11, 2018 <https://triad-city-beat.com/few-details-death-man-police-encounter>

Chapter 5

1   Staff Reports, "Greensboro identifies finalists for police chief job," *News & Record*, May 9, 2015 <https://greensboro.com/news/local_news/greensboro-identifies-finalists-for-police-chief-job/article_198b601c-c696-11e4-be45-1717ad496be1.html>

2   Sharon LaFraniere and Andrew W. Lehren, "The Disproportionate Risks of Driving While Black," *New York Times*, October 24, 2015 <https://www.nytimes.com/2015/10/25/us/racial-disparity-traffic-stops-driving-black>

3   Jordan Green, "Chief Wayne Scott, in his own words," *Triad City Beat*, March 25, 2015 <https://triad-city-beat.com/citizen-green-chief-wayne-scott-in-his-own-words>

4   Jordan Green, "GPD civil emergency unit makes impression at UNC-Chapel Hill," *Triad City Beat*, September 18 2018 <https://triad-city-beat.com/gpd-civil-emergency-unit-makes-impression-at-unc-chapel-hill>

5   Jordan Green, "Two GPD officers named as control agents for KKK imperial wizard," *Triad City Beat*, October 3, 2018 <https://triad-city-beat.com/two-gpd-officers-named-control-agents-kkk-imperial-wizard>

6   Joe Gamm, "New Greensboro police chief responds to criticism," *News & Record*, March 13, 2015 <https://greensboro.com/news/new-greensboro-police-chief-responds-to-criticism-videos/article_b30e5d0a-c8cd-11e4-9778-e3d8fcodb08a.html>

7   Brian Clarey, "Chief Wayne Scott, in context," *Triad City Beat*, August 21, 2019 <https://triad-city-beat.com/editorial-chief-wayne-scott-in-context>

Chapter 12

1   Jordan Green, "Chief explains why hog-tying death didn't violate directives," *Triad City Beat*, November 29, 2018 <https://triad-city-beat.com/chief-explains-why-hog-tying-death-didnt-violate-directives>

Chapter 14

1   Jacob Sullum, "PCP Hallucinations in Ferguson", *Reason*, August 25, 2014 <https://reason.com/2014/08/25/pcp-hallucinations-in-ferguson>

Chapter 18

1   Jordan Green, "Chief explains why hog-tying death didn't violate directives," *Triad City Beat*, November 29, 2018 <https://triad-city-beat.com/chief-explains-why-hog-tying-death-didnt-violate-directives>

Chapter 19

1   Eric Ginsburg, "Greensboro Councilwoman Denies Emails Connecting Her to Police Intelligence Squad", *Yes! Weekly*, February 13, 2013 <https://www.yesweekly.com/greensboro-councilwoman-denies-emails-connecting-her-to-police-intelligence-squad/article_8177172a-e940-11ea-9eaa-9ba055e2d6do.html>

2   Jordan Green, "Two GPD officers named as control agents for KKK imperial wizard," *Triad City Beat*, October 3, 2018 <https://triad-city-beat.com/two-gpd-officers-named-control-agents-kkk-imperial-wizard>

3   Brian Clarey, "Chief Wayne Scott, in context," Triad City Beat, August 21, 2019 <https://triad-city-beat.com/editorial-chief-wayne-scott-in-context>

4   Youtube User Lauren Eaves, "12/2/2018:#justiceformarcussmithmeeting 1/3," Youtube <https://www.youtube.com/watch?v=Poyx1cFF24I>

Chapter 21

1   Anne Skomorowsky, "How Molly Works in the Brain," *Scientific American*, March 10, 2015 <https://www.scientificamerican.com/article/how-molly-works-in-the-brain>

Chapter 22

1   Richard Barron, "Greensboro police showed no criminal negligence in death of Marcus Smith, DA says," *News & Record*, January 4, 2019 <https://greensboro.com/z-no-digital/greensboro-police-showed-no-criminal-negligence-in-death-of-marcus-smith-da-says/article_f1a0c6f4-4efa-505e-a070-97b8e3ba2983.html>

Chapter 23

1   Youtube User Ian McDowell, "Pastor angrily 'dedicates' song to Greensboro police chief at city council meeting," Youtube <https://www.youtube.com/watch?v=O_1XdgMSNpA>

Chapter 24

1 Margaret Moffett, "Recording reveals no reason for private Greensboro council meeting", *News & Record*, November 3, 2016 <https://greensboro.com/news/local_news/listen-recording-reveals-no-reason-for-private-greensboro-council-meeting/article_ca17c790-974d-53b1-80a7-7a00263e0904.html>

Chapter 25

1 John Hammer, "Time and Place of City Council Town Hall Meetings TBA," *Rhino Times* <https://www.rhinotimes.com/news/time-and-place-of-city-council-town-hall-meetings-tba>

2 Joe Killian, "Greensboro Police again face charges of profiling, brutality," *NC Newsline*, September 14, 2017 <https://ncnewsline.com/briefs/97124>

Chapter 27

1 Sayaka Matsuoka, "'Outrageous': Marcus Smith lawyers and activists respond to city's allegations of misconduct," *Triad City Beat*, May 19, 2021 <https://triad-city-beat.com/marcus-smith-lawyers-respond>

Chapter 28

1 Richard Barron, "Should Greensboro police be investigated for their conduct? A councilwoman thinks so," *News & Record*, May 26, 2021 <https://greensboro.com/news/local_news/should-greensboro-police-be-investigated-for-their-conduct-a-councilwoman-thinks-so/article_65bd0e28-be3c-11eb-b3b1-0f56a6c59a28.html>

Chapter 30

1 John Hammer, "Abuzuaiter Says Council Micromanagement Is Causing Problems," *Rhino Times*, April 20, 2022 <https://www.rhinotimes.com/news/abuzuaiter-says-council-micromanagement-is-causing-problems>

Chapter 31

1   Sayaka Matsuoka, "'I'm coming': Moments before being killed, Joseph Lopez appears to surrender in released GPD body-cam footage," *Triad City Beat*, June 9, 2022 <https://triad-city-beat.com/joseph-lopez-gpd-body-cam-footage>

2   Ian McDowell, "Video of GPD officer shooting teen depicts actions Justice Department warns against," *Yes! Weekly*, May 3, 2023 <https://www.yesweekly.com/news/video-of-gpd-officer-shooting-teen-depicts-actions-justice-department-warns-against/article_11be5b30-e9bc-11ed-a6f0-1f6f6789b2d2.html>

3   Taft Wireback, "Guilford sheriff's office gets $295,000 armored vehicle, paid for with forfeited drug-case money," *News & Record*, June 5, 2020 <https://greensboro.com/news/local_news/guilford-sheriffs-office-gets-295-000-armored-vehicle-paid-for-with-forfeited-drug-case-money/article_c1f53840-a7f1-55e7-9f80-5eed630241dc.html>

4   Janet Johnson, "Demand the Removal of Douglas Strader from Graham Police Department, April 26, 2022," Change.org <https://www.change.org/p/demand-the-removal-of-douglas-strader-from-graham-police-department>

5   *Alamance News* Staff, "In unrelated grievance: Plaintiffs in federal suit demand Graham fire police officer," *Alamance News*, July 22, 2022 <https://alamancenews.com/in-unrelated-grievance-plaintiffs-in-federal-suit-demand-graham-fire-police-officer>

6   Sayaka Matsuoka, "GSO's co-response police program answered 3,274 calls in 2021," *Triad City Beat*, December 22, 2021 <https://triad-city-beat.com/gso-co-response-police>

7   "Behavioral Health Response Team 2022 Annual Report" <https://user-kcmpnye.cld.bz/Behavioral-Health-Response-Team-2022-Annual-Report>

8   Jeffrey Billman, "Durham's New Vision for Public Safety," *The Assembly*, May 9, 2023 <https://www.theassemblync.com/newsletter/durhams-new-vision-for-public-safety>

Body camera footage

Videos of police interaction with Marcus Smith on the night of his death are available of the City of Greensboro's Youtube page, but they are not organized. The author has collected the footage under a single playlist for reference: https://youtube.com/playlist?list=PLGk1SYTFY-7atGSMAmhJvjf4PPdKgG3lR

Interviews

The author conducted the following interviews in the development of this book.

Cherizar Crippen   May 2023
Reverend Nelson Johnson   May 2023
Hester Petty   November 2022
Flint Taylor   November 2022
Lewis Pitts   October 2022
Graham Holt   October 2022
Marcus Hyde   October 2022
Reverend Wesley Morris   September 2022
Sharon Hightower   September 2022
Michelle Kennedy   August 2022
Nancy Vaughan   June 2022
Mitch Fryer   March 2022
Mary Smith   March 2022

The author conducted multiple interviews with Mary Smith, Kim Smith, Michelle Kennedy, Flint Taylor, Lewis Pitts and Reverend Nelson Johnson for articles published between December 2018 and November 2021.

INDEX

I AIN'T RESISTING

I AIN'T RESISTING

Index

I AIN'T RESISTING

I AIN'T RESISTING

I AIN'T RESISTING

Index

ACKNOWLEDGMENTS

I Ain't Resisting would not exist without the following people (as well as others not mentioned here, but to whom I remain indebted):

MARY SMITH, whose courage and persistence in the face of unimaginable loss strengthened the resolve of her and Marcus' Greensboro supporters; and KIM SMITH, whom I hope will tell the story of her brother's life, the people he touched, and the rhymes he spun.

The *News & Record's* RICHARD BARRON, who got to know the Smith family well before I did and was that gutted publication's last great reporter.

JORDAN GREEN, whose work for *Triad City Beat*, like Richard's for the *News & Record*, preceded mine for *YES! Weekly* on the Marcus Smith case, and left big shoes to fill. Jordan has moved on to *Raw Story*, where he is becoming one of this nation's foremost reporters on the perils to democracy posed by militias, insurrectionists, and white supremacists.

MICHELLE KENNEDY and MARCUS HYDE might be uncomfortable at being mentioned in the same paragraph, as even when I began writing about this tragedy, they had little good to say about each other, an animosity that only increased while they lived in the same city and spoke at council meetings. But Homeless Union of Greensboro co-founder Hyde was the first person to tell me about Marcus Smith, and the former city Greensboro City Council representative was crucial to "Hogtying, Homicide and Humanity," my second article about the death of the man whose mother said he loved Kennedy, and to many of the more than 50 I wrote afterwards.

And finally, District 1 representative SHARON HIGHTOWER, the first member of Greensboro City Council to publicly call for an investigation, and whom I wish had been deposed by plaintiff attorneys in the lawsuit. I also wish I had known and reported on what she was publicly saying in October and November of 2018, but it wasn't until I began writing this book in 2022 that I watched the videos of those meetings.

ABOUT THE AUTHOR

Although born in Wisconsin, Ian McDowell has lived most of his life in North Carolina. The son of a librarian mother and disk-jockey father, he grew up in Fayetteville and worked in that city's once-notorious downtown. He earned an MFA in Creative Writing and an MA in English Literature from the University of North Carolina Greensboro, the city in which he's lived for forty years. In his twenties, he began selling fiction to such markets as *The Magazine of Fantasy and Science Fiction* and *Asimov's Science Fiction*. Some of these stories were the genesis of his first novel, *Mordred's Curse*, published by Avon Books in 1996, followed by the sequel *Merlin's Gift* the following year. His fiction has appeared in a variety of anthologies, including *Love in Vein*, *The Year's Best Horror* and the Science Fiction Book Club's *Best Short Novels 2005*.

He came to journalism in his late forties, writing occasional articles for the Triad-based *YES! Weekly*. After surviving leukemia and a serious injury, he became a regular rather than occasional contributor to that publication.

In 2020, he won first place in investigative journalism at the 2020 North Carolina Press Association awards for his over 50 articles about the police homicide of Marcus Smith. He has also written about the case for *The Assembly* and *The Police Misconduct Civil Rights Law Review*.

DESIGN. Titles in Narkisim. Chapter numbers in Helvetica Neue Outline. Text in Warnock. The cover uses "Greensboro Skyline," made available in the public domain by Wikipedia user Beyonce245, and assets from freepik.com. Cover and interior design by Andrew Saulters. Scuppernong Editions colophon by Rachel York.

Scuppernong Editions offers the occasional publication of adventuresome, commercially questionable writing in all genres.

Scuppernong Editions
304 South Elm Street
Greensboro, NC 27401

☐ **INSIDE: VOICES FROM DEATH ROW by Michael J. Braxton, Lyle May, Terry Robinson, and George T. Wilkerson; edited by Tessie Castillo.** 'With accountability, reflection, and grace, the coauthors recount the searing stories of their lives before prison and where things went wrong. They reveal their extraordinary efforts to grow and to build meaningful lives, even under a death sentence.' —Sister Helen Prejean, author of *Dead Man Walking.*
$20. 308 pgs. 978-1-7329328-6-9

☐ **DISGUST: A MEMOIR by Stephanie Grant.** 'Starkly beautiful and infinitely true, Disgust is a deep and brilliant gaze into all it truly means to feel, to be human, to love.' —Jacqueline Woodson, author of *Red at the Bone*
$18. 170 pgs. 978-1-7329328-5-2

☐ **EVERYTHING IS PERSONAL: NOTES ON NOW by Laurie Stone.** 'A galvanic account of our era, a trumpet blare aimed at sleepwalkers...A voice unlike any other, she's a fearless thinker in an age submerged in fear.' —Emily Nussbaum, author of *I Like to Watch*
$18. 180 pgs. 978-1-7329328-2-1

☐ **THE TARBORO THREE: RAPE, RACE, AND SECRECY by Brian Lampkin.** 'Stands with books like Timothy Tyson's *Blood Done Sign My Name* as a raw and honest mix of memoir and history, reminding us of William Faulkner. The past is not dead. It is not even past. This is a book America needs now.' —Liza Wieland, author of *Paris, 7 A.M.*
$18. 108 pgs. 978-1-7329328-0-7

☐ **NO, IT'S JUST YOU: A MEMOIR IN 70 ONE-ACT PLAYS AND ONE MONTAGE by Andrew Saulters.** 'Lightly mundane.' —Ben Groh, Greensboro resident
$18. 99 pgs. 978-1-7329328-1-4

SCUPPERNONG EDITIONS, 304 S. Elm Street. Greensboro, NC 27401

Please send me the SCUPPERNONG EDITIONS books I have checked above. I am enclosing $_____ (check or money order—no currency or C.O.D.'s). In this amount I have included the list price and $4.95 to cover shipping and handling; I have also included any necessary state sales tax, according to my area of residence.

Name _____

Address _____

City _____ State _____ Zip Code _____

www.ingramcontent.com/pod-product-compliance
Lightning Source LLC
Chambersburg PA
CBHW070055030426

42335CB00016B/1900